QUEST
CI

QUESTIONS ON THE CHRISTIAN FAITH

answered from the Bible

DEREK PRIME

CHRISTIAN FOCUS PUBLICATIONS

First published
by Hodder & Stoughton 1967

This edition published 1991
by
Christian Focus Publications Ltd
Geanies House, Fearn IV20 1TW
Ross-shire, Scotland, UK.

ISBN 1 871676 827

To
ALR
and
WJG

Cover illustration
by
H.I.E.

Cover design
by
Seoris McGillivray

Printed & bound in Great Britain by
Cox & Wyman Ltd, Reading.

THE QUESTIONS

Number *Page*

THE ANSWERS

Using the Book

This book should be studied or referred to *with the Bible at hand.* The concern throughout has been to state what the Bible has to say in answer to each question. Where possible every statement has a Bible reference which should substantiate or illustrate it in some way.

The material has been set out in sections and sub-sections, both numerically and alphabetically, to make it easy for the book to be studied by sections, rather than read through hurriedly.

Read without the Bible this book will appear heavy and solid. Read with the Bible it should become alive through the power of Bible-truth.

Bible Definitions

The endeavour has been made to avoid words which would not be familiar to the reader who is only just becoming acquainted with Biblical language and phraseology. But this is not always possible and the attempt sometimes means that the full force of an idea is lost. Where a word is unusual or has a particular significance in the Bible, a brief explanation of the word and its use will be found at the end of the book in the section entitled "Bible Definitions".

BIBLE REFERENCES

(Alphabetical list of the books of the Bible and the abbreviations used)

Acts	Acts
Amos	Amos
I Chron.	I Chronicles
II Chron.	II Chronicles
Col.	Colossians
I Cor.	I Corinthians
II Cor.	II Corinthians
Dan.	Daniel
Deut.	Deuteronomy
Eccl.	Ecclesiastes
Eph.	Ephesians
Esth.	Esther
Ex.	Exodus
Ezek.	Ezekiel
Ezra	Ezra
Gal.	Galatians
Gen.	Genesis
Hab.	Habakkuk
Hag.	Haggai
Heb.	Hebrews
Hos.	Hosea
Isa.	Isaiah
Jas.	James
Jer.	Jeremiah
Job	Job
Joel	Joel
John	John
I John	I John
II John	II John
III John	III John
Jonah	Jonah
Josh.	Joshua
Jude	Jude
Judg.	Judges
I Kings	I Kings
II Kings	II Kings
Lam.	Lamentations
Lev.	Leviticus
Luke	Luke
Mal.	Malachi
Mark	Mark
Matt.	Matthew
Micah	Micah
Nahum	Nahum
Neh.	Nehemiah
Num.	Numbers
Obad.	Obadiah
I Pet.	I Peter
II Pet.	II Peter
Philem.	Philemon
Phil.	Philippians
Prov.	Proverbs
Ps.	Psalms
Rev.	Revelation
Rom.	Romans
Ruth	Ruth

I Sam.	I Samuel	*I Tim.*	I Timothy
II Sam.	II Samuel	*II Tim.*	II Timothy
S. of Songs	Song of Solomon (Song of Songs)	*Tit.*	Titus
I Thess.	I Thessalonians	*Zech.*	Zechariah
II Thess.	II Thessalonians	*Zeph.*	Zephaniah

Finding References

A few hints may be helpful for those not used to finding references in the Bible.

An example: I Thessalonians 2: 13.

The name "Thessalonians" refers to the book in the Bible. All Bibles have a list of books in the front and some have an alphabetical list as well. Look up "Thessalonians" in this list and you will find the page number. The "I" before the name indicates that there is more than one book of this name. "Thessalonians" has books "I" and "II".

The figure immediately after the name is the number of the chapter in that book and the last figure is the number of the verse.

In the Authorised or King James' Version the verses are all separated, but in the Revised Version or the New English Bible the chapters are in paragraphs but the equivalent verse number is placed in the margin. A little practice will soon make you familiar with the lay-out of the Bible.

I. DEFINING CHRISTIANITY

Question: What is Christianity?

Answer: It is the only way of knowing God aright, and of living for Him.

1. There is but one God.

(a) There have been, and are, many so-called gods; but they are false (*I Cor.* 8: 4–6).

(b) There is one God (*Eph.* 4: 6).

(c) Although God is revealed to us as a Trinity, the Lord our God is one Lord (*Deut.* 6: 4).

(d) He is the Creator (*Gen.* 1: 1 ff).

(e) He is supreme (*Rom.* 11: 36; *Rev.* 19: 6).

(f) He is the Judge of all men (*Gen.* 18: 25; *Rom.* 2: 16).

2. Men and women are not in a right relationship with God.

(a) When first created, man was in a right relationship with God; he possessed true knowledge, righteousness and holiness, for God made all things perfect (*Gen.* 1: 27, 31; *Eccl.* 7: 29).

(b) In such a condition, man enjoyed fellowship with God (*Gen.* 3: 8).

(c) The right relationship was exchanged for a wrong relationship through the fall of man, i.e. man's disobedience (*Gen.* 3).

(d) Sin came into the world through Adam, and death through sin (*Rom.* 5: 12); all men share in sin (*Rom.* 3: 23).

(e) Human sin constitutes a barrier to man's fellowship with God who is holy and righteous (*Isa.* 59: 2; *I John* 1: 5).

(f) Men are strangers to the life of God, estranged and hostile in mind to God (*Eph.* 4: 18; *Col.* 1: 21).

(g) In such a position man is incapable of knowing God and of living righteously (*Ps.* 14: 1–4; *Isa.* 64: 6; *Rom.* 7: 18).

3. Christianity proclaims what God has done through Jesus Christ to make possible man's reconciliation to God.

(a) God has no pleasure in the death of the wicked (*Ezek.* 33: 11).

(b) He loves the world (*John* 3: 16).

(c) He sent His Son into the world to save sinners (*I Tim.* 1: 15); this purpose involved His bearing the sin of sinners, and experiencing the death due to sinners (*I Pet.* 2: 24; *Isa.* 53: 5, 6).

(d) Through Christ God has made possible reconciliation, and men may be urged to be reconciled to God (*II Cor.* 5: 18, 19, 20).

(e) On repentance and faith men may enter into the benefits of this reconciliation (*Mark* 1: 15; *Acts* 17: 30; *Rom.* 5: 1 ff).

4. Having been reconciled to God, a man may know God.

(a) God then gives to the reconciled man such an understanding of Christ that he realises that to know Christ is to know God (*II Cor.* 4: 6).

(b) Christ came to reveal the Father (*John* 14: 8, 9).

(c) Christ delivered to men the words of God (*John* 14: 24).

(d) Christ is the way for us to God (*John* 14: 6).

(e) The Spirit of Christ is sent

into our hearts when we are reconciled to God that we may know God (*John* 14: 16, 17; *Rom.* 8: 15, 16; *Eph.* 1: 17).

(f) This experience of knowing God was promised when the new covenant which God would make with men was made known through the prophets (*Jer.* 31: 34).

(g) Knowing God means:

(i) A growing appreciation of the character of God (*Eph.* 1: 17; *Col.* 1: 10; *II Pet.* 3: 18; *I John* 1: 5; *I John* 4: 8).

(ii) Liberty and confidence to enter into God's presence (*Heb.* 10: 19 f).

(iii) Fellowship with the Father and with His Son Jesus Christ (*I John* 1: 3).

5. Having been reconciled to God, a man may live for God.

(a) He feels a constant urge to do so (*II Cor.* 5: 15; *Rom.* 12: 1).

(b) He possesses a new dynamic which encourages him in this new direction (*II Cor.* 5: 17; *Gal.* 2: 19, 20; *Phil.* 2: 13).

(c) The Holy Spirit who dwells within makes possible a new way of life (*Rom.* 8: 9; *Gal.* 5: 22–24).

(d) Living for God means:

(i) Negatively, not to go on sinning (*Rom.* 6: 11, 13).

(ii) But positively, to devote one's life to God (*Rom.* 6: 11, 13).

(iii) To make it one's ambition to please Him (*II Cor.* 5: 9).

(iv) To live a life of simple and straightforward obedience to the commandments of God (*I John* 2: 4, 5).

(v) To strive after holiness more and more (*I Thess.* 4: 1–4).

6. Men who know God and who live for Him find themselves restored, in some measure, to the original condition of man before the fall.

(a) Before the fall, man knew God and was righteous (*Gen.* 1: 27; 2: 15).

(b) When a man is "in Christ" there is a new creation (*II Cor.* 5: 17).

(c) That man is brought to a true knowledge of God (*Col.* 3: 10).

(d) Righteousness and holiness then become the pattern of his life (*Eph.* 4: 24).

7. The knowledge of God and the possibility of living for Him are possible through Jesus Christ alone.

(a) The key statement is *John* 14: 6: "Jesus saith . . . I am the Way, the Truth, and the Life; no man cometh unto the Father, but by me."

(b) Although there may be many ways to Christ, there is but one way to the Father.

(c) Knowledge about God may be gained by observing nature, providence and history; but all such knowledge is incomplete and insufficient (*Rom.* 1: 19, 20), and is quite different from knowing God in personal intimacy.

(d) Life lived by men without Christ is not pleasing to God (*John* 15: 5; *Eph.* 2: 3, 12).

(e) Only through Jesus Christ is possible the right relationship we so desperately need (*Acts* 4: 12).

(f) To Christ alone can we turn for the knowledge of God and for eternal life (*Matt.* 11: 27; *John* 6: 68; 17: 3).

8. It is easy to appreciate why true Christianity is so aggressive.

(a) Without saving faith in Christ, men are dead towards God, having no hope and without God in the world, lost and condemned (*Eph.* 2: 1, 12; *John* 3: 18).

(b) Christianity is unique (*John* 14: 6). The Incarnation, the perfect Life of Christ, the "once-for-all" nature of His death as a sacrifice for sins, His Resurrection, His Ascension, and His promised return are all unique facts. They are unique not only in history but also in their continuing consequences (*Acts* 2: 39). Nowhere are higher conceptions of God to be found. No one is a more sufficient Saviour than Christ.

(c) Whilst Christians should not be intolerant of the adherents of other religions, they cannot accept that these religions are in any way approved by God or properly satisfying to men (*I Thess.* 1: 9; *I John* 4: 1–3).

(d) By reason of men's desperate need and the compelling love of God Christianity must be aggressive (*Matt.* 9: 36–38; *Mark* 16: 15, 16): truth opposes error; holiness cannot compromise with sin; the love of God in the hearts of reconciled men compels them to proclaim the Christian gospel (*II Cor.* 5: 14, 20).

(e) Christianity is worth dying for (*Acts* 20: 24; *II Tim.* 1: 8–12).

2. LEARNING THE TRUTH ABOUT CHRISTIANITY

Question: Where are we to learn the truth about Christianity?

Answer: From the Bible alone.

1. Christianity presents us with particular historical facts and spiritual truths which are to be understood and believed (*I John* 1: 1–4).

For example:

(a) The deity of Christ (*John* 20: 31);

(b) His Incarnation (*I John* 4: 2, 3; *II John* 7; *John* 1: 14);

(c) His unique death for our sins (*I Cor.* 15: 3; *I John* 2: 2; 4: 10);

(d) His resurrection (*John* 20: 29; *I Cor.* 15: 4; *Acts* 2: 32);

(e) His ascension (*Acts* 7: 55, 56; *Heb.* 1: 3; 2: 9);

(f) His second coming (*I Thess.* 1: 10).

2. The record of these historical facts and the witness to these spiritual truths are found in the Bible (*Luke* 1: 1–4).

For example:

(a) The deity of Christ (*John* 1: 1–14; *Matt.* 16: 13–20);

(b) His Incarnation (*Matt.* 1: 18–25; *Luke* 1: 26–38; 2: 1–7);

(c) His death for our sins (*Matt.* 27: 26–61; *Mark* 15: 15–41; *Luke* 23: 27–49; *John* 19: 13–37);

(d) His resurrection (*Matt.* 28: 1–10; *Mark* 16: 1–13; *Luke* 24: 1–48; *John* 20: 1–29; *I Cor.* 15: 4–8);

(e) His ascension (*Mark* 16: 19; *Luke* 24: 51; *Acts* 1: 9–11);

(f) His second coming (*Matt* 24: 3–31; *I Thess.* 5· 1–3; *II Thess.* 1: 7–10).

3. The distinctive significance or interpretation of any fact or truth of Christianity is that which the Bible gives (*John* 20: 30, 31; *I Cor.* 10: 11).

(a) Many of the truths of Christianity need explanation in detail (*Luke* 24: 27; *Acts* 18: 26).

(b) Human understanding, unaided, cannot provide the satisfactory explanation (*Matt.* 16: 17; *I Cor.* 2: 14).

(c) The Scriptures were given by God to provide us with the illumination and instruction we need (*Ps.* 119: 130; *Matt.* 21: 42; *Rom.* 15: 4)—the basis on which the gospel is preached is the statements of the Scriptures (*Luke* 24: 44–47; *Acts* 10: 43; 17: 2; 18: 28; *I Cor.* 15: 3, 4).

(d) The Holy Spirit uses the Scriptures to make plain truths to which we would otherwise be blind (*Luke* 24: 27).

(e) When we fail to understand what the Scriptures say on a subject, we soon err in our judgment on spiritual matters (*Mark* 12: 24; *Matt.* 22: 29).

4. The Bible alone must be our authority in all matters of faith and conduct.

(a) The Bible is authoritative (*Matt.* 22: 31).

(b) It is inspired by God (*II Tim.* 3: 16; *II Pet.* 1: 19–21).

(c) The revelation the Bible provides is final—anything which goes against it is false (*Isa.* 8: 20; *Gal.* 1: 8, 9).

(d) The revelation God has given in the Bible—through prophets, apostles and through Christ—is at the foundation of the Church (*Eph.* 2: 20).

(e) Every opinion must be examined in the light of what the Bible says (*Acts* 17: 11).

(f) What the Bible says must be the deciding factor in any decision that has to be made (*Matt.* 4: 1–11; *Acts* 15: 14, 15).

(g) The Bible provides all that a man needs to know and tells him all he ought to be to please God (*II Tim.* 3: 15–17).

(h) If we fail to recognise the Bible's supreme authority in matters of faith and conduct, we shall find ourselves breaking God's commandments through attention to lesser authorities (*Matt.* 15: 2, 3, 6).

(i) Hollow and delusive speculations based upon traditions of man-made teaching quickly capture our attention if we neglect the Bible's authority (*Col.* 2: 8).

5. Everything points logically to the supreme authority of the Bible whenever Christianity is under consideration.

(a) Christ came to fulfil the promises made by God in the Old Testament Scriptures (*Luke* 24: 27, 44).

(b) The New Testament came into being because of the saving work of Christ (*I Cor.* 11: 25; *Luke* 1: 1–4; *Mark* 1: 1; *Rev.* 1: 19).

(c) The Spirit of Christ who caused the Old Testament Scriptures to be written caused also the New Testament Scriptures to be written (*I Pet.* 1: 11; *John* 14: 26; *Heb.* 2: 4).

3. THE BIBLE

Question: What is the Bible?

Answer: The Books of the Old and New Testaments, given by inspiration from God, containing everything which we are to believe and do, that our souls may be saved and God served.

1. The Bible is a collection of books —a library.

(a) The Old Testament is made up of the Law of Moses, the prophets, and the Book of Psalms (*Luke* 24: 44).

(b) What we call historical books the Jews reckoned among their prophetic or inspired writings: "the Psalms", as the first and longest item, was a way of referring to the final section of these inspired "Writings". The historical books record the dealings of God with His people, and provide the contemporary background of the prophets' ministries.

(c) God's messages were entrusted to the Jews in the Old Testament Scriptures (*Rom.* 3: 2).

(d) The New Testament is made up of the four gospels, which record the earthly ministry of Jesus, the Acts of the Apostles, which describes the establishment and growth of the early Church, the epistles which reveal the teaching of the apostles to the early churches, and the Book of the Revelation (sometimes called "the Apocalypse" meaning "an unveiling") which is a prophetic book, looking very much into the future.

(e) The Books of the Bible should be read as books rather than as collections of verses or texts.

(f) The Books of the Bible have come together from a variety of backgrounds:

(i) They were written by kings (e.g. David wrote many of the Psalms), prophets (e.g. Isaiah), apostles (e.g. Paul), historians (e.g. The Books of Kings), and others (e.g. Luke and his gospel and the Acts).

(ii) They were written in one of three languages, although mainly in Hebrew (the Old Testament) and Greek (the New Testament).

(iii) They were written over a period of more than a thousand years.

(iv) They originated from places as far apart as Babylon and Rome.

(v) They were written by as many as forty different individuals.

2. The books of the Bible have to do with either the Old or the New Covenant, or Testament.

(a) The books of the Old Testament may be said to have to do in general with the covenant God made with the children of Israel in the wilderness before they entered the promised land.

(b) The essential message of the Old Testament, if we have in mind the demand the covenant made for obedience, was "This do and thou shalt live" (*Lev.* 18: 5; *Luke* 10: 28)—although this manner of expressing it is a limited simplification.

(c) The books of the New Testament may be said to deal with the new covenant promised in the Old Testament (*Jer.* 31: 31–34) and fulfilled in Christ (*Matt.* 26: 28; *Heb.* 13: 20).

(d) The essential message of the New Testament is "Believe on the Lord Jesus Christ, and thou shalt be saved" (*Acts* 16: 31).

3. The Books of the Old and New Testaments share a common inspiration—the inspiration of the Holy Spirit.

(a) The New Testament speaks often of the Scriptures as a product of the creative activity of the Spirit of God. He is their primary author (*II Pet.* 1: 21; *II Tim.* 3: 16).

(b) More than 500 times in the Pentateuch alone is divine authority claimed (e.g. statements such as those found in *Deut.* 4: 5 and *Ex.* 20: 1).

(c) Christ promised the Holy Spirit's inspiration to His apostles (*John* 14: 26; 15: 26, 27; 16: 13).

(d) The apostles claimed to have His inspiration (*Acts* 2: 33; 15: 28; *I Thess.* 1: 5; 4: 8; *I Cor.* 4: 1).

(e) The apostolic writings were put on the same level as other inspired writings, i.e. the Old Testament Scriptures (*II Pet.* 3: 15; *I Thess.* 5: 27).

4. The inspiration of the Bible by the Holy Spirit accounts for the authority it is recognised to have.

(a) It does not look to the Christian Church for its authority, for it has its own authority (*I Thess.* 1: 5).

(b) The Bible is consequently worthy of our closest attention (*II Pet.* 1: 19, 21; *Josh.* 1: 7, 8).

5. Everything which God requires us to believe is found in the Bible (*Acts* 8: 26–38; *I Cor.* 15: 1–4; *John* 5: 39). Its words are not to be added to or impaired (*Deut.* 4: 2; *Rev.* 22: 18, 19).

6. Every principle which is to govern our life and conduct is to be found in the Bible (e.g. The Sermon on the Mount, *Matt.* 5: 1–7, 29; Paul's practical instructions to the Thessalonians, *I Thess.* 4: 1–12; 5: 12–22).

7. Through the good news of Christ which the Bible contains, our souls may be saved (*John* 5: 39; *II Tim.* 3: 15; *John* 20: 31).

8. By means of the Bible's instruction a man may be perfectly equipped for God's service (*Ps.* 19: 7, 8; *II Tim.* 3: 16, 17).

4. THE INSPIRATION OF THE BIBLE

Question: How do we know that the Bible is the Word of God?

Answer: The Holy Spirit endorses it as the Word of God, causing us to accept its message and to prove its power in our lives. (To this "internal" evidence there may be added many "external" evidences which give supporting testimony to the endorsement of the Holy Spirit.)

1. The Holy Spirit is connected very intimately with the Bible.

(a) All the books of the Bible owe their origin to Him (*Matt.* 22: 43 f, R.V.; *Heb.* 3: 7; *Acts* 28: 25).

(b) The writers were "borne along" by the Holy Spirit's influence (*II Pet.* 1: 21). The exercise of their natural faculties was not interfered with, yet spontaneously they produced what God planned—so perfectly so that what they said, God said (*Dan.* 9: 10).

2. As the Bible is either read or preached it is the Holy Spirit's particular right to endorse its truth to individual readers or hearers, according to His will.

(a) When the Holy Spirit chooses so to act, the message of the Bible comes over with power behind it—the Holy Spirit's power—which results in conviction (*I Thess.* 1: 5).

(b) The message of the Bible is recognised to be then what it is—the Word of God and not the word of men (*I Thess.* 2: 13).

(c) When such power is known, the call of God to the individual through the Bible, by the working of the Holy Spirit, is answered—that is to say, the message is received, and acted upon. That the promises of the gospel then become real in a person's life confirms the truth of the Bible (*I Thess.* 1: 6, 7, 8; *Ps.* 34: 4, 6, 8).

(d) The Bible finds a primary place in the individual's life as a consequence, changing it for good (*I Thess.* 1: 9, 10; 2: 14; *Ps.* 119: 9, 11).

3. The Christian's conviction that the Bible is the Word of God grows as his experience of God increases.

(a) Every promise he claims rightfully is fulfilled (*II Cor.* 1: 20).

(b) The more he learns of the Scriptures the more he finds them suitable to his need (*Ps.* 119: 49–56).

(c) He finds that the Holy Spirit speaks to him through the Bible, whether he reads in the Old or the New Testament (*Ps.* 95: 7–11; compare *Heb.* 3: 7–11, noticing verse 7—"as the Holy Ghost saith, Today if ye will hear his voice . . .").

(d) The Bible becomes more and more of a power in his life (*I Thess.* 2: 13; *Heb.* 5: 14).

4. As the Christian considers the "external" evidences that the Bible is the Word of God his conviction is strengthened.

There are many such evidences and each is worthy of thought:

(a) The Bible's age.

(b) Its preservation in spite of many attacks.

(c) Its amazing unity, although made up of 66 different books, written by over 40 authors, over a great period of time.

(d) The prophecies made in the Bible which have been fulfilled (*Deut.* 28: 64; cf. *Jer.* 30: 11; *Micah* 5: 2; *Zech.* 9: 9; 11: 12, 13).

(e) Its knowledge of human nature.

(f) Its frankness and honesty when dealing with its heroes.

(g) Its superb moral teaching: it never falls short of the highest even in the darkest hours of human history.

(h) Its power to change men's lives.

(i) The testimony of much of modern science. The evidence which science gives concerning the creation of the universe, the evidence of geology, archaeology and geography all add confirmation to the fact that the Bible is the Word of God.

(j) Most important of all the "external" evidences is Christ's repeated testimony to the Old Testament as the Word of God (e.g. *Mark* 12: 36; *Matt.* 5: 18).

5. The essential conviction that the Bible is the Word of God comes not from these "external" evidences, however, but from the Holy Spirit.

(a) Spiritual insight is given to the Christian believer (*I John* 2: 20, 27).

(b) The Holy Spirit guides the Christian into everything which is true (*John* 16: 13, 14).

(c) Christians are given an understanding which is not natural to man (*I Cor.* 2: 10–12): this fact explains the growing conviction they possess that the Bible is the Word of God.

5. THE EXISTENCE OF GOD

Question: What proof is there of the existence of God?

Answer: God is not visible to the

human eye: thus there can be no "direct" proof of God. But He has given clues to His existence and His nature both in creation and in the nature of man; and a glorious revelation of Himself in the Person of His Son, Jesus Christ. Added to these evidences, there is the witness of the Bible, and of those who have found God.

1. That men should ask this question is proof of man's sinfulness and corruption.

(a) The question demonstrates man's folly and corruption through sin (*Ps.* 14: 1).

(b) The question results from man's sinful pride and rebellion (*Ps.* 10: 4).

(c) When men do not want to be convinced of God's existence, God gives them up to their depraved reason (*Rom.* 1: 28).

(d) Their thinking ends in futility and their wisdom becomes foolishness (*Rom.* 1: 21, 22).

2. The Bible does not endeavour to answer this question—i.e. to prove God's existence—but always assumes God's existence.

(a) All the wonders of creation are recognised to be expressions of His power (*Ps.* 19: 1).

(b) All that is good is accepted as coming from Him (*Jas.* 1: 17).

3. The Bible makes plain that no one has ever seen God the Father: thus visible proof of His existence is not provided for men.

(a) No one has ever seen God (*John* 1: 18).

(b) God is not visible to the human eye (*I Tim.* 1: 17; 6: 16).

4. Although men may gain a real knowledge of God, that knowledge can be only partial in this life.

(a) Man can never fully comprehend God (*Isa.* 55: 8, 9).

(b) Man's knowledge of God in this life can be partial only (*I Cor.* 13: 9, 10, 12).

5. Nevertheless God has provided many impressive indirect proofs of His existence: He has not left Himself without witness (*Acts* 14: 17).

6. First, there is the witness of creation.

(a) Reason points to the need of a first cause, i.e. the world could not make itself: the Bible names that First Cause—God (*Gen.* 1: 1; *John* 1: 1; *Acts* 17: 24; *Ps.* 100: 3).

(b) For example, in creation we see thought (*Ps.* 139: 14), forethought (*Gen.* 2: 6), laws (*Ps.* 19: 4–6), and life (*Gen.* 7: 15; 26: 12–14). Behind such there must be a Thinker (*Gen.* 1: 3, 31; *Isa.* 55: 8, 9), an overruling Providence (*Eph.* 1: 11), a Law-Giver (*Isa.* 33: 22; *Jas.* 4: 12), and a Life-Giver (*Acts* 17: 25).

(c) God has disclosed from the beginning His everlasting power and deity in His creation: the eye of reason discerns God's characteristics in the things He has made (*Rom.* 1: 18–20).

(d) The heavens declare the glory of God, and the firmament proclaims His handiwork (*Ps.* 19: 1; *Ps.* 8: 1, 3; *Isa.* 40: 25, 26; *Jer.* 10: 10–13).

(e) In creation, God gives clues to His nature, in the kindness He shows (*Acts* 14: 17; *Matt.* 5: 45).

7. Secondly, there is the witness of man himself.

(a) The wonder of man's own

creation points to a Creator (*Ps.* 139: 14).

(b) The idea of God is written on men's hearts since man was made in God's image (*Gen.* 1: 26, 27).

(c) Man has a natural intuition that there is a God: this is seen in a natural religiousness in men, mistaken and polluted as it may become (*Acts* 17: 22, 23).

(d) Man's conscience witnesses to a law within him by nature—and where there is law there is a Law-Giver (*Rom.* 2: 14, 15).

(e) It is the fool—the corrupt man lacking understanding—who says, "There is no God" (*Ps.* 14: 1).

8. **The witness of creation and of man himself makes up what we may describe as "general revelation", that is to say, facts and understanding given to all men at all times to observe in the world, and from which they may draw logical conclusions as to God's existence. We now come to what we may describe as "special revelation", that is to say, revelation which could not have come to man by his study of nature or by the use of his own reason.**

9. **Thirdly, and most important of all the witnesses we shall mention, there is the witness of Jesus Christ.**

(a) God has revealed Himself to us in Jesus Christ His Son (*II Cor.* 4: 6).

(b) Christ made known the Father (*John* 1: 18).

(c) He is the visible image of the invisible God (*Col.* 1: 15–17).

(d) As Jesus Christ dwelt amongst men, men saw His glory, such glory as belongs to God only (*John* 1: 14).

(e) The human Jesus who could be seen, looked upon and felt, was seen to be the Son of God (*I John* 1: 1–3). The apostles and disciples needed no more proof of God's existence: through the Son they knew the Father also (*John* 14: 7).

(f) His miracles bore witness similarly to His deity (*John* 20: 30, 31).

(g) To have seen Jesus was to have seen the Father (*John* 14: 9).

10. **Fourthly, there is the witness of the Bible.**

(a) The Bible claims to be a revelation from the invisible God (*II Tim.* 3: 16). As we consider the evidences which demonstrate its divine origin so we are convinced of the existence of God.

(b) Some of the predictions it makes, claiming to come from God, are proved true. The good He promises and the evil He threatens (*Rom.* 1: 18), are found to happen in men's experience (*Isa.* 41: 23, 24). God challenges the so-called gods of the heathen to do likewise (*Isa.* 41: 22, 23).

11. **The general revelation provided by creation and the nature of man himself, and the special revelation provided by the Incarnation of Jesus Christ and the Bible are confirmed also by the witness of the Church of Jesus Christ and by the experience of individual members.**

(a) The confirming witness of the Church of Jesus Christ.

(i) The early Church had its testimony confirmed by God by means of signs, miracles and many different works of power (*Heb.* 2: 4).

(ii) The amazing growth of the Church is accounted for satisfactorily only by the power of God (*Acts* 16: 5; *Matt.* 13: 31, 32).

(iii) Its amazing life and continuance is explained by the fact that it is the Church of the living God (*I Tim.* 3: 15).

(iv) Its preservation finds a satisfactory explanation only in the promise of Christ (*Matt.* 16: 18; *Acts* 5: 38, 39).

(b) The confirming witness of individual members.

(i) They have found their search for God rewarded (*Heb.* 11: 6).

(ii) In knowing Jesus Christ they know God (*I John* 1: 1–2).

(iii) They know that the Son of God has come and given them an understanding to know God as a reality in personal experience (*I John* 5: 20).

(iv) They feel God's presence (*Acts* 23: 11; *Matt.* 28: 20; *Heb.* 13: 5).

(v) Their lives know transformation (*II Cor.* 5: 17; 3: 18).

(vi) An irrepressible testimony is theirs (*Acts* 4: 20).

12. Conclusion.

(a) If men's asking of this question —what proof is there of the existence of God?—is sincere, God will provide the answer in a manner which will leave them in no doubt (*Isa.* 55: 6; *Jer.* 29: 13; *Matt.* 7: 8).

(b) That which convinces a man is his personal experience of God through Christ and by the Spirit (*John* 20: 28; *II Tim.* 1: 12).

6. THE BEING OF GOD

Question: What is God in Himself?

Answer: God is Spirit: invisible, without body, personal, great beyond human estimation, life-giving, and supremely powerful.

1. God is Spirit.

(a) *John* 4: 24—"God is a Spirit: and they that worship Him must worship Him in spirit and in truth"—is the nearest approach we get to a definition of the Being of God.

(b) Being Spirit, God has no body; a spirit has not flesh and bones (*Luke* 24: 39).

2. He is invisible.

(a) Being Spirit, God is invisible: no man has ever seen Him or can see Him (*I Tim.* 6: 15, 16).

(b) God is not discernible by our physical senses (*John* 1: 18).

(c) It was on the grounds of the fact that the people saw no form of God on the day that He spoke to them at Horeb that they were instructed not to make any graven image of God for themselves (*Deut.* 4: 15).

3. He is personal.

(a) He is a Personal Spirit, revealing Himself to Moses, for example, as "I AM THAT I AM" (*Ex.* 3: 14).

(b) Personal fellowship may be enjoyed with Him:

(i) He spoke to Adam (*Gen.* 2: 16; 3: 9 ff);

(ii) He revealed Himself to Noah (*Gen.* 6: 13 ff);

(iii) He entered into covenant with Abraham (*Gen.* 12: 1–3);

(iv) He conversed with Moses, as a friend with friend (*Ex.* 33: 11);

(v) He makes His abode with believing men and women (*John* 14: 23);

(vi) The Christian enjoys fellowship with Him (*I John* 1: 3).

4. He is very great.

(a) As the Lord, He is unique (*Isa.* 45: 6).

(b) He speaks with supreme authority (*Heb.* 1: 2).

(c) He alone has immortality inherent in Himself (*I Tim.* 6: 16)—see 6 (a) below.

(d) He is infinite: heaven and the highest heaven cannot contain Him (*I Kings* 7: 27).

(e) There is no one to whom He may be likened or compared (*Isa.* 40: 18).

(f) There are no limits or bounds to be fixed to any of His characteristics, for example:

(i) So far as space is concerned, He is everywhere (*Jer.* 23: 24; *Ps.* 139: 7–10);

(ii) So far as time is concerned, He is eternal (*Ps.* 90: 2, 4; *Isa.* 40: 28; *Hab.* 1: 12);

(iii) So far as knowledge is concerned, He knows all things (*Ps.* 139: 2–5; 147: 5; *I John* 3: 20).

(g) In the light of His greatness, we can see the relevance of the second commandment: "Thou shalt not make unto thee any graven image, or any likeness of any thing that is in heaven above, or that is in the earth beneath, or that is in the water under the earth" (*Ex.* 20: 4).

5. God is clearly beyond our complete understanding.

(a) He dwells in the high and holy place (*Isa.* 57: 15).

(b) His judgments are unsearchable, His ways are untraceable, and His knowledge is beyond our estimation (*Rom.* 11: 33–34; *I Cor.* 2: 16).

(c) He dwells in unapproachable light (*I Tim.* 6: 16).

(d) We do not know God here as He is; we are like people seeing a reflection in a mirror dimly (*I Cor.* 13: 12).

6. He has life-giving power in Himself.

(a) Being the source of all being and life, all things trace their beginning from Him (*Gen.* 1: 1).

(b) God's existence depends upon no one besides Himself; He said to Moses, "I AM THAT I AM" (*Ex.* 3: 14).

(c) He has life-giving power in Himself (*John* 5: 26).

(d) He gives to all men life and breath and everything (*Acts* 17: 25).

7. He does what He pleases.

(a) He does whatever He pleases everywhere (*Ps.* 115: 3; 135: 6; *Dan.* 4: 35).

(b) His will always prevails; His purposes are always fulfilled (*Isa.* 46: 10).

(c) None can resist His will, or say to Him, "What doest Thou?" (*Rom.* 9: 19; *Dan.* 4: 35).

(d) He does with His creatures whatever He pleases: the nations are as nothing before His power (*Isa.* 40: 15, 17).

(e) His dominion is an everlasting dominion, and His kingdom endures from generation to generation (*Dan.* 4: 34).

7. THE ATTRIBUTES OF GOD

Question: What is God like?

Answer: He is holy, righteous, loving, good, wise, all-knowing, eternal, unchanging, and independent of all His creation.

1. God is holy.

(a) The holiness of God is His most outstanding characteristic because it marks Him as quite different and distinct from all His creatures (*Ps.* 99: 3; *Isa.* 40: 25; *Hos.* 11: 9).

(b) Each Person of the Godhead is said to be holy (*John* 14: 26; 17: 11; *Acts* 4: 30).

(c) Holiness is the initial feature of God's character with which men are confronted (*Ps.* 24: 3; *Isa.* 6: 3).

(d) He is majestic in holiness (*Ex.* 15: 11); there is none holy like Him (*I Sam.* 2: 2).

(e) His holiness is such that He cannot overlook wickedness and dishonesty (*Micah* 6: 10–13); He is of purer eyes than to behold evil and cannot look on wrong (*Hab.* 1: 13).

(f) He desires that His spiritual children should share His holiness (*Heb.* 12: 10; *I Pet.* 1: 15, 16).

2. God is righteous.

(a) He is righteous, and His righteousness is always the same (*John* 17: 25; *Zeph.* 3: 5).

(b) He is just and righteous in all that He does (*Isa.* 30: 18)—even in the bringing of calamity upon His people (*Dan.* 9: 14).

(c) Righteousness and justice are at the foundation of His government (*Ps.* 97: 2).

(d) He is the righteous Judge (*Ps.* 7: 11), who always does right (*Gen.* 18: 25), and who will judge the world with righteousness (*Ps.* 96: 13).

(e) He is justified in His sentence and blameless in His judgment (*Ps.* 51: 4).

(f) He does not overlook anything His children do for Him and the love they show to Him (*Heb.* 6: 10).

3. God is loving.

(a) Everything about God displays His love (*Ps.* 25: 10): indeed He is love (*I John* 4: 8, 16).

(b) He has revealed Himself as a God merciful and gracious, slow to anger and abounding in steadfast love and faithfulness (*Ex.* 34: 6; *Ps.* 51: 1; *Joel* 2: 13; *Jonah* 4: 2; *Micah* 7: 18).

(c) His love is so great that it is said to extend to the heavens (*Ps.* 36: 5).

(d) His love for His people cannot be brought to an end; where human love would end, His continues (*Hos.* 11: 8–9).

(e) His love is the basis of the redemption He provides (*Hos.* 3: 1, 2).

(f) His love is seen supremely in His sending of His Son into the world to be the propitiation for our sins (*I John* 4: 8, 9, 10).

4. God is good—by which we mean that He is in every way all that He as God should be; He is absolutely perfect.

(a) He is good (*II Chron.* 30: 18; *Ps.* 86: 5; 106: 1; 107: 1; 118: 1), and alone so (*Mark* 10: 18).

(b) His goodness is seen in His creation (*Gen.* 1: 4, 10, 12, 18, 21, 25, 31; *I Tim.* 4: 4).

(c) His goodness is seen in what He does (*Ps.* 119: 68; 104: 24–31).

(d) His goodness is seen in His gifts (*Jas.* 1: 17; *Ps.* 85: 12; 145: 9; *Neh.* 9: 20; *Acts* 14: 17).

(e) The commandments and the directions He gives to men are good (*Rom.* 7: 12; *Ps.* 119: 39; *Heb.* 6: 5).

(f) The promises He gives are good (*I Kings* 8: 56).

(g) The will and purpose He gives for our life is good (*Rom.* 12: 2), and no good thing does He withhold from those who walk uprightly (*Ps.* 84: 11).

(h) The work which He begins in Christians' lives at their regeneration is a good work (*Phil.* 1: 6).

(i) Even when God needs to discipline Christians it is always for their good (*Ps.* 119: 67, 71; *Heb.* 12: 10).

(j) There is no limit to the good He gives to His children in Christ (*Rom.* 8: 32; *Eph.* 1: 3).

5. **God is wise.**

(a) He is the source of wisdom (*Dan.* 2: 22, 23; *Isa.* 31: 2; *Job* 12: 13); it belongs to Him (*Dan.* 2: 20).

(b) His wisdom is seen in creation (*Prov.* 3: 19, 20; *Jer.* 10: 12; *Ps.* 104: 24).

(c) His wisdom is seen in the natural processes of the earth (*Isa.* 28: 23–26).

(d) His wisdom is seen in the working out of human history (*Isa.* 28: 29; 31: 2).

(e) He gives wisdom to the wise and knowledge to those who have understanding (*Dan.* 2: 21).

(f) His wisdom and understanding are beyond measurement, and certainly beyond man's power to investigate and understand (*Ps.* 147: 5; *Job* 28: 12–21; *Rom.* 11: 33).

6. **God knows all things.**

(a) Knowing all things, none can offer advice to Him (*I Cor.* 2: 16).

(b) He knows all things and nothing is hid from Him (*Hos.* 5: 3).

(c) No creature is hidden from His scrutiny (*Heb.* 4: 13; *Prov.* 15: 3; 5: 21); He is acquainted with all our ways (*Ps.* 139: 3).

(d) Everything lies naked and exposed to God (*Heb.* 4: 13).

(e) If hell and destruction are before the Lord, how much then are the hearts of men before Him (*Prov.* 15: 11).

7. **God is eternal.**

(a) His years have no end (*Heb.* 1: 11, 12); He is the living God (*Rev.* 7: 2).

(b) He is the eternal "I AM" (*Ex.* 3: 14), the first and the last (*Isa.* 44: 6).

(c) From everlasting to everlasting He is God (*Ps.* 90: 2), and He inhabits eternity (*Isa.* 57: 15).

(d) With Him one day is like a thousand years, and a thousand years like one day (*II Pet.* 3: 8; *Ps.* 90: 4).

(e) When the everlasting hills and eternal mountains disappear He remains (*Hab.* 3: 6).

8. **God is unchanging.**

(a) He does not change (*Mal.* 3: 6).

(b) In the midst of change, He is the same (*Heb.* 1: 12).

(c) With Him there is no variation or shadow of inconsistency (*Jas.* 1: 17).

(d) He is unchangeable in His purposes and promises (*Heb.* 6: 17); once He has spoken, He does what He has said (*Num.* 23: 19).

(e) His purposes stand for ever, and His plans last from age to age (*Ps.* 33: 11).

9. **God is independent of all His creation.**

(a) He made Himself known to Moses as "I AM WHO I AM" (*Ex*. 3: 14).

(b) He makes His decisions independently of anyone (*Dan*. 4: 35; *Rom*. 9: 19, 20; 11: 33, 34; *Ps*. 115: 3).

(c) He is independent in all His qualities and abilities (*Isa*. 40: 18–23).

8. THE TRINITY

Question: What is meant by saying that God is a Trinity?

Answer: The one true God is one in every way, in nature, will and being; but one in three distinct Persons—Father, Son and Holy Spirit.

(The word 'Trinity' is not found in the Bible. Nevertheless it sums up what the Bible teaches throughout concerning the mystery of God's Being. The term was first used to preserve the truth concerning the Being of God against the false teaching of heretics.)

1. There is one God.

(a) There is but one living and true God, or divine Being (*Deut*. 6: 4; *Mark* 12: 29; *Rom*. 3: 30; *I Tim*. 2: 5; *Jas*. 2: 19).

(b) Before Him was no god formed; nor shall there be any after Him (*Isa*. 43: 10). He is the first and the last (*Isa*. 44: 6).

(c) There is none besides Him (*Deut*. 4: 35; *Isa*. 44: 6).

2. God exists in three Persons: the Father, the Son and the Holy Spirit.

(a) Since the beginnings of human history God has revealed Himself as a Trinity: indications of the truth of the Trinity are found in the Old Testament, and in the earliest books.

(b) On occasions God speaks using the first person plural (*Gen*. 1: 26; 11: 7; *Isa*. 6: 8).

(c) The form of God's blessing is threefold (*Num*. 6: 24–26).

(d) A distinction is made between the Lord and the angel of the Lord, who Himself is God, to whom all divine titles are given and divine worship offered (*Gen*. 16: 10–13; 18: 13–14, 19, 25, 33; 22: 11 ff; 48: 15, 16; *Ex*. 3: 2, 6, 14; 13: 21; 14: 19; 23: 20, 21; *Josh*. 5: 13–15; *Judg*. 6: 11 ff; 13: 3 ff).

(e) As the revelation of the Old Testament is continued, the distinction between the Lord and the angel of the Lord becomes clearer. This messenger of the Lord (*Mal*. 3: 1) is called the Son of God (*Dan*. 3: 25). His personality and divinity are clearly revealed (*Zech*. 3: 1). He is of old, even from everlasting (*Micah* 5: 2), the Mighty God (*Isa*. 9: 6), the Lord of David (*Ps*. 110: 1), who was to be born of a virgin (*Isa*. 7: 14), and bear the sins of many (*Isa*. 53).

(f) With regard to the Holy Spirit, He is represented in the first chapter of Genesis as the source of order and life in the created universe (*Gen*. 1: 2). In the books that follow in the Old Testament, He is represented as inspiring the prophets (*Micah* 3: 8; cf. *II Pet*. 1: 21), giving wisdom, strength and goodness to statesmen and warriors, and to the people of God (*Ex*. 31: 3; *Num*. 11: 17, 25; *Deut*. 34: 9; *Judg*. 3: 10; 11: 29; *I Sam*. 10: 6; 16: 13).

(g) And then, of course, there is the ample evidence of the fact of the Trinity throughout the New Testament, and the particular evidence of the baptismal formula (*Matt.* 28: 19) and the apostolic benediction (*II Cor.* 13: 14).

3. The Father, the Son and the Holy Spirit are three distinct Persons: that is to say, these Persons are not simply different modes of appearance God uses in His relationship to us.

(a) The Father says "I" (*John* 12: 28); the Son says "I" (*John* 17: 4); the Spirit says "I" (*Acts* 13: 2).

(b) The Father says "Thou" to the Son (*Mark* 1: 11); the Son says "Thou" to the Father (*John* 17: 2); the Father and the Son use the words "He" and "Him" in reference to the Spirit (*John* 14: 26; 15: 26).

(c) Although the work of the Father and the Son is one, Jesus said, "My Father worketh hitherto, and I work" (John 5: 17), implying that their being—in some mysterious way beyond our understanding—is distinct.

(d) The Father loves the Son (*John* 3: 35); the Son loves the Father (*John* 14: 31); the Spirit testifies of the Son (*John* 15: 26).

(e) Some acts are referred to the Father, Son and Spirit: for example, creation and preservation. The Father created the world (*Isa.* 40: 28); the Son created the world (*John* 1: 3); the Spirit created the world (*Gen.* 1: 2; *Job* 33: 4). The Father preserves all things (*Neh.* 9: 6); the Son upholds all things (*Heb.* 1: 3); the Spirit is the source of all life (*Ps.* 104: 30).

(f) Other acts are mainly referred to the Father, others to the Son, and others to the Spirit: for example, the work and plan of redemption. The Father elects and calls, the Son redeems by His blood, and the Spirit sanctifies (*I Pet.* 1: 2).

4. There is a particular order of relationship between the Persons of the Trinity.

(a) The Father is first (*John* 5: 26, 27; *Eph.* 1: 3).

(b) The Son is second: He is begotten of the Father and is sent by Him (*Ps.* 2: 7; *John* 3: 16; *Heb.* 1: 5; *I John* 4: 14).

(c) The Spirit is third: He proceeds from the Father and the Son (*John* 14: 17; 15: 26; 20: 22).

5. The order of relationship does not imply that the Father, the Son and the Holy Spirit do not possess true and equal divinity: their true and equal divinity is insisted upon.

(a) The Father is God (*I Cor.* 8: 6; *Eph.* 4: 6).

(b) The Son is God (*John* 1: 14, 18; 20: 28, 31; *Phil.* 2: 6; *Tit.* 2: 13).

(c) The Holy Spirit is God (*Acts* 5: 3, 4; *II Cor.* 3: 18).

(d) In the Bible all the divine characteristics are considered as belonging to the Father, Son and Holy Spirit: for example, holiness (*Ex.* 15: 11; *Acts* 2: 27; 1: 5); love (*John* 3: 16; *Eph.* 3: 19; *Gal.* 5: 22); omnipotence (*Job* 42: 2; *Isa.* 9: 6; *I Cor.* 2: 4 and *Rom.* 1: 4); omniscience (*Heb.* 4: 13; *John* 21: 17; *I Cor.* 2: 10); omnipresence (*Jer.* 23: 23, 24; *Matt.* 28: 20; *Ps.* 139: 7–10).

6. The Trinity is a mystery—quite beyond our comprehension—to be accepted and believed.

(a) We cannot delve into God's secrets which He has not chosen to reveal (*Rom.* 11: 33–36; *I Tim.* 6: 16).

(b) Nor can the angels of heaven fathom the mystery of His being (*Isa.* 6: 2, 3).

(c) By means of the Scriptures we are given sufficient understanding of the work of the Trinity, in creation, redemption, and sanctification to be saved and to be brought to eternal glory (*II Tim.* 3: 15–17; *Col.* 1: 11–14).

9. THE CREATION

Question: What is the Christian explanation of creation?

Answer: The God and Father of our Lord Jesus Christ is the creator of all things. God the Son and God the Holy Ghost were active in the creation; and God has ordained that all creation shall ultimately belong to the Son. In the final analysis, acceptance of the truth of the absolute creation of all things by God is a matter for faith rather than scientific proof.

1. Genesis 1 is the foundation of any Christian explanation of creation.

(a) Many of the problems people have about creation are resolved when it is realised that Genesis 1 is an account of God's creation in poetic rather than scientific terms, an account which is concerned with the fact of creation rather than with providing scientific explanation.

(b) The emphasis is upon what God accomplished in a period of six days by successive creative acts:

Day One: Light (*Gen.* 1: 3–5);
Day Two: Firmament and division of the waters (*Gen.* 1: 6–8);
Day Three: Dry land and vegetation (*Gen.* 1: 9–13);
Day Four: The light-giving bodies (*Gen.* 1: 14–19);
Day Five: Birds and fishes (*Gen.* 1: 20–23);
Day Six: Animals and man (*Gen.* 1: 24–31).

(c) We cannot state dogmatically what is meant by the word "day", as used in Genesis 1—it is sometimes used of an indefinite period (*Ps.* 105: 8) or of a very long period of time (*II Pet.* 3: 8).

(d) The Genesis account of creation is clearly designed to be simple, to be intelligible for men at all stages in human history, describing the truth of God's complex creation in but few words.

2. God is the Creator.

(a) The Lord created all things (*Ps.* 33: 6; 102: 25; *Isa.* 40: 26; 44: 24; 45: 12; *Acts* 17: 24; *Rev.* 4: 11; 10: 6).

(b) He created the heavens (*Neh.* 9: 6; *Isa.* 42: 5; 45: 18).

(c) He created the earth and all that is on it (*Neh.* 9: 6; *Ps.* 90: 2; *Isa.* 42: 5; 45: 18).

(d) All being comes from God (*I Cor.* 8: 6): He gives life and breath to all things (*Isa.* 42: 5; *Acts* 17: 24, 25).

(e) From one forefather He has created every race of men to live over the face of the whole earth (*Acts* 17: 26).

(f) He sustains all that He has made (*Neh.* 9: 6; *Isa.* 40: 26, 28), for the entire creation is dependent upon His power for its existence (*Acts* 17: 28; *Col.* 1: 17).

3. The work of creation is said to have belonged both to the Son and the Holy Spirit.

(a) During the creative period, it was the Holy Spirit who moved upon "the face of the waters", bringing forth the order God purposed (*Gen.* 1: 2; *Job* 26: 13).

(b) It was, however, through Christ that everything was made, whether spiritual or material, seen or unseen (*John* 1: 3; 1: 10; *Col.* 1: 16; *Heb.* 1: 2).

(c) For Christ is both the First Principle and the Upholding Principle of the whole scheme of creation (*Col.* 1: 17; *Heb.* 1: 3).

(d) God the Father has ordained that to the Son the whole of creation shall ultimately belong (*Heb.* 1: 2).

4. Essential facts about God's creation.

(a) The implication throughout is that God's creation was from nothing by the power of His Word (*Gen.* 1: 1; *Ps.* 33: 6, 9; *Heb.* 11: 3).

(b) God performed His work of creation independently of any creature (*Job* 38: 4 ff; *Isa.* 44: 24), and God remains independent of His creation (*Rom.* 9: 5).

(c) God did not need to create the world or man; it was an act of His free and sovereign will (*Prov.* 16: 4; *Acts* 17: 25; *Rev.* 4: 11).

(d) God created the world for the display of His own glory (*Col.* 1: 16; *Rev.* 4: 11); and thus His eternal power and divinity have been plainly discernible through the things which He has made from the very beginning (*Rom.* 1: 20).

(e) The Bible makes no attempt to reveal or to explain how God performed the creation: the absolute creation of all things by God is, in the final analysis, something which we believe because we accept the revelation of God (*Heb.* 11: 3).

(f) The God of creation is the God of redemption (*II Cor.* 4: 6).

10. THE PROVIDENCE OF GOD

Question: Is God in control of everything?

Answer: God controls all things, working out everything in agreement with the counsel and design of His own will.

1. God's control extends to the whole universe.

(a) He is the only Sovereign, King of kings, and Lord of lords (*I Tim.* 6: 15): His throne is in the heavens, and His kingdom rules over all (*Ps.* 103: 19).

(b) He keeps in being the whole universe by His word of power (*Neh.* 9: 6; *Heb.* 1: 3).

(c) The government of the entire universe is with Him (*Deut.* 10: 14; *Ps.* 135: 6; *Dan.* 4: 35).

2. God's control of nature follows.

(a) All natural forces are in His control (*Ps.* 29).

(b) The elements are at His command (*Ps.* 68: 9; *Jonah* 1: 4).

(c) All the processes of nature are at His direction (*Gen.* 8: 22; *Ps.* 107: 33, 34, 38; *Jer.* 31: 35).

3. God's control of His creatures follows.

(a) His care, for example, extends to the smallest of His creatures:

He gives the beasts their food (*Ps.* 147: 9).

(b) Not a single sparrow falls to the ground without His knowledge (*Matt.* 10: 29).

(c) He can appoint all His creatures to perform His will (*Jonah* 1: 17; 2: 10): even for ravens to convey bread and meat to His servants (*I Kings* 17: 6).

4. God's control of men—and of evil men—follows.

(a) There are occasions when God, desiring to show His wrath and to make known His power, has put up with evil men due for destruction, in order to make known the riches of His glory to those whom He has purposed to save (*Rom.* 9: 22, 23).

(b) Sometimes God sees to it that the worst of men are allowed to be exalted in order that they may work for God without their knowing it (*Isa.* 10: 5, 7).

(c) He uses even the enemies of His people to discipline them in their disobedience (*Judg.* 2: 14, 15, 21–23; 3: 12).

(d) On the other hand, He can harden the hearts of His people's enemies so that either they fall into His people's hands or even destroy themselves (*Josh.* 11: 20; *Judg.* 7: 22).

5. God's control of nations follows.

(a) God fixed the bounds of the peoples of the earth (*Deut.* 32: 8).

(b) He can make a nation large or small (*Obad.* 2).

(c) In the affairs of the world, and its rulers, the Lord puts down one leader and lifts up another (*Ps.* 75: 7; *I Sam.* 16: 1).

(d) He uses heathen nations to accomplish the disciplining of His disobedient people (*Isa.* 5: 26; *Amos* 3: 9–11; 6: 14; *Hab.* 1: 12).

(e) So far as it has suited His purposes, He has allowed nations to walk in their own ways (*Acts* 14: 16).

(f) Behind the strange, gracious actions of unbelieving rulers towards God's people at various times is the working of God in their hearts without their knowledge (*Ezra* 1: 1): for example, Tiglath-pileser (*Isa.* 10: 6, 7); Cyrus (*Isa.* 41: 2–4); Artaxerxes (*Ezra* 7: 21)—each pursuing his own chosen course, served the furtherance of God's will, though in their personal living they were disobedient, self-willed and sinful.

6. God's control of history follows.

(a) His dominion is everlasting and His kingdom endures from generation to generation (*Dan.* 4: 34): thus all the events of human history are under His direct control (*Rev.* 9: 15).

(b) He fixes the epochs of human history and the limits of men's territory (*Acts* 17: 26).

(c) God is at work in unrecognised events and processes to bring about His purposes of blessing: it was the Lord who sent Joseph ahead of his brothers to Egypt (*Ps.* 105: 16–22); it was the Lord who turned the hearts of the Egyptians to hate God's people (*Ps.* 105: 25); it was the Lord who called Cyrus, a heathen ruler, "His anointed" because He was going to use him to do His will for His people (*Isa.* 44: 28–45: 4).

(d) The outstanding example of God at work in an event—unrecognised at first—to do His will was the Cross (*Acts* 4: 28; cf. 2: 23).

(e) In all the events of history God is working out His purpose of calling into one body, the Church, men and women of every nation and people, saved through Christ (*Eph.* 3: 3–11).

7. God's control of all circumstances follows.

(a) God, not chance, decides what happens in the affairs of men (*Prov.* 16: 33; cf. *Jonah* 1: 7).

(b) Behind every circumstance is the Lord (*Amos* 3: 6).

(c) He can shorten life or lengthen it (*Ps.* 102: 23; *Job* 1: 21).

(d) The Lord brings both happiness and calamity (*Isa.* 45: 7); success and victory in battle (*I Sam.* 11: 13) and the power to get wealth (*Deut.* 8: 18) are from Him, as too is the power to bring illness or to remove it (*Deut.* 7: 15).

(e) Ordinary daily needs are within His concern and control (*Matt.* 6: 30, 33).

(f) The will of God may be worked out in what appears to be a complete accident (*I Kings* 22: 28, 34).

8. God's special control of affairs on behalf of His people follows.

(a) God's care extends to all individuals, and especially to His people (*I Pet.* 5: 7).

(b) He delivers His people from trouble (*Ps.* 23: 5; 34: 7; 107: 2).

(c) He can hand His people over to their enemies for a period to discipline them if need be (*Judg.* 3: 8; 4: 2; 6: 1).

(d) God is in complete control when His people are persecuted (*Acts* 8: 1, 4; *Phil.* 1: 28, 29).

(e) He gives a sure footing in life to the righteous (*Ps.* 33: 18, 19).

(f) He supplies every need of His children according to His riches in glory by Christ Jesus (*Phil.* 4: 19), guaranteeing that everything in life will be worked out for the spiritual and eternal good which God has in view (*Rom.* 8: 28).

9. God's control of Satan is clearly involved, and is taught.

(a) The Lord can put a restraint upon Satan as He will (*Job* 1: 12).

(b) He gives Satan, at times, power to do his wicked worst, but God is always in control (*Rev.* 9: 1; 20: 7).

II. WAR AND SUFFERING

Question: If God controls all things, why are there wars and suffering?

Answer: Wars, suffering, and such like, are permitted by God insofar as they may serve to fulfil His purposes; His final and sure purpose is that they shall cease.

1. God's control does not conflict with human responsibility.

(a) His control does not involve Him in human sin: men remain free agents, morally responsible for their decisions (*Deut.* 30: 15–20).

(b) God is unchanging in His holiness, justice and goodness: it is inconceivable that in anything that He does He could do anything other than that which is right (*Gen.* 18: 25)—He is eternally self-consistent (*Mal.* 3: 6).

(c) The blame for evil belongs completely to the sinner (*Luke* 22: 22; *Acts* 2: 23).

2. God's control in relation to wars.

(a) War is assumed to be a necessary human experience in this evil world (*Judg.* 3: 1, 2; *Luke* 21: 9; *Matt.* 24: 6).

(b) Wars are the result of men forsaking the Lord and pursuing false gods (*Judg.* 5: 8).

(c) The Lord permits nations to labour for no good purpose, making their scheme profitless as it suits His purposes (*Hab.* 2: 13).

(d) He permits wars in order to call men to repentance, for wars can be a punishment and a warning voice to unbelievers (*Rev.* 9: 13–21), although men and women in general refuse to learn the lessons of war, and repent (*Rev.* 9: 18 ff).

(e) Wars shall cease after the coming of the Day of the Lord and the ushering in of His kingdom (*Isa.* 2: 4; *Micah* 4: 1–8).

3. God's control in relation to suffering.

(a) In the sufferings of the righteous, who have no immunity from suffering (*Eccl.* 9: 2), the mysterious purposes of God are worked out perfectly (*Job*).

(b) Tragedy, accident, suffering are not automatically to be assumed to be the consequences of the individual sufferer's sin (*Luke* 13: 2, 4; *John* 9: 2, 3).

(c) Suffering of some sort or another is clearly taught to be an indispensable part of discipleship of Christ (*Acts* 9: 16; *II Tim.* 4: 5; *Heb.* 11: 33–38; *Rev.* 1: 9).

(d) Suffering has a place in God's loving discipline of His children (*Prov.* 3: 11, 12; *Heb.* 12: 5–11).

(e) While impenitent men are not sanctified through suffering (*Rev.* 16: 8, 9), believers are restored to the Lord by means of it often after straying from Him (*Ps.* 119: 67).

(f) Suffering is to be patiently endured by the Christian for very good reasons (*II Cor.* 1: 6):

(i) Suffering accepted submissively, though not understood, glorifies God and brings blessing in the end (*Job* 1: 21, 22; 2: 10; 42: 1–6, 10);

(ii) Christ is able to help us in our suffering (*Heb.* 2: 18);

(iii) Suffering is temporary, and is tempered by the Lord's mercy (*Lam.* 3: 31–33);

(iv) God sets a limit on the suffering, knowing how much we can endure (*I Cor.* 10: 13);

(v) No kind of suffering or difficulty can separate the believer from Christ (*Rom.* 8: 35–39).

(g) The Christian may even rejoice in his sufferings because of the confidence he has of the benefits which shall come from them (*Rom.* 5: 3–5):

(i) Proof of the genuineness of his faith (*I Pet.* 1: 7);

(ii) Improvement in Christian character (*Jas.* 1: 2–4);

(iii) Knowledge that fellowship with God is his greatest possession (*Ps.* 73: 14, 23–26; *Hab.* 3: 17–19);

(iv) The discovery of God's comfort (*II Cor.* 1: 7);

(v) The encouragement of others through our own experience of God's comfort (*II Cor.* 1: 4);

(vi) A deeper understanding of life and its meaning (*Eccl.* 7: 3);

(vii) Preparation for the glory to come (*I Pet.* 4: 13);

(viii) Good to others spiritually (*Phil.* 1: 12–14; *Gal.* 4: 13).

(h) The Lord can use suffering so

much to a person's good that he comes to look back upon it with tremendous thanksgiving (*Ps.* 119: 71).

4. Thus the completeness of God's control is plain.

(a) God accomplishes all things according to the counsel of His will (*Eph.* 1: 11).

(b) The control of God over everything is really beyond our minds to comprehend (*Ps.* 92: 5–9).

(c) It is so complete that He can laugh at all His enemies would seek to do (*Ps.* 2: 4; *Mal.* 1: 4, 5).

(d) He does what He pleases, and He does not have to answer to His creatures for what He does (*Ps.* 115: 3; *Dan.* 4: 35; *Rom.* 9: 20).

5. The completeness of God's control will be demonstrated at the Day of Judgment.

(a) The judgment of the wicked is certain: the Lord is on high for ever (*Ps.* 92: 7–9).

(b) God will adequately punish evildoers and vindicate the righteous on the day of judgment (*Rom.* 2: 4–11; 12: 19; cf. *Ps.* 37: 14, 15; *Mal.* 3: 13–4: 1).

(c) Evil is not punished as quickly as we anticipate, only because God is patient and gives many opportunities to men for repentance (*Rom.* 2: 4; *II Pet.* 3: 8, 9; *Rev.* 2: 21).

(d) The seeming prosperity of the wicked, therefore, is a temporary thing; they are not to be envied (*Ps.* 37: 1, 2, 9, 10).

6. The Christian's reaction to God's control of all things.

(a) Our response should be to declare, "Great is the Lord" (*Mal.* 1: 5).

(b) No matter how desperate the circumstances, we should consider God's love and say, "If God be for us, who can be against us?" (*Ps.* 107: 43; *Rom.* 8: 31).

(c) The basis for all fear is removed (*Isa.* 10: 24–27; *Matt.* 10: 31).

(d) We may look to God for vindication in His time (*Ps.* 40: 13–15; cf. *I Pet.* 2: 23).

(e) We should submit to all circumstances, ready to learn what God is going to teach through them (*Ps.* 39: 9), learning at least contentment in them (*Phil.* 4: 11): because we always have Him (*Heb.* 13: 5).

(f) We should pray for those in authority, being in subjection to them, as ordained of God (*I Tim.* 2: 1–3; *Rom.* 13: 1).

(g) When we do not understand God's seeming delays to remedy wrong, we should say, "I will quietly wait" (*Hab.* 3: 16; *Jas.* 5: 7–8).

12. SIN

Question: What is sin?

Answer: Sin is basically rebellion against God. Arising from the corruption of the human heart, it is the cause of our separation from God, and the reason for our deserving God's wrath. Sin is man's greatest problem.

1. Sin is basically rebellion against God.

(a) Sin is doing wrong (*Dan.* 9: 5).

(b) Sin is acting wickedly (*Dan.* 9: 5); it is doing evil in the sight of the Lord (*Ps.* 51: 4).

(c) Sin is turning aside from God's commandments and ordinances (*Dan.* 9: 5)—what the Bible calls "transgression" (*Ps.* 51: 1).

(d) Sin is falling short of God's glory (*Rom.* 3: 23).

(e) Sin is ignoring God's Word as it has come to us through the messengers He has provided (*Dan.* 9: 6; *Heb.* 3: 13).

(f) Sin is lawlessness (*Hos.* 4: 2; *I John* 3: 4).

(g) Sin is rebellion (*Dan.* 9: 5)—the result of hostility to God (*Rom.* 8: 7).

(h) The essence of sin is to be against God (*Ps.* 51: 4).

(i) Sin entered the world by man wanting things which belong to God alone (*Gen.* 3: 5).

(j) Sin ignores God's authority (*Gen.* 2: 16, 17; 3: 6).

(k) Sin casts doubts upon God's character (*Gen.* 3: 4).

(l) Sin does not accept the wisdom of God (*Gen.* 3: 4, 5).

2. Sin is the result of the corruption of the human heart.

(a) From the heart flows the springs of life (*Prov.* 4: 23), e.g. as a man thinks in his heart so is he (*Prov.* 23: 7).

(b) Sin begins in the heart (*Matt.* 5: 28).

(c) All the evil things in men's lives come from within (*Mark* 7: 21, 22, 23).

(d) God, who searches the mind and tries the heart, declares that the human heart is deceitful above all things, and desperately wicked (*Jer.* 17: 9, 10).

3. Sin is the cause of our separation from God.

(a) Our sin is known to God when it is hidden perhaps from everyone else (*Ps.* 51: 4).

(b) Sin brings confusion of face before God (*Dan.* 9: 7).

(c) Sin separates us from God (*Deut.* 31: 17, 18; *Ps.* 78: 59–61; *Isa.* 59: 1–2; *Amos* 3: 2, 3; *Micah* 3: 4).

(d) Sin makes impossible, therefore, the enjoyment of fellowship with God (*Gen.* 3: 8; *I John* 1: 6), for it puts us at a distance from God (*Ps.* 51: 11).

4. Sin is that which brings down God's wrath upon us.

(a) We gain an understanding of sin when we appreciate God's holiness (*Isa.* 6: 3, 5).

(b) God knows the precise extent of our sin (*Amos* 5: 12).

(c) Living according to the passions of our flesh, and following the desires of our body and mind, we are by nature the children of wrath (*Eph.* 2: 3).

(d) Sin draws forth God's wrath (*Rom.* 1: 18; 3: 5); the wrath of God rests on the sinner by reason of his sin (*John* 3: 36).

(e) God's wrath against sin will be revealed on the Day of Judgment—the Day of His wrath (*Rom.* 2: 5, 6).

(f) Sin leads to destruction (*Matt.* 7: 13).

5. Sin is man's greatest problem.

(a) Sin's pathway is all too easy to tread (*Matt.* 7: 13).

(b) Sin can so deceive us that we flatter ourselves that it will never be found out (*Ps.* 36: 2); but sin surely finds us out (*Ex.* 2: 12 ff).

(c) Sin is like leaven: it spreads its corruption (*I Cor.* 5: 6).

(d) All the time sin is persisted in, there can be no restoration to God (*Hos.* 5: 4).

(e) We need to be delivered from the wrath to come (*Rom.* 5: 9; *I Thess.* 1: 10).

(f) Sin must be dealt with if men are to have fellowship with God (*Heb.* 2: 17; *I Pet.* 3: 18).

13. THE FALL

Question: What is meant by the fall of man?

Answer: By the fall of man we mean that event in history by which sin came into the world through one man and death through sin.

1. The fall was preceded by temptation.

(a) Yielding to deception Eve fell into sin (*I Tim.* 2: 14).

(b) By the devil's cunning, man's thoughts were corrupted and he lost his single-hearted devotion to God (*II Cor.* 11: 3).

(c) Our first parents were tempted to doubt God's Word (*Gen.* 3: 6).

(d) They became proud and independent, willing to accept the temptation expressed in the words "Ye shall be as gods" (*Gen.* 3: 5).

2. Disobedience was the cause of the fall.

(a) Having doubted God's Word, our first parents disbelieved it (*Gen.* 3: 4).

(b) Having disbelieved God's Word, they disobeyed it (*Gen.* 3: 6).

(c) They disobeyed God's clear command by eating the fruit of the tree of the knowledge of good and evil (*Gen.* 2: 16, 17; 3: 6).

(d) This act constituted rebellion against God's authority (*Gen.* 2: 17).

3. The immediate consequence of the fall.

(a) Man's attitude to God immediately changed: Adam and Eve hid themselves from the presence of the Lord God (*Gen.* 3: 8)—an awareness of guilt and separation from God had come.

(b) Man ceased to be a spiritual being in the way in which he had been previous to his disobedience: he is unspiritual (*Jude* 19); he cannot understand spiritual things (*I Cor.* 2: 14); he is naturally earth-bound and sensual (*Jas.* 3: 15); he is without God (*Eph.* 2: 12).

(c) Man's sin brought the penalty of death upon all (*Gen.* 2: 17; 3: 19).

(d) Man's experience of the wonder of God's creation was immediately spoiled: childbearing became associated with pain (*Gen.* 3: 16); daily work became a matter of toil (*Gen.* 3: 17, 18).

(e) Man's sin had immediate effect on all the creation over which he had been given charge (*Gen.* 1: 28; 3: 17).

(f) Continuing trouble came to all who followed after our first parents:

(i) Murder (*Gen.* 4: 8, 23);
(ii) Polygamy (*Gen.* 4: 19);
(iii) Revenge (*Gen.* 4: 24);
(iv) Immorality (*Gen.* 6: 2);
(v) Increasing wickedness (*Gen.* 6: 5).

4. The continuing consequences of the fall.

(a) All the immediate consequences

of the fall listed above continue.

(b) As a result of the fall, man is astray from God and has lost his purpose in living (*Isa.* 53: 6).

(c) He loves darkness rather than light, because his deeds are evil (*John* 3: 19, 20).

(d) He no longer does God's will, although he was made for this purpose (*Rom.* 3: 23).

(e) He loses the dignity which was his by his original creation the more he moves away from God (*Rom.* 1: 22, 23).

(f) Instead of being glad at what truth he still knows about God, man suppresses it because it makes him too uncomfortable (*Rom.* 1: 18, 20, 21).

14. ORIGINAL SIN

Question: What is original sin?

Answer: Adam was the responsible head of the human race, and thus his sin is imputed to all. We are born fallen creatures, and we go astray from God from birth.

1. Adam represented all men and so his sin is imputed to us all.

(a) Adam represented all mankind (*Rom.* 5: 12–19; *I Cor.* 15: 22, 45–49).

(b) It was through Adam that sin entered the world (*Rom.* 5: 12).

(c) The wrongdoing of Adam brought death upon all men (*Rom.* 5: 15).

(d) The wrongdoing of Adam established the reign of death (*Rom.* 5: 17).

(e) The result of Adam's sin was condemnation for all men (*Rom.* 5: 18).

(f) By the disobedience of Adam—one man—the many were made sinners (*Rom.* 5: 19): his sin is reckoned to us all.

(g) The basis on which God deals with us with regard to Adam is the basis on which He deals with us with regard to Christ: just as through Adam we were made sinners, so through Christ we may be made righteous (*I Cor.* 15: 22, 45–49).

2. Being born fallen creatures, we go astray from birth.

(a) We are made in the image of Adam rather than in the image of God (*Gen.* 5: 3; cf. *I Cor.* 15: 48, 49).

(b) We are brought forth in iniquity and conceived in sin (*Ps.* 51: 5).

(c) We go astray from birth (*Ps.* 14: 3; 58: 3; *Isa.* 48: 8; *Rom.* 3: 11).

(d) There is not a righteous man on earth who does good and never sins (*Eccl.* 7: 20; *I Kings* 8: 46).

(e) Purity and righteousness are impossible to those who know only human birth (*Job* 15: 14; 25: 4).

(f) The Scriptures represent us as all under the bondage of sin (*Gal.* 3: 22).

(g) Our will is stubborn and evil (*Jer.* 16: 12).

(h) Our minds are impure: they are corrupted alike in reason and conscience (*Tit.* 1: 15; *Eph.* 4: 18).

(i) Spiritual things are folly to us, by nature (*I Cor.* 2: 14).

(j) Our heart is evil from our youth (*Gen.* 8: 21; 6: 5; *Jer.* 17: 9, 10; *Matt.* 15: 19).

(k) We are corrupt (*Gen.* 6: 12), not always able to understand our own actions (*Rom.* 7: 15).

(l) Knowing only the life of the flesh—that is to say, life lived without the knowledge of God—we set our minds on the things of the flesh (*Rom.* 8: 5; *John* 3: 6; *Rom.* 7: 18; 8: 7; *Eph.* 2: 3).

(m) If a man does not do right habitually, he is identifiable as a child of the devil (*I John* 3: 8, 10; *John* 8: 44). (The Bible does not teach the universal fatherhood of God, except in the general physical sense that God is the Creator of all.)

(n) We are, by nature, the children of wrath, deserving God's dreadful judgment (*Eph.* 2: 3; *John* 3: 36).

(o) By reason of our situation described above, it is impossible for us to please God whilst we remain in this position (*Rom.* 8: 8).

15. HUMAN EXISTENCE

Question: Why do I exist?

Answer: The original purpose of man's creation ceased to be fulfilled when man rebelled against God. Unreconciled, men cannot adequately answer this question. Reconciled, men discover themselves to exist in order to know God, to do His will, to glorify Him, and to enjoy Him for ever.

1. Why do I exist?

(a) This is one of those fundamental questions to which we see the answer but dimly; the full answer will be revealed and appreciated in the life to come (*I Cor.* 13: 12).

(b) The question can be answered adequately by God alone: we are assured that everything He made, including man, was made for a particular end (*Prov.* 16: 4).

(c) The question is extremely relevant in view of the futility of human life from so many points of view (*Ps.* 103: 15–16; *Jas.* 4: 14).

2. God's purposes for man in his creation give the first clues to the correct answer to the question, "Why do I exist?"

(a) We are here because God created the world, and He created man to inhabit it (*Gen.* 1: 26–28; 2: 7).

(b) Man was created to possess the earth (*Gen.* 1: 28):

(i) He was to make the earth serve him (*Gen.* 1: 28);

(ii) He was to rule all other creatures (*Gen.* 1: 28);

(iii) He was to cultivate God's creation (*Gen.* 2: 15; *Ps.* 104: 14);

(iv) He was intended to enjoy God's creation (*Ps.* 104: 14, 15).

(c) Man was created to know God:

(i) He was made in God's image, and in this was unique amongst all of God's creatures (*Gen.* 1: 27; *Ps.* 8: 5 f);

(ii) He was made to have fellowship with God (*Gen.* 3: 9; *Amos* 4: 13);

(iii) It was intended that he should find his highest satisfaction in having God Himself as his friend (*Ps.* 27: 1, 4);

(iv) He was created to live in devoted dependence upon God (*Luke* 10: 27; *Matt.* 4: 4).

(d) Man was created to do God's will:

(i) He was to obey God (*Gen.* 2: 16, 17; 3: 13; *Eccl.* 12: 13);

(ii) He was to live by faith and obedience (*Gen.* 2: 15–17);

(iii) He was made for God's pleasure, as was all of God's creation (*Heb.* 2: 10; *Rev.* 4: 11; *Gen.* 1: 31).

(e) Man was created with a capacity to enjoy God for ever:

(i) Man is not merely a physical creature (*Matt.* 4: 4);

(ii) Man has an eternal soul (*Mark* 8: 36).

(f) In view of God's creation of man the answer to the question "Why do I exist?" is "I am here to enjoy the earth, to know God, to do His will, and to enjoy Him for ever."

(g) But when man rebelled against God he lost his way and ceased to know the wonder of God's purposes for human life.

(i) Man is like a sheep gone astray (*Ps.* 119: 176; *Isa.* 53: 6).

(ii) Instead of worshipping the Creator, he worships more readily the created thing (*Rom.* 1: 25).

(iii) Yet there remains within man that which makes him feel after God; but he cannot find God without God's help (*Job* 11: 7).

(iv) Man's greatest need is to be reconciled to God (*II Cor.* 5: 20).

(v) On account of the saving work of Christ in dying for sinners, men may be reconciled to God and discover the full wonder of God's purpose for life, which was lost in the beginning (*II Cor.* 5: 17–19).

3. The question, "Why do I exist?" is very relevant to men and women who are not reconciled to God through Christ.

(a) The Lord is forbearing toward men, not wishing that any should perish: we are here to be given an opportunity of reaching repentance (*II Pet.* 3: 9) before His final judgment descends upon a world which ignores God and is unconcerned to know the answer to this question (*II Pet.* 3: 10).

(b) We are here to sow, by means of our lives, in order that we may reap an everlasting harvest—for good or ill (*Gal.* 6: 7).

4. The question has very positive answers when we are reconciled to God—for then we are in a position to enter into God's full purpose for life.

(a) We are here to know God (*John* 17: 3).

(b) We are here to know and fulfil God's perfect plan for our life (*Rom.* 12: 2).

(c) We are here to be agents for extending Christ's Kingdom (*Mark* 16: 15; *II Cor.* 5: 20).

(d) We are here to be made like Christ in character (*II Cor.* 3: 18).

(e) We are here to please God (*II Cor.* 5: 9).

(f) We are here to reflect God's glory (*Matt.* 5: 48; *I Pet.* 1: 16).

(g) Our chief purpose in life is to glorify God (*I Cor.* 10: 31).

(i) To glorify God is to appreciate Him (*Ps.* 92: 8); to adore Him (*Ps.* 29: 2); to love Him (*Deut.* 6: 5); to subject ourselves to Him (*Matt.* 2: 11; *Jas.* 4: 7).

(ii) Our desire is that God should be glorified in everything (*I Pet.* 4: 11).

(iii) We are here to glorify God in our bodies (*I Cor.* 6: 20): whatever we do—eating or drinking or anything else—should be done to bring glory to God (*I Cor.* 10: 31).

(h) Our glorious anticipation is of enjoying God for ever (*Ps.* 73: 25; *I Thess.* 4: 17): in the life to come we shall be satisfied with beholding God's likeness (*Ps.* 17: 15; *I Pet.* 1: 8).

16. THE LAW OF GOD

Question: Why has God given us His law—as, for example, in the ten commandments—if it is impossible for us to keep it?

Answer: While it is indeed impossible for us to keep the law of God perfectly, God has given it to mankind as a revelation of His righteousness, of His demands upon His creatures, and as a restraint upon the rebellion of mankind. By revealing to us our inability to please God, and the condemnation we deserve, God's Law enables us to see our need of Christ, and of the justification made possible by His cross.

1. The Law and the Ten Commandments.

(a) The word "law" is used in many senses. It may refer to the Old Testament as a whole (*Rom.* 3: 19), or just part of the Old Testament (*Matt.* 5: 17; 7: 12), or even the first five books of the Bible—the Pentateuch (*Luke* 24: 44). Sometimes it is used of those commandments given by God through Moses (*Rom.* 5: 13, 20; *Gal.* 3: 17, 19, 21). Often the term is used to describe the law of God as the expression of God's will (*Rom.* 3: 20; *Gal.* 3: 13).

(b) The fact recognised from the beginning was that it is God's right to command (*Gen.* 2: 16).

(c) Men have a law in themselves insofar as their own consciences endorse the existence of God's law, even though they may be ignorant of the law of God as it is set forth in the Bible (*Rom.* 2: 14, 15).

(d) The law of God was given to Adam and to Noah (*Gen.* 2: 16, 17; 9: 6; *Rom.* 5: 12–14), and the law of God, as we know it, came four hundred and thirty years after the promises of God to Abraham (*Gal.* 3: 17).

(e) The law was given to the Israelites (*Ex.* 20: 1–17; *Ps.* 78: 5) through the ministry of angels (*Acts* 7: 38; *Gal.* 3: 19; *Heb.* 2: 2) and a human intermediary, Moses (*Ex.* 31: 18; *John* 7: 19; *Josh.* 1: 7).

(f) The ten commandments are a comprehensive summary of the law of God: the first table of the law expresses man's duty toward God (*Ex.* 20: 3–11), and the second his duty toward his fellow men (*Ex.* 20: 12–17).

(g) The law is found for us, therefore, in the Scriptures (*Jas.* 2: 8).

(h) The law is a unity, expressing the undivided will of the supreme Lawgiver (*Jas.* 2: 11).

(i) The law makes demands upon men—it calls for works, for action (*Gal.* 2: 15, 16).

(j) The law is holy, just, good (*Rom.* 7: 12), spiritual (*Rom.* 7: 14), and royal—royal because it belongs to God's kingdom, and is given by the King of kings and the Lord of lords (*Jas.* 2: 8).

(k) Love is the fulfilling of the law (*Rom.* 13: 8, 10): the commandments of God relating to our fellow human beings are summed up in the commandment, "You shall love your neighbour as yourself" (*Rom.* 13: 9; *Gal.* 5: 14; *Jas.* 2: 8), and love for God Himself is seen in love for our fellowmen (*I John* 4: 20–21).

2. The law is meant to be kept.

(a) God requires that we should keep the whole of His law (*Gal.* 3: 21; *Jas.* 2: 10, 11).

(b) Thus the prophets conscientiously set the law of God before the people of God (*Dan.* 9: 10), and Jesus made it plain that He had not come to abolish the law but to complete it (*Matt.* 5: 17–19).

(c) The law of God is to be regarded as the voice of God speaking to us, and to transgress that law is to disobey God's voice (*Dan.* 9: 9, 11).

(d) It is man's duty to keep God's law (*Eccl.* 12: 13), and the right attitude to it is one of submission (*Rom.* 8: 7).

3. We cannot of ourselves keep God's law.

(a) The law requires perfect obedience (*Deut.* 27: 26; *Gal.* 3: 10; *Jas.* 2: 10).

(b) It requires the obedience of the heart (*Ps.* 51: 6; *Matt.* 5: 28; 22: 37).

(c) While God's image in man was unmarred by sin, men and women were able to keep God's law (*Gen.* 1: 26), and were sensitive to it, but now they have become callous (*Eph.* 4: 19).

(d) Fallen man finds it impossible to submit himself rightly to God's law (*Rom.* 8: 7); his nature finds it uncongenial (*Rom.* 7: 14).

(e) Man cannot render perfect obedience to the law of God (*I Kings* 8: 46; *Eccl.* 7: 20; *Rom.* 3: 10).

(f) Because the law is a unity, whoever otherwise keeps the whole law but fails in one point is none the less a law-breaker (*Jas.* 2: 10).

(g) We sin against the law (*Gal.* 2: 17, 18)—and all have transgressed it (*Rom.* 3: 9, 19).

(h) The law hushes every mouth, and holds the whole world accountable to God (*Rom.* 3: 19).

4. The law is not—and never has been—the basis upon which men have been justified.

(a) The law is not to be relied upon for justification because it brings a curse if full obedience is not rendered (*Gal.* 3: 10).

(b) Men cannot, therefore, be justified by the law (*Acts* 13: 39; *Rom.* 3: 20, 28; *Gal.* 2: 16; 3: 11). (It needs to be said, however, that when we are justified by God, it is in complete harmony with the law—*Rom.* 3: 31.)

(c) The law can produce no promise, only a threat of wrath to come (*Rom.* 4: 15): it has no power to bestow life (*Gal.* 3: 21).

(d) The law possessed only a dim outline of the benefits Christ would provide and did not actually bring any of those benefits to individuals (*Heb.* 10: 1): for example, by the works of the law no man receives the Spirit of God (*Gal.* 3: 2, 5).

(e) Thus the law has never been the basis upon which men have been justified or reckoned righteous—as, for example, in the case of Abraham (*Gal.* 3: 6, 7).

(f) The splendour of the law is completely outshone by the splendour of the gospel (*II Cor.* 3: 10).

5. The penalty for disobedience to God's law is death.

(a) It is a dreadful thing to reject the law of the Lord of hosts (*Isa.* 5: 24).

(b) If we do not fulfil the law of God, we sin, and that same law convicts us as transgressors (*Jas.* 2: 10).

(c) To reject God's law and not to keep God's statutes is to merit God's judgment (*Amos* 2: 4) and wrath (*Rom.* 4: 15).

(d) God's law which was meant to be a direction to life, we find to be a sentence to death (*II Cor.* 3: 6; *Rom.* 7: 10).

6. God's law is a schoolmaster to bring us to Christ.

(a) The law provided a preparatory discipline until Christ appeared to make possible the fulfilment of God's promise of the gospel.

(b) An obvious purpose of the law is the restraint of the lawless and the disobedient (*Gal.* 3: 23; *I Tim.* 1: 9).

(c) The real function of the law is to make men recognise and be conscious of sin (*Rom.* 3: 20): it is the straight-edge of the law which shows us how crooked we are (*Rom.* 7: 7).

(d) For example, we should never have felt guilty of the sin of coveting if we had not heard the law saying, "Thou shalt not covet" (*Rom.* 7: 7).

(e) The law was like a strict schoolmaster in charge of men until they could go to the school of Christ and learn to be justified by faith in Him (*Gal.* 3: 24, 25).

(f) Once they have such faith in Christ, they are free from the law's custodianship (*Gal.* 3: 25).

7. Christ redeems men and women from the necessity of keeping the law as the condition of justification and acceptance with God.

(a) Man's complete failure to obey God's law in its entirety makes it necessary for his salvation to depend, not on his own righteousness, but upon the righteousness of another—Jesus Christ (*Phil.* 3: 9; *Isa.* 64: 6).

(b) Christ became man for the purpose of removing sin—that is to say, the consequences of the breaking of God's law (*Heb.* 9: 28; *I John* 3: 5).

(c) Christ has redeemed us from the curse of the Law's condemnation by Himself becoming a curse in our place when He was crucified (*Gal.* 3: 13).

(d) Christ means the end of the struggle for righteousness by the law for everyone who believes in Him (*Rom.* 10: 4).

8. The law of God and the Christian life.

(a) The Christian is to recognise that the law is good in itself and has a legitimate function, particularly too as it is directed against any and every action which contradicts the wholesome teaching of the gospel (*I Tim.* 1: 8–11).

(b) The law is of continuing significance for the Christian: it is written on his heart, and set in his understanding—even as the Old Testament anticipated (*Heb.* 8: 10; *Jer.* 31: 31–34).

(c) The commandments of God are not burdensome (*I John* 5: 3).

(d) The Christian recognises that his first obligation is to love the Lord his God with all his heart and soul and strength and mind, and his neighbour as himself (*Matt.* 22: 37–40; *Rom.* 13: 10), and such love involves obedience to God's commandments (*I John* 5: 2, 3).

17. THE FIRST COMING OF CHRIST

Question: Why did Christ come?

Answer: As promised in the Old Testament Scriptures, Christ came into the world to save sinners by His death upon the Cross, according to the deliberate will and plan of God, that the way should be open for sinners to obtain a right relationship with God and the gift of eternal life.

1. Christ Himself declared certain purposes for which He did not come.

(a) He did not come to call the righteous (*Mark* 2: 17; *Matt.* 9: 13; *Luke* 5: 32).

(b) He did not come to judge the world (*John* 3: 17; 12: 47).

(c) He did not come to abolish the law and the prophets (*Matt.* 5: 17).

(d) He did not come to be served and waited upon (*Mark* 10: 45).

2. Christ came because it was the Father's will.

(a) He came from heaven (*John* 6: 38).

(b) He did not come of His own accord (*John* 7: 28).

(c) He was sent into the world (*John* 4: 34; cf. 3: 16).

(d) He came not to do His own will (*John* 6: 38).

(e) He came from the Father (*John* 8: 42; 16: 28; 17: 8).

(f) He came to do the Father's will (*John* 4: 34; 6: 38; 8: 29; *Luke* 2: 49).

(g) His aim throughout His earthly ministry was to do the will of the Father (*John* 5: 30).

3. Christ came to fulfil the Scriptures.

(a) He came as the One promised in the Old Testament as the Messiah and Saviour (*Luke* 7: 20; *John* 6: 14; 11: 27).

(b) He came to fulfil all the promises God had made about the coming One (*Matt.* 11: 3, 4, 5, 6): to announce good news to the poor, to proclaim release for prisoners and recovery of sight for the blind, to set at liberty the oppressed, to proclaim the year of the Lord's favour (*Luke* 4: 18, 19).

(c) Thus He came first to His own people—the Jewish people—to whom He had been promised (*John* 1: 11).

(d) Most of all He came to fulfil the Scriptures which show that the Messiah had to suffer and rise from the dead (*Mark* 14: 49; *Isa.* 53; *Acts* 8: 30–35; 17: 3).

4. Christ came to reveal the Father to men.

(a) He came to make the Father known—His grace and truth—for no one has ever seen God (*John* 1: 17, 18).

(b) He came to bear witness to the truth about God (*John* 18: 37).

(c) He came to complete the law, or, expressing the fact in another way, to reveal more completely what God requires of men (*Matt.* 5: 17).

(d) He came to give to men the

words of the Father (*John* 3: 34; 7: 16; 8: 26; 14: 24).

(e) He came to speak what the Father had commanded Him to say—and His words were the words of eternal life (*John* 12: 49, 50).

(f) One of the reasons why Christ is called "the Light" is that He revealed the Father (*John* 3: 19).

5. Christ came to save sinners—this is the stress of the Bible.

(a) He came into the world to save sinners (*I Tim.* 1: 15; *Mark* 2: 17).

(b) Acting on the principle that it is the sick who need a doctor and not the well, He came to call sinners to repentance (*Luke* 5: 32; *Matt.* 9: 12, 13).

(c) On account of His intent to save sinners, He spent His time with them, much to the disgust of the self-righteous (*Matt.* 11: 19).

(d) He came to seek and to save the lost (*Matt.* 18: 11; *Luke* 15: 1–32; 19: 10; *John* 10: 16).

(e) He came to be the Saviour of the world (*John* 12: 47; *I John* 4: 14)—to make it possible for God to save those in danger of perishing (*John* 3: 16).

(f) He came that men might believe on Him and be saved (*John* 6: 29; 3: 16, 17).

6. Christ came, therefore, to die.

(a) He made it clear to His disciples that He had to go to Jerusalem, there to suffer much from the elders, chief priests and scribes, to be put to death, and to be raised again on the third day (*Mark* 8: 31; *Matt.* 16: 21; *Luke* 9: 22)—all in accord with what was written of Him in the law of Moses, and in the prophets and Psalms (*Luke* 24: 44–47; 22: 37; *Isa.* 53: 12).

(b) He came into the world with the deliberate intention of dying upon the Cross (*John* 12: 27; *Acts* 2: 23).

(c) He came to give His life a ransom for many (*Mark* 10: 45).

(d) He came to be lifted up on the Cross as the serpent was lifted up by Moses in the wilderness (*John* 3: 14; 12: 34).

(e) He came to give His own flesh for the life of the world (*John* 6: 51).

(f) He was continually aware of the terrible suffering which awaited Him at the Cross (*Luke* 12: 50).

(g) The whole programme of His earthly life moved towards the Cross as its climax (*John* 7: 6, 8, 30; 8: 20; 12: 23, 27; 13: 1; 17: 1; *Luke* 24: 7).

(h) He came to be the propitiation for our sins (*I John* 4: 10).

7. Christ came that through His death for sinners, men might have a right relationship with God, and eternal life.

(a) He came that those who accept Him may receive a right relationship with the Father (*Matt.* 10: 40; *Luke* 10: 16; *John* 13: 20).

(b) He came that, by means of the Cross, He might be the way to God for us (*John* 14: 6).

(c) He came to proclaim the good news of peace through the reconciliation by the Cross (*Eph.* 2: 17).

(d) He came to bring spiritual life to men (*John* 5: 40; 6: 51, 58; 10: 10; 20: 31; *I John* 4: 9).

(e) He came so that everyone who has faith in Him as the crucified and risen Messiah should possess eternal life (*John* 3: 14, 15; 6: 40, 51, 58; 17: 3).

18. THE DEITY OF CHRIST

Question: How do we know that Christ is God?

Answer: The deity of Christ, confirmed by His perfect life and unique ministry and triumphantly attested by His Resurrection, is vigorously affirmed by the prophets, the apostles and the accumulative testimony of the Bible and by other direct and indirect means.

1. We have Christ's own claims to deity.

(a) There were occasions when He openly claimed to be the Messiah (*Mark* 14: 61–64; *Luke* 22: 66–71; *John* 4: 25, 26).

(b) To claim Messiahship was to claim deity (*Ps.* 2: 6–12; *Isa.* 9: 6; *Zech.* 13: 7).

(c) The Jews recognised this implication of Jesus' claim to Messiahship (*John* 10: 33).

(d) He made unique claims for Himself (*John* 6: 35; 8: 12; 10: 7, 9; 10: 11; 11: 25; 14: 6; 15: 1).

(e) He declared Himself to be one with the Father (*John* 10: 30; 5: 18).

(f) He accepted the declaration of Thomas, "My Lord and my God" (*John* 20: 28, 29).

2. Everything about His life serves to substantiate His claims to deity.

(a) There is the evidence of His supernatural conception and birth (*Luke* 1: 26–56; 2: 1–51; *Matt.* 1: 18–24).

(b) There is the evidence of His sinless life:

(i) He committed no sin and no guile was found on His lips (*I Pet.* 2: 22).

(ii) He could ask a question which only a perfect man would rightly dare to ask, "Which of you convicts Me of sin?" (*John* 8: 46).

(iii) Pilate's wife called Him "That just man" (*Matt.* 27: 19).

(iv) Judas said, "I have betrayed innocent blood" (*Matt.* 27: 4).

(v) The dying thief declared, "This man hath done nothing amiss" (*Luke* 23: 41).

(vi) The Roman soldier in charge of the crucifixion declared, "Certainly this man was innocent" (*Luke* 23: 47).

(vii) No amount of provocation caused Him to act wrongly (*I Pet.* 2: 23).

(c) There is the evidence of His remarkable insight and knowledge:

(i) He needed no evidence from others about a man, for He Himself could tell what was in a man (*John* 2: 24, 25);

(ii) He knew His betrayer from the beginning (*John* 6: 70, 71; 13: 10, 11);

(iii) He anticipated Peter's denial and restoration (*Luke* 22: 31–34).

(d) There is the evidence of His unique teaching: the authority of His teaching astonished all who heard Him (*Matt.* 7: 28, 29; *John* 7: 32, 45, 46). The prophets, for example, said, "Thus says the Lord", whereas Jesus said, "Verily I say to you . . ."

(e) There is the evidence of His miracles:

(i) These were never selfish or merely spectacular (*Matt.* 4: 5–7).

(ii) Those who witnessed the miracles sensed themselves to be in the presence of God (*Mark* 1: 27; *Luke* 5: 26; 7: 16; 9: 43).

(iii) The miracles were "signs" of Christ's deity (*John* 20: 30–31). The Jewish exorcists invoked the name of the Lord, but Jesus commanded, and evil spirits, the wind and the sea obeyed Him (*Mark* 1: 27; 4: 41).

(f) There is the overwhelming evidence of Christ's resurrection:

(i) All the gospel writers record it in detail (*Matt.* 28: 1–20; *Mark* 16: 1–20; *Luke* 24: 1–53; *John* 20; 21).

(ii) Both Peter and Paul make mention of it in their letters (*I Pet.* 1: 3, 21; *I Cor.* 15).

(iii) The apostolic preaching emphasised the Resurrection as the chief witness to Christ's deity (*Acts* 2: 32; 3: 15, 26; 4: 33).

(iv) God the Father declared Christ to be His Son by the resurrection, thus endorsing every claim Christ had made (*Rom.* 1: 4).

3. To the evidence of Christ's claims and unique life to His deity, there must be added the witness of the prophets, including John the Baptist.

(a) Some of the prophetic psalms spoke of a divine Messiah (*Ps.* 2: 6–12; cf. *Heb.* 1: 5; *Ps.* 45: 6, 7; cf. *Heb.* 1: 8, 9; *Ps.* 110: 1; cf. *Heb.* 1: 13).

(b) Isaiah spoke of the Messiah whose name should be called Wonderful, Counsellor, Mighty God, Everlasting Father, and Prince of Peace (*Isa.* 9: 6).

(c) Jeremiah declared that the Messiah would be called "The Lord is our righteousness" (*Jer.* 23: 5, 6; cf. *I Cor.* 1: 30).

(d) Micah speaks of the Messiah as One whose origins have been of old, from everlasting (*Micah* 5: 2).

(e) Zechariah records God speaking of the Messiah as His fellow (*Zech.* 13: 7).

(f) John the Baptist not only described his ministry as making straight the way of the Lord (*John* 1: 23; cf. *Isa.* 40: 3) but bore witness that Jesus was the Son of God (*John* 1: 34).

4. We have also the witness of the apostles to the deity of Christ.

(a) Peter's confession, "Thou art the Christ, the Son of the living God" (*Matt.* 16: 16), marked a vital stage in the training of the apostles.

(b) The apostles saw Christ's glory as He lived among them, such glory as befits the Father's only Son (*John* 1: 14; *I John* 1: 1).

(c) John bears witness:

(i) "The Word was made flesh and dwelt among us" (*John* 1: 14; cf. 1: 1–4);

(ii) John identifies the glory of the Lord which Isaiah witnessed (*Isa.* 6) as the glory of Christ (*John* 12: 41);

(iii) The truth of Christ's deity was the great fundamental for John (*John* 20: 31; *I John* 5: 20).

(d) Peter bears witness:

(i) He heard the testimony of God the Father concerning Jesus Christ His Son (*II Pet.* 1: 16–18);

(ii) He speaks in trinitarian terms of the Father, the Son and the Holy Spirit (*I Pet.* 1: 2).

(e) Paul bears witness:

(i) The first truth he proclaimed after his conversion was Jesus "is the Son of God" (*Acts* 9: 20).

(ii) The Church, he declares, was purchased by God "with His own blood" (*Acts* 20: 28).

(iii) In Christ dwells the whole fulness of deity bodily (*Col.* 2: 9).

5. Finally, we have the witness of the Bible itself.

(a) References to God in the Old Testament are in the New Testament applied to Christ.

Examples:

(i) Christ is the Lord (*Isa.* 40: 3; cf. *Matt.* 3: 3);
(ii) Christ is the First and the Last (*Isa.* 44: 6; *Rev.* 1: 17);
(iii) Christ is the Judge (*Eccl.* 12: 14; cf. *I Cor.* 4: 5).

(b) The works of God are ascribed to Him:

(i) The work of creation was His (*John* 1: 3; *I Cor.* 8: 6; *Col.* 1: 16; *Heb.* 1: 2);
(ii) The work of preservation in providence is His also (*Heb.* 1: 3).

(c) The characteristics which belong only to God are ascribed to Christ:

(i) He is everywhere present (*Matt.* 28: 20);
(ii) He is all-powerful (*Phil.* 3: 21; *Rev.* 1: 8);
(iii) He knows all things (*John* 16: 30; 21: 17; *Rev.* 2: 23);
(iv) He is unchanging (*Heb.* 13: 8);
(v) He forgives sins (*Col.* 3: 13; *Mark* 2: 7, 10).

Conclusions.

1. The deity of Christ throws amazing light upon the love of God: God Himself came to redeem men (*II Cor.* 5: 19).

2. Christ is worthy of our worship: all of God's angels worship Him (*Heb.* 1: 6), as does the whole of heaven (*Rev.* 5: 12).

3. His deity gives unique value to His death: by His death we may be redeemed for God and set free from all wickedness (*Rev.* 5: 9; *Tit.* 2: 14).

4. Christ is the object of the Christian's faith: men are urged to believe on the Lord Jesus Christ and be saved (*Acts* 16: 31).

5. The Church is built upon the fact of Christ's deity (*Matt.* 16: 18).

6. The Christian's relationship to Christ is the most important reality in his life (*Phil.* 3: 7–10).

19. THE INCARNATION

Question: How do we know that Christ is both God and man?

Answer: In both the Old and the New Testaments Christ is declared to be both God and man, united in one person; many infallible proofs of the truth of this mystery are provided.

1. The Old Testament prophecies spoke of the coming Messiah, or Christ, as both God and man.

(a) The Psalms provide many examples of such prophecies (*Ps.* 2; 22; 45; 72; 110).

(b) Christ's human and divine nature was portrayed by Isaiah (*Isa.* 9: 6, 7).

(c) The prophecies concerning the Messiah, which took for granted His deity, spoke also of His body, or His humanity (*Isa.* 50: 6).

(d) Micah prophesied that the Christ to be born was One whose "goings forth have been from of old, from everlasting" (*Micah* 5: 2).

2. The New Testament speaks of Christ as both God and man.

(a) Christ, who is God, was made

man, without ceasing to be God (*John* 1: 1–3, 14)—He bore the human likeness, He was revealed in human form (*Phil.* 2: 8).

(b) As the apostle John expresses it, the Word became flesh and dwelt among men, full of grace and truth; and men beheld His glory, glory as of the only Son from the Father (*John* 1: 14).

(c) The testimony of the apostles was that the man Christ Jesus was the Word, the Son of God (*I John* 1: 1–3).

(d) That Christ became flesh did not mean that His deity was any the less: in Him the whole fulness of deity dwells bodily (*Col.* 2: 9).

3. Christ's virgin conception points to the fact of His perfect deity and perfect humanity.

(a) He was born of a human mother, without any human father (*Luke* 2: 6, 7; *Gal.* 4: 4).

(b) He became flesh through being conceived by the power of the Holy Spirit in the womb of Mary (*Matt.* 1: 20); the Holy Spirit came upon her, and the power of the Most High overshadowed her; these facts explain the holiness of the child, and His identity as the Son of God (*Luke* 1: 35).

(c) The virgin conception had been promised by God through the prophet Isaiah (*Isa.* 7: 14; 8: 8; *Matt.* 1: 23); thus through this event God began to fulfil His promises made throughout the centuries that He would Himself visit and redeem His people (*Matt.* 1: 21 ff; Luke 1: 31 ff, 68–75; 2: 10 f, 29–32).

4. We are given ample proof of Christ's deity.

(a) Passages of Scripture in the Old Testament speaking of the Lord Jehovah are applied to Christ in the New Testament (*Num.* 21: 5, 6, cf. *I Cor.* 10: 9; *Ps.* 102: 25–27, cf. *Heb.* 1: 10; *Isa.* 6: 1–10, cf. *John* 12: 40, 41; *Isa.* 8: 13, 14, cf. *Luke* 2: 34; *Rom.* 9: 33; *Isa.* 40: 3, 4, cf. *John* 1: 23; *Isa.* 45: 22, 23, cf. *Rom.* 14: 11, *Phil.* 2: 10, 11; *Mal.* 3: 1, cf. *Matt.* 11: 10).

(b) Works and activity which particularly belong to God are said to belong to Christ: for example, creation (*John* 1: 3; *I Cor.* 8: 6; *Heb.* 1: 2); the sustaining of the universe (*Heb.* 1: 3; *John* 5: 17); and miracles (*John* 20: 30; cf. *John* 2: 11).

(c) Characteristics which belong to God alone are said to belong to Christ: for example, He is everywhere (*Matt.* 28: 20; *John* 14: 23; *Eph.* 3: 17); He is eternal (*John* 1: 1; *Rev.* 1: 11; *Micah* 5: 2); He is unchanging (*Heb.* 1: 11, 12; 13: 8); He knows all things (*John* 21: 17; *Rev.* 2: 23); He has majesty and glory equal to His Father (*John* 5: 23; *Rev.* 5: 13; *Phil.* 1: 2; 2: 6, 9, 10).

(d) The names given to Him bear witness to His deity: for example, He is definitely called God (*John* 1: 1; 20: 28; *Acts* 20: 28; *Rom.* 9: 5; *Phil.* 2: 6; *Heb.* 1: 8; *I Tim.* 3: 16); He is called the Son of God (*John* 1: 18; *Rom.* 8: 3); He is called Lord (*I Cor.* 8: 5, 6)—"Lord" being the word used in the Greek translation of the Old Testament to render the name of God, "Jehovah".

5. We are given ample proof of His humanity.

(a) God sent His own Son in the likeness of sinful flesh—the word "likeness" implies that Jesus was similar to sinful men in His earthly life, yet not absolutely like them (*Rom.* 8: 3; *Phil.* 2: 7), because He Himself was without sin (*Heb.* 4: 15).

(b) He shared our flesh and blood (*Heb.* 2: 14).

(c) He had all that is essential in a man: a body (*Luke* 24: 39; *Heb.* 2: 17; 10: 5; *I John* 1: 1); a soul (*Matt.* 26: 38; *Mark* 14: 34); and as a consequence a will (*Matt.* 26: 39), affections (*Mark* 3: 5; *Luke* 10: 21; *John* 11: 5), and particular abilities (*Luke* 2: 52).

(d) He knew tiredness (*John* 4: 6), thirst (*John* 4: 7; 19: 28), tears (*John* 11: 33 ff; *Heb.* 5: 7), and all the weaknesses of the flesh, with one exception (*Heb.* 4: 15).

(e) He shared fully in all our experiences, especially in the realm of temptation, except that He never sinned (*Heb.* 4: 15; *II Cor.* 5: 21; *I Pet.* 2: 22).

(f) Possessing a human body Christ endured bodily suffering (*I Pet.* 4: 1); He was put to death in the flesh (*I Pet.* 3: 18).

6. It was only by Christ being both God and man that salvation could be obtained for sinful men and women.

(a) Christ's body was a fundamental part of God's plan of salvation (*Heb.* 10: 5).

(b) God the Father caused Christ to be made flesh of a pure virgin, to live amongst men, that He might be obedient unto death, the death of the Cross (*Isa.* 50: 6; *John* 1: 14; *Luke* 1: 35; *Phil.* 2: 8; *I Tim.* 3: 16).

(c) The reconciliation which God purposed was accomplished by Christ's death in His body of flesh and blood (*Col.* 1: 22; *Eph.* 2: 15, 16).

(d) The new and living way for sinners into the presence of God by the blood of Christ was possible solely by means of Christ's taking flesh upon Himself (*Heb.* 10: 19, 20).

(e) It was by becoming a human being, that, going through death as a man, He destroyed him who had the power of death, that is, the devil, and set free those who lived their whole lives a prey to the fear of death (*Heb.* 2: 14, 15).

(f) Through taking human nature upon Him, He has made it possible for sinners to escape from the corruption that is in the world, and become partakers of the divine nature (*II Pet.* 1: 4).

(g) It was necessary that Christ should be man that the nature which had offended should suffer, and make satisfaction, so that Christ might be in every way a fit and sufficient Saviour for men (*Heb.* 2: 10–17); by becoming man He could mediate between God and men (*I Tim.* 2: 5).

(h) It was necessary that Christ should be God that He might be able to save absolutely those who come to God through Him (*Heb.* 7: 25).

7. Christ's perfect deity and perfect humanity are essentials of the Christian faith.

(a) Fundamental to the Christian faith is the fact that Christ, the Son of God, truly came "in the flesh" (*I John* 4: 2; *II John* 7).

(b) Any denial of the reality of Christ's "flesh", that is to say, that He was not truly a man, is heresy

(*I John* 2: 22–25; 4: 1–6; 5: 5–12; *II John* 7, 9 ff).

8. The fact of Christ being the Word made flesh—what we call "The Incarnation"—is beyond the understanding of the human mind.

That Christ is truly God and perfect man is a mystery, revealed to us in the Scriptures, yet beyond our complete understanding, being something which causes even the angels to admire the wisdom and goodness of God (*I Tim.* 3: 16; *I Pet.* 1: 12).

20. THE CROSS

Question: What happened when Christ died upon the Cross?

Answer: He offered up Himself as a sacrifice, bearing the punishment due to sinners, fulfilling the plan of God whereby men may be reconciled to Himself through Christ.

1. The Cross cannot be understood unless the plight of man in his sin is realised.

(a) Men are in danger of perishing (*John* 3: 16).

(b) Men have sinned against God (*Rom.* 3: 23).

(c) Sin has separated men from God (*Isa.* 59: 2).

(d) Sin has brought death upon men (*Rom.* 5: 12; 6: 23).

(e) Men are under the wrath of God (*John* 3: 36; *Eph.* 2: 3).

2. The Cross was no accident but the deliberate will and plan of God (*Acts* 2: 23).

(a) Before the world was founded God the Father determined that His Son should fulfil the function of a Saviour for sinners (*I Pet.* 1: 20).

(b) The Father and the Son entered into a compact and a covenant: the Son was to accomplish the work assigned to Him (*John* 12: 27; 17: 2, 4), and the Father promised that as a result a great number of men and women from all nations should be given to Him as His inheritance (*Ps.* 2: 7–8) and He should be supreme Head to the Church (*Eph.* 1: 22; *Phil.* 2: 7, 9; *Heb.* 12: 2).

(c) The world was prepared for the great event of the Cross by many symbols and illustrations.

(i) The Old Testament sacrifices all looked forward to the coming of Jesus and His death upon the Cross for sinners (*Heb.* 9: 24; 10: 4, 10, 11, 12; *John* 1: 29, 36).

(ii) The Passover Lamb was a picture of Jesus also (*Ex.* 12: 21–23; *I Cor.* 5: 7) and Jesus used the feast of the Passover to establish the Lord's Supper as a reminder of the meaning of His death (*Luke* 22: 7–23).

3. The initiative in the Cross was God's.

(a) Loving the world so much God gave His Son (*John* 3: 16).

(b) It was the will of God to bruise Him (*Isa.* 53: 10).

(c) The bitter experience of the Cross was received by the Son from the Father (*Matt.* 26: 39, 42).

(d) The design of the whole plan of expiating sin by Christ's sacrificial death was the Father's (*Rom.* 3: 25).

4. Christ willingly died upon the Cross.

(a) From before the time the world was founded Christ had committed

Himself willingly to the Cross (*Isa.* 50: 4–6; *Heb.* 10: 5–10).

(b) He laid down His life (*John* 10: 11, 18).

(c) He poured out His soul to death (*Isa.* 53: 12).

(d) He gave Himself up as an offering and a sacrifice (*Eph.* 5: 2).

5. Christ bore the punishment due to sinners.

(a) He bore the sin of many (*Isa.* 53: 12; *I Pet.* 2: 24).

(b) He bore the wrath of God against sin which sinners deserve (*John* 3: 36; *Rom.* 1: 18; *I John* 2: 2; 4: 10—"propitiation" means the putting away of wrath).

(c) He bore the curse of the law which sinners through their disobedience deserve to experience—death and separation from God (*Gal.* 3: 10, 13; *Isa.* 59: 2; *Rom.* 5: 12; *Mark* 15: 34).

(d) He bore the pains of hell which the sinner deserves (*Ps.* 18: 5; *Mark* 15: 33, 34).

6. We cannot overemphasise either the worth or the eternal character of Christ's sacrifice.

(a) The punishment He suffered was sufficient to satisfy for the transgressions of all because He who suffered was not only a man, but God also. He was of infinitely more value than all those who had offended (*Rom.* 5: 9; *Heb.* 9: 13, 14).

(b) His sacrifice was final—once and for all—and utterly sufficient for all time (*I Pet.* 3: 18; *Heb.* 9: 26; 10: 11, 14).

7. The benefits achieved by Christ's death.

(a) The justice of God was satisfied (*Isa.* 53: 11).

(i) The punishment sin deserves has been allotted and carried out (*Isa.* 53: 4–6; *II Cor.* 5: 21).

(ii) God has shown Himself just and may justify any man who puts his faith in Jesus (*Rom.* 3: 26; *II Cor.* 5: 21).

(b) Redemption from the power of sin, death and hell was made possible for sinners:

(i) The price of redemption has been paid in full by Christ (*Matt.* 20: 28; *Mark* 10: 45; *I Tim.* 2: 6)—the price being His own precious blood (*Acts* 20: 28; *I John* 1: 7).

(ii) Christ has utterly overcome and defeated Satan, death and the powers of hell, that hold men captive. The devil's power is broken (*Heb.* 2: 14). As a consequence the power of death is broken too (*John* 5: 24; *Heb.* 2: 14; *I Cor.* 15: 55–57). Furthermore, hell need not be men's destination (*I Thess.* 1: 10).

(c) The new covenant which God had promised was confirmed.

(i) It was promised when Adam sinned (*Gen.* 3: 15).

(ii) Both Christ and the covenant were promised to Abraham (*Gen.* 12: 3; *Gal.* 3: 8, 16).

(iii) Yet more details were promised through the prophets (*Jer.* 31: 31–34; 32: 40).

(iv) This new covenant could come into operation only by the mediation of Jesus (*Heb.* 8: 6, 10–12).

(v) A testament or a covenant demands a death—a testament is operative only after a death—and Christ made valid the new covenant by the shedding of His blood (*Heb.* 9: 14–26; 13: 20).

(d) Grace and glory are assured

for all who enter into this new covenant:

(i) Having given His Son to die such a death, there is nothing which God will fail to lavish upon those who are saved by it (*Rom.* 8: 32; *Heb.* 4: 16).

(ii) Every spiritual benefit in this life and in that to come is assured (*Eph.* 1: 3 ff).

(iii) Eternal life is the gift of Christ to those who are saved by His death (*John* 17: 2; 14: 1–6).

(e) These benefits may be summed up in the word "reconciliation". Through God's work in Christ of reconciling the world to Himself, men's sins and misdeeds need no longer be held against them (*II Cor.* 5: 18, 19); united to Christ a man may receive a new life altogether (*II Cor.* 5: 17) and be declared righteous by God (*II Cor.* 5: 21).

8. Only by Christ's death may we be reconciled to God.

The message of the gospel is plain: be reconciled to God through Christ (*II Cor.* 5: 18, 20).

21. THE RESURRECTION

Question: What is the significance of the Resurrection of Christ?

Answer: God the Father raised Christ from the dead, in fulfilment of the Scriptures and of Christ's promises, declaring Christ to be His Son, and His acceptance of Christ's redemptive work, guaranteeing the justification, spiritual life and final resurrection of all believers.

1. The fact of the Resurrection is at the core of the gospel.

(a) The Resurrection was the work of the Father (*Acts* 2: 24; 3: 15; 10: 40; *Eph.* 1: 20; Col. 2: 12) by the power of the Spirit (*Rom.* 8: 11; *I Pet.* 3: 18).

(b) The centrality of the Resurrection is seen in the trouble to which the New Testament goes, and the Gospels especially, to give the facts concerning our Lord's appearances. Jesus appeared to Mary Magdalene (*Mark* 16: 9; *John* 20: 18), the women (*Matt.* 28: 9), Simon Peter (*Luke* 24: 34), two disciples (*Luke* 24: 13–31), all the apostles, except Thomas (*John* 20: 19, 24), Thomas himself (*John* 20: 26), the apostles at the Sea of Tiberias (*John* 21: 1), the apostles in Galilee (*Matt.* 28: 16, 17), about 500 brethren (*I Cor.* 15: 6), James (*I Cor.* 15: 7), all the apostles (*Luke* 24: 51; *Acts* 1: 9; *I Cor.* 15: 7), Paul (*I Cor.* 15: 8).

2. The fact of the Resurrection was central in the witness of the apostles.

(a) "We are witnesses" was their theme (*Acts* 2: 24; *Acts* 3: 15; *I Cor.* 15: 14, 15).

(b) To be an apostle a man had to be a witness to Christ's Resurrection (*Acts* 1: 22).

(c) The distinctive characteristic of their preaching was the power with which they bore witness to the Resurrection of Christ (*Acts* 4: 30, 33).

(d) They knew and preached a living Christ (*Acts* 25: 19; *II Tim.* 2: 8).

3. The Old Testament Scriptures demanded that the Resurrection should take place.

(a) The Messiah was not to be allowed to experience corruption (*Ps.* 16: 10; *Acts* 13: 34, 35).

(b) Everything written about Christ in the Law of Moses, the prophets and the Psalms demanded fulfilment (*Luke* 24: 44; *John* 20: 9; *Acts* 26: 22, 23).

4. Christ had foretold His Resurrection.

(a) At the beginning of His ministry He had hinted at it (*John* 2: 19–22).

(b) When Peter confessed Jesus as the Messiah, the first clear revelation about the Resurrection was given to the disciples (*Matt.* 16: 21).

(c) The experience of the Transfiguration was not to be reported until after the Resurrection (*Mark* 9: 9).

(d) Jesus clearly foretold His Resurrection to the disciples (*Matt.* 20: 19; *Mark* 14: 28).

5. The Resurrection was necessary to demonstrate irrefutably the truth of all Christ's claims.

(a) By His life, words and miracles Jesus had made many claims (*Luke* 11: 20; *John* 14: 6; 11: 25; 10: 18).

(b) From the lips of a mere man such claims would have been blasphemous (*Matt.* 26: 63–66). If such a one died and remained dead as other men then the charge of imposter would be true but if He rose again from the dead the truth of His claim—that He was from God and was the Son of God—would be vindicated. (*Matt.* 27: 63–66; cf. *Acts* 5: 38, 39, applying the latter words for the moment to the Resurrection.)

6. The Resurrection was necessary to give final proof of Christ's deity.

(a) The Resurrection was a declaration of the Father, as promised in the Old Testament, that Jesus is His Son (*Ps.* 2: 7; *Acts* 13: 33).

(b) By raising Christ to life again by the power of the Holy Spirit, God the Father patently marked Christ out as His Son—the Son of God, the Second Person of the Trinity (*Rom.* 1: 4).

(c) It was impossible for death to keep Christ in its grip (*Acts* 2: 24)—of God alone could such a claim be justly made.

7. Without the Resurrection we would not know that Christ's death achieved its objects so far as sin is concerned.

(a) Without it the gospel would be null and void (*I Cor.* 15: 14).

(b) Without it there would be no hope of forgiveness (*I Cor.* 15: 17).

(c) Without it men would be utterly lost with no possibility of salvation (*I Cor.* 15: 19).

(d) By the Resurrection the acquittal from every charge of all who believe is declared (*Rom.* 4: 25; 8: 34).

8. The Resurrection was necessary to provide a solid basis for faith.

(a) Christ showed Himself alive by many infallible proofs (*Acts* 1: 3).

(b) God's acceptance of Christ's work is demonstrated by the Resurrection (see 7, above): through Christ men may approach God with confidence (*I Pet.* 1: 21).

(c) The Resurrection gives our faith substance (*Rom.* 10: 9, 10; *I Cor.* 15: 17).

9. The Resurrection was necessary to give a living hope.

(a) The Christian's hope or assurance arises from Christ's Resurrection: through His Resurrection we receive new life (*I Pet.* 1: 3; *Rom.* 6: 4; *Col.* 2: 12).

(b) Believers have a living hope regarding the resurrection of the dead, for God who raised up Christ shall raise up them also (*I Cor.* 15: 20, 23; *Acts* 26: 23; *I Cor.* 6: 14; *II Cor.* 4: 14).

(c) Believers have a living hope regarding the resurrection of the body, for Christ's Resurrection is the pattern of theirs (*Luke* 24: 35, 39, 43; *John* 20: 20, 27; *Phil.* 3: 21; *Rom.* 6: 5; *I Cor.* 15: 49).

10. The Resurrection was necessary in order to demonstrate that Christ may be known today.

(a) Paul proved the truth of this experience in his day, at first to his great amazement (*Acts* 9: 1–9).

(b) Paul then made the knowing of Christ and the experiencing of the power of His Resurrection the objective of his life (*Phil.* 3: 10).

11. The Resurrection was necessary to give assurance of the just judgment of the world.

(a) Men wrongly condemned Christ; God the Father vindicated Him by the Resurrection, thereby judging those who dealt with Christ so falsely (*Acts* 2: 22–24).

(b) God will have the world judged and justly judged by Christ—He has given assurance of this by the Resurrection (*Acts* 17: 31).

12. The Resurrection was necessary to illustrate that the last word is always with God.

Men called Christ a "deceiver"; God the Father—by the Resurrection—declared Him "My Son" (*Matt.* 27: 63–66; *Ps.* 2: 7; *Rom.* 1: 4).

22. THE ASCENSION

Question: What happened when Christ ascended to heaven?

Answer: Christ returned to the Father and was glorified—the final proof of His completed sacrificial work. He entered then upon His work as priest and king upon the throne—no longer needing to offer atoning sacrifice to God—giving gifts to His Church, and guaranteeing her security and final presence with Him in heaven. He waits now for the time of His final victory.

1. The Ascension.

(a) The Ascension was a vital link in a chain of fulfilled prophecy, promised both in the Old Testament (*Ps.* 110: 1; *Acts* 2: 32–36) and by Christ Himself (*Matt.* 26: 64; *John* 6: 62; 7: 33; 14: 28; 16: 5; 20: 17).

(b) It took place forty days after the Resurrection (*Acts* 1: 3).

(c) It took place at the Mount of Olives (*Luke* 24: 50; cf. *Mark* 11: 1; *Acts* 1: 12).

(d) It was witnessed by the apostles, after He had talked with them (*Mark* 16: 19) and lifted up His hands to bless them (*Luke* 24: 50, 51).

(e) He was lifted up, and a cloud took Him out of their sight (*Acts* 1: 9).

(f) The return of Christ will be after the pattern of the Ascension (*Acts* 1: 11).

2. What the Ascension was.

(a) It was an act of God's power (*Eph.* 1: 19–22).

(b) It was the necessary completion of Christ's death and resurrection: it proved the full acceptance by God of His single sacrifice for sins for all time (*Heb.* 10: 12); it marked Christ out as Lord, even as the Resurrection marked Him out as the Son of God (*Phil.* 2: 9–11; *Acts* 2: 34–36; cf. *Rom.* 1: 4).

(c) It was the visible ascent of Christ, according to His human nature, from earth to heaven (*Mark* 16: 19; *I Pet.* 3: 22): He was exalted to the place in the universe He had laid aside when He humbled Himself to assume our humanity (*Eph.* 4: 9, 10).

(d) It marked Christ's return to the Father: He went to Him who had sent Him into the world (*John* 6: 62; 7: 33; 14: 28; 16: 5; 20: 17).

(e) It included a further glorification of the human nature of Christ: He carried His humanity with Him back to heaven (*Heb.* 2: 14–18; 4: 14–16), and He was highly exalted and glorified in doing so (*Acts* 2: 33; *John* 7: 39; *I Tim.* 3: 16), the Father honouring Him with the highest possible honour (*Eph.* 1: 20–22).

3. The significance of the Ascension.

(a) God the Father's acceptance of His Son into glory declared decisively and finally His acceptance of Christ's sacrifice for our sins (*Heb.* 1: 3; 9: 12; 10: 11–14).

(b) Christ entered upon His work as a royal priest upon the throne, no longer needing to offer atoning sacrifice to God (*Heb.* 7: 26; 8: 1; 10: 21); He entered into heaven to appear now before God on our behalf, representing our cause before the Father (*Heb.* 9: 24).

(c) Christ, demonstrated by the Ascension to be Lord (*Matt.* 28: 18; *Acts* 2: 36), entered upon His work as king; He is seated at the right hand of God (*Matt.* 26: 64; *Acts* 2: 33; *Rom.* 8: 34; *Col.* 3: 1; *Heb.* 1: 3; 10: 12; 12: 2; *I Pet.* 3: 22), a picture of the unique position the Father has given Him of kingly power and authority over angels, authorities and powers in heaven and on earth (*Heb.* 1: 13; *Dan.* 7: 13, 14; *Matt.* 26: 64; *Eph.* 1: 21, 22; 4: 10; *Col.* 1: 16–18; *I Pet.* 3: 22).

(d) Christ ascended to receive, as conqueror, the gifts promised Him for His Church (*Eph.* 4: 8; *Ps.* 68: 18): He ascended to send forth the Holy Spirit (*John* 7: 39; 16: 7; *Acts* 2: 33).

(e) The Ascension of Christ and the consequent outpouring of the Spirit made possible the numerous gifts of the Spirit which the Church enjoys (*Eph.* 4: 8, 11–13).

(f) Christ ascended to prepare a place for Christians (*John* 14: 2): He is their forerunner, preparing the way for them (*Heb.* 6: 20; cf. *Acts* 7: 56).

(g) Christians are already set with Christ in heavenly places, for they are made to share by grace, through faith, the Resurrection and Ascension of Christ (*Eph.* 2: 6): their citizenship is now in heaven and their thoughts and affections should be set there (*Phil.* 3: 20; *Col.* 3: 1, 2).

(h) In Christ's Ascension Christians have the assurance of a place in heaven (*II Cor.* 4: 14; *John* 14: 19) and of their own glorification (*Phil.* 3: 21): God's purpose in giving Christians a share in the Resurrection and Ascension of Christ is that in the coming ages He might show the immeasurable riches of His grace in kindness toward them in Christ Jesus (*John* 17: 24; *Eph.* 2: 7).

4. What Christ does at God's right hand.

(a) He lives for ever, holding a permanent priesthood (*Rev.* 1: 18; *Heb.* 7: 24).

(b) He rules and protects His Church as its Head (*Eph.* 1: 22, 23), helping the members in need (*Heb.* 2: 18; 4: 15), and giving the power to do great works (*John* 14: 12).

(c) He governs the universe, and to the end that God's purposes for the Church may be fulfilled (*Heb.* 1: 3; *Eph.* 1: 5–14).

(d) He intercedes for His people on the basis of His completed sacrifice (*Rom.* 8: 34): He is our Advocate with the Father (*I John* 2: 1).

(e) He waits for the time of His final victory: all His enemies shall be subdued (*Ps.* 110: 1; *Acts* 2: 35; *I Cor.* 15: 24–26; *Heb.* 10: 13).

(f) His Ascension in power is the prelude to His coming in power as the divine Judge (*Dan.* 7: 13, 14; *Matt.* 26: 64; *John* 14: 28; *Acts* 10: 42; *II Thess.* 1: 6–10).

23. THE HOLY SPIRIT

Question: Who is the Holy Spirit?

Answer: He is the Lord and Giver of Life, the third Person of the Trinity to be worshipped and glorified with the Father and the Son. He is most commonly presented to us as the Executor of God's purposes, whether in creation, revelation or redemption.

1. He is unique.

There is but one Spirit (*I Cor.* 12: 13; *Eph.* 4: 4).

2. He is a Person—not simply an influence or a power.

(a) He is spoken of as "He" and not as "It" (*John* 16: 13).

(b) He is spoken of as a Person—the Comforter or Advocate (*John* 14: 16, 26; 15: 26; 16: 7).

(c) He may be grieved (*Isa.* 63: 10; *Eph.* 4: 30).

(d) He is affronted by the apostate (*Heb.* 10: 29).

3. He is God.

(a) He is the Spirit of the living God (*II Cor.* 3: 3; *I Pet.* 4: 14).

(b) Sovereignty is ascribed to Him (*I Cor.* 12: 11).

(c) Old Testament references to God are revealed in the New Testament to have been references to the Holy Spirit (*Ex.* 17: 7; cf. *Heb.* 3: 7–9; *Isa.* 6: 3, 8–10; cf. *Acts* 28: 25–27; *Ps.* 78: 17, 21; cf. *Acts* 7: 51).

(d) The qualities ascribed to the Holy Spirit are the qualities ascribed everywhere to God alone: He is everywhere present (*Ps.* 139: 7–13; *I Cor.* 12: 13); He knows all things (*I Cor.* 2: 10); He has all power (*Luke* 1: 35; *Rom.* 8: 11; 15: 19).

(e) To lie to the Spirit is to lie to God (*Acts* 5: 3, 4, 5).

(f) He is to be obeyed (*Gal.* 5: 16–24).

(g) Blasphemy against Him is the worst of all sins (*Matt.* 12: 31 ff; *Mark* 3: 28 f; *Luke* 12: 10).

(h) His intercession is according to the will of God (*Rom.* 8: 27).

(i) To affront the Spirit is to deserve the severest judgment (*Heb.* 10: 29).

4. He is the Third Person of the Trinity.

(a) He is one with the Father and the Son (*Matt.* 28: 19; *II Cor.* 13: 14; *I Cor.* 12: 4–6; *Eph.* 4: 4–6).

(b) He is sent by both the Father and the Son and He acts for them both (*John* 15: 26).

5. He was the Agent of God's first creation.

(a) He was active in creation, bringing order out of chaos (*Gen.* 1: 2).

(b) By God's Spirit the heavens were made beautiful (*Job* 26: 13).

(c) Man was made by the Spirit of God (*Job* 33: 4; cf. *Gen.* 2: 7; *Ps.* 104: 29, 30).

6. He is the Author of the Scriptures.

(a) He inspired the Scriptures (*II Tim.* 3: 16): men impelled by the Holy Spirit spoke and wrote from God (*II Pet.* 1: 21; *Acts* 1: 16).

(b) The Scriptures are His testimony (*Heb.* 10: 15).

(c) He compelled the prophets to speak (*Ezek.* 11: 5; *Zech.* 7: 12; *Micah* 3: 8).

(d) He inspired men to prophesy (*Luke* 1: 67; 2: 26, 27, 29–32).

(e) He revealed to the apostles and prophets the truth concerning Christ and the gospel at the time determined by God (*Eph.* 3: 5, 6).

(f) He speaks today through the Scriptures (*Heb.* 3: 7).

7. He was active with regard to the Incarnation.

(a) By His power the virgin conception was accomplished (*Luke* 1: 35).

(b) Mary was found with child by the Holy Spirit (*Matt.* 1: 18, 20).

(c) The Spirit descended upon Jesus in a special manner at His baptism (*Mark* 1: 10 f).

(d) The Spirit led and directed Christ during His ministry (*Matt.* 4: 1; *Mark* 1: 12).

(e) The Spirit equipped Christ for His ministry (*Luke* 4: 1, 18; *Acts* 10: 38).

(f) Christ possessed the Spirit in a measureless manner (*John* 3: 34).

(g) Christ's works of power were by the power of the Spirit of God which was His (*Luke* 11: 20; cf. *Matt.* 12: 28; *Acts* 10: 38).

(h) The Spirit gave Christ joy during His earthly life and ministry (*Luke* 10: 21).

(i) The Spirit raised Christ from the dead (*Acts* 2: 24; cf. *I Pet.* 3: 18; *Heb.* 13: 20; cf. *Rom.* 1: 4).

8. He is the Agent of God's new creation in Christ—the Church.

(a) The Holy Spirit's activity in God's new creation is all-important:

(i) He puts the redeemed in possession of the results of the Father's love and the mediation of Christ (*II Cor.* 3: 8; *John* 7: 39);

(ii) Justification takes place through the name of the Lord Jesus and the Spirit of God (*I Cor.* 6: 11; *I Pet.* 1: 2);

(iii) Through the Spirit the redeemed are brought into the one body, the Church, this act being described as a baptism (*I Cor.* 12: 13);

(iv) The Spirit is the Author of the new birth (*John* 3: 5, 6; *II Cor.* 5: 17). Whereas the written law condemns to death, the Spirit gives life (*II Cor.* 3: 6; *Gal.* 5: 25). Where the Spirit is there is life (*Ezek.* 37: 1–14; *Rom.* 8: 2, 11; *John* 6: 63).

(b) The Holy Spirit is directly associated with the extension of God's new creation—the Church (*Matt.* 28: 19; cf. *Acts* 1: 4, 8):

(i) He ensures that messengers are raised up and men sent forth to proclaim the gospel (*Matt.* 9: 38; cf. *Acts* 13: 2, 4; 16: 6, 7, 10; 20: 28);

(ii) He accompanies the preaching of the gospel with His power (*I Pet.* 1: 12);

(iii) He shows men their need of salvation by convicting them of sin (*John* 16: 8–11);

(iv) He bears witness to Christ (*John* 15: 26), and by His influence men are enabled to say "Jesus is Lord" (*I Cor.* 12: 3);

(v) Given to every believer as a result of Christ's work (*John* 7: 39), He binds believers together in one body in spiritual unity (*Eph.* 4: 3, 4);

(vi) For the care of the Church the Spirit raises up guardians or pastors (*Acts* 20: 28);

(vii) He allots varying gifts to Christians (*Rom.* 12: 6–8);

(viii) In each Christian the Spirit desires to manifest Himself in some particular way, for some useful purpose (*I Cor.* 12: 4–11);

(ix) The Spirit's purpose in all this is to equip God's people for work in Christ's service, to the building up of the body of Christ (*Eph.* 4: 11–13).

24. THE HOLY SPIRIT AND THE CHRISTIAN

Question: What is the relationship of the Holy Spirit to the Christian?

Answer: The Holy Spirit is the gift of the Father and the Son to the believer to live within him: giving him spiritual life; assuring him of his sonship; and communicating to him the benefits of the gospel.

1. The Holy Spirit is Christ's promised gift to the believer.

(a) Christ asked the Father that the Spirit might be the believer's possession (*John* 14: 16).

(b) The Spirit is sent by Christ from the Father (*John* 15: 26; 16: 7).

(c) He is called sometimes "the Spirit of Christ" (*Acts* 16: 7; *Rom.* 8: 9; *I Pet.* 1: 11).

(d) He is received not by keeping the law but by believing the good news made known through Jesus Christ (*Gal.* 3: 2, 3, 14).

2. The Holy Spirit works in the believer the miracle of the new birth.

(a) Unless a man is born anew by the Holy Spirit he cannot see the kingdom of God (*John* 3: 3, 5).

(b) The life of the Christian is begun in the Spirit (*Gal.* 3: 3).

(c) If a man does not have the Spirit of Christ he does not belong to Christ (*Rom.* 8: 9).

3. The Holy Spirit is, therefore, the source of the believer's spiritual life (*Gal.* 5: 25).

(a) By nature men are spiritually dead (*Eph.* 2: 1).

(b) The Spirit brings spiritual life to dead men (*Eph.* 2: 1 f; cf. *Ezek.* 37: 14; *Rom.* 8: 2, 11; *John* 6: 63).

4. The Holy Spirit testifies with the Christian's spirit that he is a child of God (*Rom.* 8: 16).

(a) He makes the believer sure of his union with Christ (*I John* 3: 24; 4: 13).

(b) The Spirit cries in our hearts as the Spirit of God's Son, "Abba! Father!" (*Gal.* 4: 6).

5. The Holy Spirit dwells within the Christian believer.

(a) The possession of the Spirit is the Christian's distinguishing mark (*Rom.* 8: 9).

(b) The Christian's body is the shrine of the indwelling Holy Spirit (*I Cor.* 3: 16 f; 6: 19; cf. *Isa.* 57: 15; *II Tim.* 1: 14).

(c) By reason of the Spirit abiding with him, and in him, the Christian knows Him (*John* 14: 17).

(d) The Spirit dwells within the Christian for ever (*John* 14: 16 f).

6. The Holy Spirit sanctifies the Christian.

(a) The Holy Spirit makes the Christian holy—He sets him apart for God (*II Thess.* 2: 13; *I Pet.* 1: 2).

(b) The Holy Spirit is completely contrary in His desires to the desires of the Christian's lower nature (*Gal.* 5: 16), and He proceeds to fight against this lower nature (*Gal.* 5: 17).

(c) The Holy Spirit enables the Christian to put to death the deeds of the body—those activities of his lower nature—which displease God (*Rom.* 8: 13).

(d) By the power of the Spirit the Christian's character is transformed (*Gal.* 5: 22 f).

7. The Holy Spirit produces the character of Christ in the Christian.

(a) The Holy Spirit purposes to transfigure the Christian into the Lord's likeness, from splendour to splendour (*II Cor.* 3: 18).

(b) Love, joy, peace, patience, kindness, goodness, fidelity, gentleness, and self-control are His fruit (*Gal.* 5: 22, 23).

(c) We would expect the Holy Spirit to produce these characteristics for He is the Spirit of Christ (*Acts* 16: 7; *Rom.* 8: 9; *Gal.* 4: 6; *Phil.* 1: 19; *I Pet.* 1: 11).

8. The Holy Spirit strengthens the Christian.

(a) His resources are available to him (*Phil.* 1: 19).

(b) He upholds him (*Acts* 9: 31).

(c) He gives continuous help in times of difficulty and opposition (*I Pet.* 4: 14).

9. The Holy Spirit helps the Christian to pray.

(a) He helps him to pray at all times (*Eph.* 6: 18).

(b) He inspires prayer by the love He places in the Christian's heart for his fellow-believers (*Rom.* 15: 30).

(c) He prompts the Christian's "groanings"—those inner feelings which cannot find expression in words—for He is in them, and He conveys their meaning to the Father (*Rom.* 8: 26).

10. The Holy Spirit instructs the Christian, interpreting to him the Scriptures.

(a) The Holy Spirit explores everything: even the depths of God's own nature (*I Cor.* 2: 11).

(b) The Spirit alone knows what God is (*I Cor.* 2: 11).

(c) The Spirit reveals to the Christian things which would otherwise be hidden to him (*I Cor.* 2: 10).

(d) The Spirit makes known to the Christian all that God of His own grace gives him (*I Cor.* 2: 12).

(e) The Spirit bears witness pre-eminently to Christ (*John* 15: 26).

(f) The Spirit gives the Christian discernment (*I Cor.* 2: 14).

(g) The Spirit guides the Christian into all the truth (*John* 16: 13).

(h) The Spirit speaks to him today in the Scriptures (*Heb.* 3: 7).

11. The Holy Spirit gives power to the Christian's endeavours in witness.

(a) He gives power to witness and to fulfil the Lord's command to evangelise (*Matt.* 28: 19; cf. *Acts* 1: 4, 8).

(b) He makes preaching to carry conviction by spiritual power (*I Cor.* 2: 4 f).

12. The Holy Spirit guides the Christian.

(a) He guides the Christian into the way of victory over sin (*Gal.* 5: 16).

(b) He leads and directs the Christian in his service for God (*Acts* 16: 6, 7; *Rom.* 8: 14).

(c) He prompts right action at particular times (*Luke* 2: 27).

(d) He guides as to the right solution of difficult problems (*Acts* 15: 28).

13. The Holy Spirit imparts gifts to the Christian for the service of God (*Rom.* 12: 6–8).

(a) He equips the Christian to help in the task of building up Christ's Church (*Eph.* 4: 11–13).

(b) He gives the right gift or gifts for all varieties of service and the many forms of work there are (*I Cor.* 12: 4, 5, 6).

(c) He enables the Christian to fulfil a useful purpose within the Church (*I Cor.* 12: 7).

14. The Holy Spirit communicates the spiritual benefits of the gospel to the Christian.

(a) He makes God's love to flood his heart (*Rom.* 5: 5).

(b) He communicates joy (*Rom.* 14: 17; *I Thess.* 1: 6).

(c) He makes the Christian to overflow with the joy of the Christian hope (*Rom.* 15: 13; *Gal.* 5: 5).

15. The Holy Spirit is God's pledge to the Christian of what is to come to him in the future (*II Cor.* 1: 22).

(a) God has shaped the Christian for a wonderful future in glory (*II Cor.* 4: 16–5: 5).

(b) The Christian is reborn by the Spirit to a great and wonderful inheritance which nothing can destroy or spoil or wither (*I Pet.* 1: 4; *Eph.* 1: 14).

(c) The Spirit is the pledge that the Christian shall enter upon this inheritance (*Eph.* 1: 14).

16. The Christian's appropriation of the help of the Holy Spirit.

(a) The Holy Spirit's illumination is given in answer to prayer (*Eph.* 1: 16, 17).

(b) The Holy Spirit is given in His fullness to the Christian as the Christian seeks such from God (*Luke* 11: 13).

(c) As the Christian lives in obedience to God, so he knows more and more of the Spirit (*Acts* 5: 32).

(d) The Christian is to let the Spirit direct the course of his life (*Gal.* 5: 25).

25. DEFINING A CHRISTIAN

Question: What is a Christian?

Answer: A Christian is one who, having understood the ABC of the gospel of Christ, has received

Christ, has taken his stand upon Him, and experiences salvation through Him.

1. The gospel which has to be understood.

(a) The appointed time, concerning which the prophets in the Old Testament had spoken and to which the people of God had looked forward, has come. Through Christ, God has visited and redeemed His people (*Acts* 2: 16–21).

(b) This act of God, intervening in human history, is to be seen in the life of Jesus Christ, the Messiah, sent by God, rejected, and put to death by men, and raised up by God on the third day (*Acts* 2: 32, 36).

(c) By His death and resurrection Jesus Christ has conquered sin and death and opened the kingdom of heaven to all believers. In no one else is there to be found salvation (*Acts* 4: 12).

(d) The proofs of God's present power in the world are to be found in the fact of the resurrection and the evidences of the Holy Spirit's working in the Church (*Rom.* 1: 4; *Eph.* 1: 19, 20; *Acts* 4: 33).

(e) This is but the beginning of God's kingdom. Christ will come again as Judge, and God's kingdom will be finally established (*Acts* 3: 20, 21; 17: 30, 31; *II Thess.* 1: 7–10).

(f) Therefore all men everywhere should repent and be baptised in the name of Jesus the Messiah for the forgiveness of their sins, and thus receive the gift of the Holy Spirit (*Acts* 2: 38).

2. Fundamental to a person's understanding of the gospel is his appreciation, therefore, of at least the following truths:

(a) Jesus is the Christ, the Son of God (*John* 20: 31; *Acts* 8: 37).

(b) Christ's purpose in coming into the world and in dying upon the cross was to save sinners (*I Tim.* 1: 15).

(c) Christ's resurrection was God the Father's declaration of Christ as His Son and His satisfaction with His work (*Rom.* 1: 4).

(d) To enter into the benefits of Christ's work—to know forgiveness, the gift of God's Spirit and a place in His kingdom—repentance and open confession of Christ are required (*Acts* 2: 38).

(e) A Christian recognises his personal sinfulness (*Rom.* 7: 24).

(f) A Christian knows his personal indebtedness to Christ in that He gave His life a ransom for him (*Mark* 10: 45; *Gal.* 2: 20; *I Pet.* 2: 24).

3. The benefits the gospel promises.

(a) Deliverance from condemnation (*John* 3: 18; *Rom.* 8: 1).

(b) Justification (*I Cor.* 6: 11).

(c) The gift of the Holy Spirit (*I Cor.* 2: 12).

(d) Eternal life (*John* 3: 16, 36).

(e) Reconciliation with God (*II Cor.* 5: 18–21).

(f) Membership of the people of God (*I Pet.* 2: 9, 10).

(g) Membership of the kingdom of God (*Col.* 1: 13).

(h) The resurrection of the body (*I Cor.* 6: 14).

(i) Endless fellowship with Christ (*John* 14: 4; *I Thess.* 4: 17).

4. A Christian is one who, having

understood the ABC of the gospel, has received Christ.

(a) The words "believe" and "receive" are more or less identical (*John* 1: 12; *I Cor.* 15: 1, 2).

(b) The call to believe on the Lord Jesus Christ for salvation comes home to the individual with the conviction and power of the Holy Spirit (*I Cor.* 2: 1–5; *I Thess.* 1: 5).

(c) The call of God to believe on the Lord Jesus Christ is responded to (*Acts* 16: 31, 34; *I Cor.* 1: 9, 23, 24; *Rom.* 10: 9).

(d) Christ is received into the life, and spiritual birth takes place by the Holy Spirit (*John* 1: 12, 13; 3: 3, 7).

5. A Christian is one who, having understood the ABC of the gospel, has received Christ, and takes his stand upon Christ.

(a) He recognises that being bought with a price, he does not belong to himself any more (*I Cor.* 6: 20; 7: 23).

(b) The word "stand" speaks of assurance: he knows that he has eternal life (*I John* 5: 13; cf. *I John* 2: 3, 5; 3: 14; 4: 13).

(c) The expression "taking a stand" implies action: his stand is seen first by baptism (*Acts* 2: 38, 41; *I Cor.* 1: 13), and the confession of his lips that Jesus is Lord (*Rom.* 10: 9).

(d) He takes his stand by identifying himself with all who have similarly received the gospel (*Acts* 2: 41–47; *I Cor.* 1: 2; 6: 1, 2).

(e) He recognises himself to be a member of the body of Christ, the Church (*I Cor.* 12: 13, 27).

(f) He recognises himself to be God's—dedicated to God in Christ (*I Cor.* 1: 2; 6: 11).

(g) He loves the Lord Jesus Christ and shows that love by obedience (*I Cor.* 16: 22; *John* 14: 21).

(h) He waits expectantly for Christ (*I Cor.* 1: 7; 11: 26; 16: 22; *I Thess.* 1: 10).

6. A Christian is one who, having understood the ABC of the gospel, has received Christ, and having taken his stand upon Christ, experiences salvation through Christ.

(a) When the Christian first believed, he experienced salvation, e.g. he was washed, sanctified and justified (*I Cor.* 6: 11), he was enriched by Christ (*I Cor.* 1: 5); he found the cross the power of God (*I Cor.* 1: 18), and Christ became to him all he needed (*I Cor.* 1: 30).

(b) But salvation is also the Christian's present experience: he continues to call on the name of the Lord Jesus (*I Cor.* 1: 2); he continues to receive God's grace (*I Cor.* 1: 5; 15: 10; 16: 23); he continues to be enriched by Christ (*I Cor.* 1: 5).

(c) He is delivered from his old state of sin (*I Cor.* 15: 17); he is freed from the power of sin (*Rom.* 8: 2; *I Cor.* 6: 12; 8: 9).

(d) He knows the power of the Spirit in his life (*I Cor.* 6: 19, 20; 12: 7).

(e) He is kept by Christ (*I Cor.* 1: 8; *I Pet.* 1: 5).

7. Being a Christian.

(a) Belief in God alone does not make a man a Christian (*Jas.* 2: 19).

(b) Being a Christian is not a matter of being born in the right country or belonging to the right race (*John* 1: 13).

(c) Being a Christian is not just being zealously religious, for one can be such without being a Christian (*Rom.* 10: 2, 3).

(d) Being a Christian is not simply trying one's best to please God by good works (*Eph.* 2: 9).

(e) A Christian knows that what matters is not self-achieved righteousness gained by obedience to the law, but rather that genuine righteousness which God gives as we put our faith in Christ (*Phil.* 3: 9).

(f) The word "Christian" began as a description of the disciples of Christ (*Acts* 11: 26; 9: 1).

(g) A Christian is not self-made, but Christ-made (*II Cor.* 5: 17; *John* 3: 3, 7).

(h) All Bible definitions or descriptions of a Christian have one thing in common: they all imply a personal relationship to Christ (*I Cor.* 1: 9; *I John* 1: 3; *Col.* 3: 1).

(i) The name "Christian" is something which the Christian is to live up to (*I Pet.* 4: 16).

(j) When a man is a Christian, he would that all might become Christians too (*Acts* 26: 29; *Rom.* 10: 1).

26. REGENERATION

Question: What is regeneration?

Answer: It is the supernatural work of the Holy Spirit by which those who were dead in trespasses and sins are made spiritually alive.

1. Regeneration deals with men's dead spiritual state.

(a) Men are by nature dead in trespasses and sins (*Eph.* 2: 1).

(b) Human nature is sinful (*Rom.* 8: 3).

(c) Human life is governed very much by man's lower nature and its desires (*Rom.* 8: 4, 5).

(d) Whilst men's lives are governed by their lower nature, besides being in a state of hostility to God, they cannot please God (*Rom.* 8: 7, 8).

(e) Spiritual things are folly and beyond the grasp of unregenerate man (*I Cor.* 2: 14).

(f) Regeneration deals with this dead condition of men (*Eph.* 2: 1) —they are made alive.

2. Men's dead spiritual state is beyond the power of men to deal with.

(a) With lives governed by their lower nature men cannot please God (*John* 3: 6; *Rom.* 8: 7, 8).

(b) Deeds done by men in righteousness are not sufficient to accomplish the task of giving spiritual life (*Tit.* 3: 5).

(c) Men can do no more about it than they can change the colour of their skin or animals their fur (*Jer.* 13: 23).

3. Regeneration is the supernatural work of the Holy Spirit.

(a) It is supernatural because it is due to the immediate power of Almighty God—witnessed, for example, in Paul's regeneration (*Acts* 9: 1–9; *I Cor.* 15: 8; *Gal.* 1: 15, 16).

(b) The Holy Spirit makes men spiritually alive (*Eph.* 2: 1).

(c) He acts according to the will of God the Father (*John* 1: 13; *II Cor.* 5: 18; *Gal.* 4: 6; *Tit.* 3: 5; *Jas.* 1: 18).

(d) He acts on the grounds of Christ's saving work by His death and resurrection (*Tit.* 3: 6; *I Pet.* 1: 2, 3).

(e) The Spirit's work of regeneration is a work of tremendous power—of creative power (*II Cor.* 4: 6; 5: 17).

(f) His work is as sovereign, mysterious and irresistible as that of the wind (*John* 3: 8).

(g) It is as dramatic as birth (*John* 3: 3) and resurrection (*Eph.* 2: 5; *Col.* 2: 13).

(h) The unenlightened human mind finds the new birth impossible to understand because of its supernatural character (*John* 3: 4).

4. Various descriptions are given of this work of the Spirit.

(a) It is spoken of as a birth (*John* 3: 3, 6, 7, 8; *Jas.* 1: 18; *I Pet.* 1: 23).

(b) It is spoken of in terms of adoption: by it men become the children of God (*John* 1: 12, 13; *Rom.* 8: 15, 16).

(c) It is spoken of as a new creation (*II Cor.* 5: 17).

(d) It is spoken of as renewal (*Tit.* 3: 5).

(e) It is spoken of as passing out of death into life (*I John* 3: 14; 4: 7).

5. Regeneration is a necessity if men are to enter heaven.

(a) Unless a man is born anew, he cannot see the kingdom of God (*John* 3: 3).

(b) Only through being born anew can a man have "a living hope" (*I Pet.* 1: 3).

6. The Holy Spirit uses various means to bring to fulfilment His work of regeneration in men's lives.

(a) The word of truth—i.e. the inspired Scriptures—is His main instrument.

(b) The living and abiding Word of God is imperishable seed which brings forth spiritual life under the power of the Spirit (*I Pet.* 1: 23).

(c) The preaching of the gospel is the most frequent means, therefore, He uses to bring His work to light (*I Pet.* 1: 25).

(d) The Holy Spirit accompanies true gospel preaching with life-giving power (*I Cor.* 2: 2–5; *I Thess.* 1: 5, 6).

(e) He uses men, therefore, who preach the gospel (*I Cor.* 4: 15; *II Cor.* 5: 20).

7. There may be visible evidences sometimes that the Holy Spirit's work of regeneration is taking place but these evidences are for the most part beyond observation (*John* 3: 8).

(a) Conviction of sin is frequently seen to be present (*John* 16: 8–11; *Acts* 2: 37).

(b) It is as the regenerate man looks back after his regeneration that he realises that God was at work in his life before ever he realised it (*Gal.* 1: 11–16).

8. The work of regeneration may be said to have taken place when a man has saving faith in Christ (*John* 1: 12, 13; *II Thess.* 2: 13).

(a) Faith is more the effect of regeneration than the cause of it, insofar as it is the Holy Spirit who brings men to faith in Christ: He opens men's hearts to give heed to the message of the gospel (*Acts* 16: 14).

(b) Faith and regeneration, however, may take place at more or less the same time (*Acts* 2: 37–41; 8: 26–38).

9. The effects of the work of regeneration in a man's life.

(a) The most important truth is that he has a new life implanted in him by the Holy Spirit: the Holy Spirit enters the soul and abides there as a principle of a new life (*Rom.* 7: 6; 8: 9).

(b) He is made clean, or sanctified by the Spirit (*Tit.* 3: 5).

(c) He is renewed spiritually (*Tit.* 3: 5); he has newness of life (*Rom.* 6: 4).

(d) He has a new heart—a heart which wants to obey God (*Ezek.* 11: 19, 20).

(e) He is a new creation—the old has passed away, the new has come (*II Cor.* 5: 17; *Gal.* 6: 15).

(f) This new creation is seen in good works produced in the life, which are pleasing to God (*Eph.* 2: 10).

(g) God is at work in the man (*Phil.* 2: 13; *Heb.* 13: 21).

(h) The man is no longer enslaved by sin (*Rom.* 6: 6).

(i) He receives a new nature—the divine nature (*II Pet.* 1: 4)—created after the likeness of God in true righteousness and holiness (*Eph.* 4: 24; *Col.* 3: 10; *Rom.* 8: 29).

(j) This inner nature is renewed every day (*II Cor.* 4: 16).

(k) As a result of this new life and nature, he can appreciate spiritual things because he has spiritual discernment (*I Cor.* 2: 14; *II Cor.* 4: 6).

(l) He possesses a new appetite for spiritual things (*I Pet.* 2: 1, 2).

(m) He delights in the law of God in his inmost self (*Rom.* 7: 22).

(n) He may be said to know God (*Jer.* 24: 7; *Col.* 3: 10).

(o) He hates sin because his new nature cannot sin and is opposed to sin (*I John* 3: 9; 5: 18—notice here that the verb "to sin" is in the present tense, and speaks of continual and habitual action. John is not saying that the regenerate man cannot sin but rather that he cannot consistently and deliberately do so).

(p) He is preserved from the evil one (*I John* 5: 18) and will be presented faultless before God (*Phil.* 1: 6; *Jude* 24).

(q) He becomes, together with all the regenerate, the first-fruits of a new creation (*Jas.* 1: 18)—the kingdom of God (*John* 3: 3).

(r) He possesses this as a living hope through the resurrection of Jesus Christ from the dead—life after death, eternal life and an inheritance in heaven (*I Pet.* 1: 3–5).

(s) Three outstanding proofs of regeneration are given by John in his first epistle: the regenerate man believes that Jesus is the Christ (*I John* 5: 1), practises righteousness, i.e. does right things as a practice (*I John* 2: 29; 3: 9; 5: 18), and loves his Christian brethren (*I John* 4: 7).

27. CONVERSION

Question: What is conversion?

Answer: Conversion is turning from sin, to be the servant of the living and true God, through repentance and personal faith in Jesus Christ. It is a work in which God takes the initiative, and in which He requires

man's response as the gospel is understood.

1. Conversion is turning with sincerity to God.

(a) It is the turning of the life to the living God, our Creator (*Acts* 14: 15).

(b) It is the acknowledgment of God in a manner not practised previously (*Gal.* 4: 8, 9).

(c) Conversion conveys literally the idea of a turning *from* and a turning *to*: repentance and faith correspond to these two ideas (*I Thess.* 1: 9).

(d) Conversion must be of the heart to receive the benefits which God promises (*Deut.* 4: 29; *Acts* 15: 8).

2. Conversion is a possibility for men and women on the grounds of Christ's work on behalf of sinners.

(a) Conversion is for sinners (*Ps.* 51: 13).

(b) God sent His Son into the world so that it might be possible for sinners to be converted from their wickedness (*Luke* 24: 46, 47; *Acts* 3: 26; 5: 31).

3. Conversion's negative aspect is repentance.

(a) Conversion comes about as transgressors are taught God's ways (*Ps.* 51: 13).

(b) It is accompanied by an understanding of who God is and what He demands (*Jer.* 24: 7).

(c) It comes about when a man realises the ways of God and the contrast of his own ways (*Ps.* 119: 59).

(d) It means turning from wickedness (*Acts* 3: 26).

(e) It means turning from idols (*I Thess.* 1: 9), from vain worship and confused conceptions of God (*Acts* 14: 15).

(f) It means turning from darkness and the power of Satan (*Acts* 26: 18).

(g) It means ceasing to stray from God (*I Pet.* 2: 25).

(h) Repentance is an essential part of conversion (*Acts* 3: 19; 26: 20).

4. Conversion's positive aspect is faith in Christ.

(a) Conversion takes place when Christ is revealed to a person (*Gal.* 1: 16).

(b) It is the result of being confronted with the Person and claims of Christ (*Acts* 9: 5, 6).

(c) It is the expression of faith in Christ (*Acts* 11: 21).

(d) It means recognising Christ as the Shepherd and Guardian of one's soul and returning to Him (*I Pet.* 2: 25).

5. Conversion is a necessity for entry into the kingdom of heaven.

(a) Unless we are converted and become as little children, we cannot enter the kingdom of heaven (*Matt.* 18: 3).

(b) Essential blessings necessary for entry into the kingdom of heaven come by conversion alone:

(i) Forgiveness (*Mark* 4: 12; *Acts* 3: 19);

(ii) The cleansing of the heart (*Acts* 15: 9);

(iii) Deliverance from the wrath to come (*I Thess.* 1: 10);

(iv) A place amongst those who are sanctified by faith in Christ (*Acts* 26: 18).

6. Conversion marks the beginning of the Christian life in a person's experience.

(a) The converted person is a new creature (*II Cor.* 5: 17).

(b) At conversion an individual receives the gospel, takes his stand upon it, is saved by it, and holds it fast (*I Cor.* 15: 1, 2).

(c) He receives the forgiveness of sins (*Acts* 26: 18).

(d) He receives the gift of the Holy Spirit (*Acts* 15: 8).

(e) He begins to serve the living and true God (*I Thess.* 1: 9).

(f) He is committed to obedience to God (*Deut.* 30: 2).

(g) He discovers that God has a purpose for his life (*Gal.* 1: 16).

(h) He witnesses by means of baptism to what has happened in his life (*Acts* 2: 38; 8: 36–38; 9: 18; 16: 15; 16: 33).

7. The initiative in conversion is God's.

(a) Conversion is God's work (*John* 6: 44; *Acts* 11: 18; 21: 19; *II Tim.* 2: 25).

(b) It is God's work in us (*Jer.* 24: 7; *Acts* 8: 29; 16: 14; *Phil.* 1: 6).

(c) God sometimes uses unpleasant circumstances to bring conversion about in the lives of men and women (*Ps.* 78: 34).

(d) It is the result of God's grace to us (*Acts* 11: 21, 23; *Gal.* 1: 15).

(e) It takes place at God's will and choice (*Acts* 9: 3 ff; 15: 7; *Gal.* 1: 15).

(f) It is the consequence of the work of God the Holy Spirit (*Acts* 10: 44 ff).

(g) It is a blessing from God (*Acts* 3: 26).

(h) The praise is God's (*Gal.* 1: 24).

8. Conversion reveals the response God requires from man as he hears the gospel.

(a) Conversion is the step God requires of us if He is to restore us to Himself (*John* 12: 40).

(b) Man responds to God's command in conversion (*Acts* 17: 30).

(c) Conversion means becoming like children before God—completely submissive to what He commands we must do if we would enter His kingdom (*Matt.* 18: 3).

9. Conversion is the great work which God uses His servants to help bring about in the world amongst men.

(a) Conversion follows upon hearing the word of the gospel and believing (*Acts* 15: 7).

(b) God uses His messengers to bring conversion about in the lives of men (*Acts* 26: 18).

(c) Preaching has a vital place in conversion: God uses it to turn men to Himself (*Luke* 1: 16; *Acts* 26: 18).

(d) Conversion takes place as the messengers of the gospel are welcomed and their message obeyed (*I Thess.* 1: 9).

(e) Conversion may come about through the testimony of converted men to God's mercy and salvation (*Ps.* 51: 13).

(f) Conversion is the work of Christ which He is pleased to accomplish through His servants in the lives of those to whom they proclaim the message of repentance and faith (*Acts* 11: 21; *Rom.* 15: 18; *I Thess.* 1: 9).

10. Conversion is commanded by God.

(a) Men are exhorted to repent,

and to turn to God, so that their sins may be wiped out (*Acts* 3: 19).

(b) The delay in God's judgment of the world springs from His desire that men may heed His warnings and obey His command to be converted (*II Pet.* 3: 8, 9).

28. REPENTANCE

Question: What is repentance?

Answer: Repentance is turning from sin to God, as a result of a change of mind and heart about sin.

1. The necessity of repentance.

(a) God commands it on the part of all men (*Acts* 17: 30).

(b) Unless men repent, they will perish (*Luke* 13: 3, 5).

(c) Repentance is the first response demanded of men if they are to respond to the gospel of Jesus Christ (*Acts* 2: 38).

(d) Repentance is the first condition God imposes if men are to find Him (*Zech.* 1: 3, 4; *Acts* 20: 21).

(e) Repentance is a condition of cleansing (*Isa.* 6: 5).

(f) Repentance is a condition of forgiveness (*Luke* 24: 47; *Acts* 3: 19; 26: 18).

(g) Repentance is a condition of salvation (*Acts* 26: 18).

(h) Repentance is a condition of entry into the kingdom of heaven (*Matt.* 4: 17).

(i) Repentance is a condition of eternal life (*Acts* 11: 18).

(j) Repentance is a condition for escaping the judgment of God upon sin (*Acts* 17: 30, 31).

2. Repentance is turning from sin to God.

(a) Repentance is the result of the eyes of the mind being opened to understand the sinner's need before God (*Acts* 26: 18).

(b) Repentance is associated with the idea of turning (*Acts* 3: 19; 26: 20).

(c) Repentance is turning away from dead works (*Heb.* 6: 1); it is turning from wicked ways (*II Chron.* 7: 14); it is turning from iniquities to give heed to God's truth (*Dan.* 9: 13); it is turning away from sin to God (*Ezek.* 33: 11).

(d) Repentance involves the recognition of sin as failure to keep God's statutes (*Mal.* 3: 7).

(e) Repentance means seeing how awful sin is in God's sight (*Ps.* 51: 4), and recognising the affliction of the human heart which is sin (*I Kings* 8: 38).

(f) Conviction of sin is necessary for repentance to take place (*Acts* 2: 37, 38).

(g) Repentance involves a real sorrow and grief on account of sin (*Luke* 22: 62; *II Cor.* 7: 9, 10).

(h) Repentance brings such a sense of shame (*Ezra* 9: 6–15; *Jer.* 31: 19) that a man despises himself for his sin (*Job* 42: 6).

(i) Repentance is the wicked forsaking his way, and the unrighteous man his thoughts and returning to the Lord, that He may have mercy on him (*Isa.* 55: 7).

(j) Repentance means inevitably a fundamental break with the past (*Luke* 9: 23 f; 14: 26, 33).

3. Characteristics of true repentance.

(a) Unfortunately false repentance is a possibility: Saul (*I Sam.* 15: 24–30) and Ahab (*I Kings* 21: 27–29) provide examples of false repentance.

(b) True repentance springs from a recognition of God as the Lord (*Jer.* 3: 22).

(c) It is seen in grief for sin (*Joel* 2: 12; *II Cor.* 7: 9).

(d) It is rational and openly declared (*Hos.* 14: 2).

(e) It is accompanied by confession, renunciation and dedication (*Hos.* 14: 1–3, 8).

(f) It is wholehearted (*Joel* 2: 12, 13; *Hos.* 7: 14).

(g) It is humble (*Jonah* 3: 6; *II Chron.* 7: 14; *Jas.* 4: 9, 10).

(h) It is obviously a work and a gift of God (*Acts* 11: 18).

4. Motives for repentance.

(a) The character of God is a tremendous encouragement to repentance. He is gracious and merciful, slow to anger, and abounding in steadfast love (*Joel* 2: 13).

(b) God's patience should encourage repentance (*II Pet.* 3: 9).

(c) God's kindness is meant to lead men to a change of heart about sin (*Rom.* 2: 4).

(d) God pleads with men to repent (*Isa.* 30: 15).

(e) Repentance is never despised by God (*Jonah* 3: 9; *Luke* 15: 7, 10).

(f) Christ came to call sinners to repentance (*Matt.* 9: 13).

(g) Repentance is called for in the light of what God has accomplished for sinners through Christ's saving work (*Acts* 3: 18, 19; 5: 31).

(h) Repentance is the first part of conversion, and faith in the Lord Jesus Christ is the second (*Acts* 20: 21; *Mark* 1: 15).

5. Evidences of repentance.

(a) True repentance brings no regret but leads to salvation (*II Cor.* 7: 10).

(b) Practical reformation is assumed (*Judg.* 6: 25–27; *Luke* 19: 8).

(c) Actions follow which give proof of a change of mind about sin (*Joel* 2: 12; *Acts* 26: 20), especially restitution where necessary (*Ezek.* 33: 14, 15).

(d) Repentance yields appropriate fruit (*Matt.* 3: 8; *Luke* 13: 6–9).

29. FAITH

Question: What is faith?

Answer: Faith is both a decisive act and a sustained attitude. It begins as an act, by which a person abandons reliance on himself to merit salvation, has a firm conviction as to the truth of God's promises of mercy in Jesus Christ, and depends sincerely upon them. After this, faith becomes a habit of that person's life.

1. Faith rests on certain facts which the apostles were careful to preach (*I Cor.* 11: 23; 15: 1–3; *I Thess.* 2: 13; 4: 1, 2).

2. These facts are easy to determine.

(a) Jesus is the Christ, the Son of God (*John* 20: 31; *Acts* 9: 20).

(b) He died for our sins (*I Pet.* 2: 24).

(c) He was buried and was raised

to life again on the third day (*I Pet.* 1: 3; *Rom.* 4: 25).

(d) His death and resurrection took place according to the manner in which God had promised beforehand in the Old Testament Scriptures (*I Cor.* 15: 3, 4).

(e) On the grounds of what Christ accomplished men may receive forgiveness and the gift of the Holy Spirit (*Acts* 2: 38, 39).

3. These facts have to be received (*I Cor.* 15: 1).

(a) The facts themselves have to be understood (*Acts* 17: 2, 3; 18: 4, 19).

(b) Intellectual assent has to be given to them (*Acts* 28: 27; *Luke* 24: 45).

4. A stand has to be taken then upon these facts (*I Cor.* 15: 1).

(a) This stand involves a personal confession of Christ as the Son of God (*Matt.* 16: 16; *Acts* 8: 37; *Rom.* 10: 10).

(b) A personal belief that Christ died for our sins (*Gal.* 2: 20; *I Tim.* 1: 15).

(c) A personal belief that God raised Christ from the dead (*Rom.* 10: 9).

(d) Thus faith moves beyond the facts to trusting a Person—the Lord Jesus Christ (*Acts* 16: 31; *John* 1: 12; *John* 3: 16).

5. The stand which is taken upon these facts—significantly known as "the faith" (*Jude* 3)**—involves the abandonment of all confidence in human merit and works for the obtaining of salvation.**

(a) No confidence in externals, whether of race, social status, religious zeal, or legal rectitude is allowed (*Phil.* 3: 3–8).

(b) No confidence in one's good deeds is permissible (*Tit.* 3: 5).

6. When a person comes to true faith in Christ, faith becomes then a sustained attitude of that person's life.

(a) Faith gives substance to his hopes (*Heb.* 11: 1).

(b) Faith makes him certain of realities he cannot see (*Heb.* 11: 1).

(c) Faith is his guide (*II Cor.* 5: 7).

(d) He is defended in the battles of the Christian life by the shield of faith (*Eph.* 6: 16).

(e) He fights the good fight of faith (*I Tim.* 6: 12).

7. Such a habit of faith in a person's life makes a tremendous difference to his life. The men and women of faith, described in Hebrews 11, who did not fully know "the faith" of the gospel, provide helpful illustrations.

(a) Faith makes a man offer only his best to God—Abel (*Heb.* 11: 4).

(b) Faith makes a man reckon walking with God the most important thing in life—Enoch (*Heb.* 11: 5).

(c) Faith makes a man concerned for the saving of his household—Noah (*Heb.* 11: 7).

(d) Faith makes a man obey God, even blindly sometimes—Abraham leaving Haran (*Heb.* 11: 8).

(e) Faith makes a man live after the manner of a refugee in the world, holding lightly to its possessions—Abraham and his immediate descendants (*Heb.* 11: 9, 10, 13–16).

(f) Faith makes a man change his

mind about things thought impossible—Sarah (*Heb.* 11: 11, 12).

(g) Faith makes a man render implicit obedience to God no matter what He demands—Abraham and Isaac (*Heb.* 11: 17–19).

(h) Faith makes a man concerned for the spiritual well-being of the generations to follow—Isaac blessing Jacob and Esau (*Heb.* 11: 20).

(i) Faith gives a man confidence in the face of death—Jacob and Joseph (*Heb.* 11: 21, 22).

(j) Faith makes a man co-operative actively with the purposes of God as he knows them—Moses' parents (*Heb.* 11: 23).

(k) Faith makes a man live a life which is different and separate from the standard set by the world—Moses (*Heb.* 11: 24, 25).

(l) Faith takes away fear of man—Moses as to Pharaoh (*Heb.* 11: 27).

(m) Faith leads to the activity which comes from obedience—the Passover and the crossing of the Red Sea (*Heb.* 11: 28, 29).

(n) Faith brings victory and success—Jericho (*Heb.* 11: 30).

30. THE AWAKENING OF FAITH

Question: How do we come to saving Christian faith?

Answer: By the effective working of the Holy Spirit in our hearts, as the gospel is made known to us, calling us, without reference to our merits, from the dominion of darkness and transferring us to the kingdom of God's dear Son.

1. As the facts of the faith (see Question: What is faith?) are presented to us, the Holy Spirit convinces us of their truth.

(a) He is the Spirit of truth (*John* 16: 13).

(b) God's message is received, not as the word of men, but as what it truly is, the very Word of God (*I Thess.* 2: 13).

2. As we recognise the truth of the facts of the faith, the Holy Spirit enables us to apply them to ourselves.

(a) He uses the Law of God to reveal to us our sin (*Gal.* 3: 21–24; *Rom.* 7: 7).

(b) And thus He brings us to conviction of sin and repentance (*John* 16: 8–11; *Acts* 2: 37, 38).

3. Having convinced us of our sin, the Holy Spirit makes plain the remedy for our sin.

(a) The good news of Jesus and the benefits of His death and resurrection come home to the heart with strong conviction (*I Thess.* 1: 5).

(b) He glorifies Jesus in the eyes of the sinner, for He draws upon what is Christ's and discloses it to him (*John* 16: 14).

4. The result is faith built not upon human wisdom but upon the power of God (*I Cor.* 2: 5).

(a) Faith has come about not through the force of subtle arguments of men, but through the power of the Holy Spirit (*I Cor.* 2: 4).

(b) The Lord has added to the number of those whom He is saving (*Acts* 2: 40, 41; cf. 2: 47).

(c) No longer does the individual belong to the dominion of darkness but to the kingdom of God's dear Son (*Col.* 1: 13).

5. This effective working of the Holy Spirit in our hearts to bring us faith in Christ is without reference at all to our merits (*Tit.* 3: 5; *Rom.* 4: 5; *Tit.* 1: 1; *II Thess.* 1: 11).

31. JUSTIFICATION

Question: What is justification?

Answer: Justification is the free and undeserved act of God, by which He reckons to a sinner, through faith, the righteousness of Christ, declaring the sinner just and right before Him.

1. Justification has to do with the justice and righteousness of God.

(a) He is the just God and everything He does shows His justice (*Rom.* 3: 25, 26).

(b) He is the Lord and Judge of all the earth (*Gen.* 18: 25), who always does right.

(c) His righteousness is seen in His judgment and condemnation of those who disobey His laws (*Ps.* 7: 11; *Isa.* 5: 16; *Acts* 17: 31; *Rom.* 2: 5).

2. Men and women are unrighteous before God.

(a) No living person is righteous before the Lord (*Ps.* 143: 2).

(b) All have sinned and come short of the glory of God (*Rom.* 3: 23).

3. Theoretically, the Law of God is a means of justification.

(a) By perfect obedience to the Law of God an individual could be justified before God (*Rom.* 2: 13; 10: 5; *Lev.* 18: 5; *Jas.* 2: 10).

(b) But, in fact, all men everywhere have broken God's Law (*Rom.* 10: 5; cf. 9: 31)—it has served to bring an awareness of sin (*Rom.* 3: 20).

(c) The endeavour to keep the Law of God, therefore, can bring about neither righteousness before God nor justification (*Rom.* 3: 21; *Gal.* 2: 16, 21; 3: 11).

(d) Works or acts of obedience can neither satisfy God's justice, fulfil His Law nor stand up to His standard (*Ps.* 130: 3, 4; 143: 2; *Isa.* 64: 6; *Luke* 17: 10).

(e) The thought of God entering into judgment with man is, therefore, terrifying (*Ps.* 143: 2).

4. God alone could deliver man from the condemnation which rightly awaits him; and the situation required an amazing solution.

(a) Clearly, the wrong that was in men's and women's lives could not be righted by their obedience to the Law of God (*Rom.* 3: 21; 9: 31, 32; *Job* 9: 2, 3, 20; 25: 4).

(b) Whatever way God determined for righting the wrong that was in man, had to be adequate for all, without distinction; and it had to be consistent with His own justice (*Rom.* 3: 21, 22, 26).

(c) The answer was the gospel: it is the revelation of God's plan for imparting righteousness to sinful men (*Rom.* 1: 16, 17).

(d) The wonder of God's new covenant is that a man may be reconciled to God (*II Cor.* 5: 20), all the demands of God's law having been satisfied (*II Cor.* 3: 9).

(e) The Law and the prophets gave witness in advance of this way of justification which God purposed (*Rom.* 3: 21).

(f) Abraham is an example of God's justifying grace: he believed God, and it was reckoned to him as righteousness (*Gen.* 15: 6; *Rom.* 4: 3).

5. Justification, therefore, is necessarily an act of God, being beyond the power of man to accomplish.

(a) It is a legal term, meaning to acquit (*Rom.* 8: 33; cf. *Deut.* 25: 1; *Prov.* 17: 15).

(b) While God is the Judge, He is also the justifier (*Rom.* 3: 26, 30; 4: 5; 8: 33; *Gal.* 3: 8).

(c) The amazing thing is that He justifies the ungodly (*Rom.* 4: 5): for His own sake, He blots out their transgressions and will not remember their sins (*Isa.* 43: 25).

6. Justification depends upon what Christ has done for sinners.

(a) The grounds of it are what Christ accomplished for sinners (*Acts* 13: 39).

(b) God could justify the ungodly only through Christ's dying, at the right time, for the ungodly (*Rom.* 5: 6).

(c) He sets Christ before us as the One whose sacrificial death has atoned for our guilt and removed the judgment soon to happen which our rebellion against God has brought upon us (*Rom.* 3: 24, 25).

(d) Christ redeemed us from the curse of the Law, having become a curse for us (*Gal.* 3: 13).

(e) God caused Christ, who Himself knew nothing of sin, actually to *be* sin for our sakes, so that in Christ we might be made righteous with the righteousness of God (*II Cor.* 5: 21; *Isa.* 53: 5).

(f) Thus Jesus Christ, acting on behalf of sinners, has satisfied the claims of God's law and justice (*Gal.* 4: 4, 5), and has put away their sins by His blood (*Rom.* 3: 25; 5: 9).

(g) By justifying men on the basis of Christ's sacrificial death God demonstrates both His justice and His love (*Rom.* 3: 25, 26).

7. On the basis of Christ's sacrificial death, God reckons to believers the righteousness of Christ.

(a) Of Christ's righteousness there was no doubt (*Matt.* 3: 17; *I Pet.* 3: 18): justification is by the imputing of His righteousness to the sinner (*Rom.* 3: 22; 5: 18; *I Cor.* 1: 30; *II Cor.* 5: 21).

(b) To be justified is to receive the righteousness of Christ, for which alone the Lord accepts us as holy and righteous (*Isa.* 43: 25; *Rom.* 3: 23–26; 4: 5; *Phil.* 3: 9).

(c) God pronounces us to be free from all guilt and declares us to be righteous as He sees us in the righteousness of Christ (*Rom.* 3: 26).

(d) Christians are described as the righteous as a consequence (*I Pet.* 4: 18).

8. Justification is a free gift from God.

(a) Men and women are justified by God's free grace alone (*Rom.* 3: 24).

(b) The righteousness God bestows through Christ is a gift (*Rom.* 5: 17; *Phil.* 3: 9).

(c) Consequently, all room for human pride is removed (*Rom.* 3: 27).

9. The means of our entering into justification is by faith.

(a) The righteousness God offers is to be apprehended by faith

(*Rom.* 1: 17; 3: 22, 26; 4: 3 ff, 13; 9: 30; 10: 4, 6, 10).

(b) Justification depends upon faith to be effective (*Acts* 13: 39; *Rom.* 3: 25, 28; 4: 5).

(c) It is with the heart that men have faith which leads God to accept them as righteous (*Rom.* 10: 10).

(d) Faith, therefore, is reckoned as righteousness (*Gen.* 15: 6; *Ps.* 106: 31; *Rom.* 4: 3, 5 f, 9, 11, 22; *Gal.* 3: 6).

10. The benefits justification brings.

(a) The first benefit of justification is peace with God (*Rom.* 5: 1).

(b) It is to be acquitted of everything for which there was not acquittal under the law of Moses; it means the forgiveness of sins (*Acts* 13: 38, 39).

(c) It frees us from condemnation (*Isa.* 50: 8, 9; 54: 17; *Rom.* 8: 33, 34).

(d) No one can bring a charge against those whom God justifies (*Rom.* 8: 33).

(e) Being justified, the believer can rejoice in deliverance from the wrath of God to come (*Rom.* 5: 9).

(f) God has so justified the believer that he has nothing to fear at God's judgment seat (*Rom.* 8: 1).

(g) The peace justification brings carries with it access to God (*Rom.* 5: 2).

(h) Justification brings us into union with God and makes us sons and heirs of God (*Gal.* 3: 26; 4: 4 ff; *Rom.* 8: 14 ff).

(i) It is on the basis of his justification that the believer is in Christ, and knows Christ, together with all the benefits Christ has gained for him (*Phil.* 3: 9, 10; *Rom.* 8: 32).

(j) Justification brings tremendous joy: the joy of the hope of sharing the glory of God (*Rom.* 5: 2); joy in sufferings because we know God's good purposes are fulfilled in them for His children (*Rom.* 5: 3); and, supremely, joy in God Himself (*Rom.* 5: 11).

(k) Justification assures the believer that he will have eternal life (*Rom.* 8: 10; *Tit.* 3: 7).

(l) Justification means that absolutely nothing can separate us from the love of God in Christ Jesus our Lord (*Rom.* 8: 31–39).

(m) It is the basis of true happiness (*Rom.* 4: 6, 7; *Ps.* 32: 1, 2).

(n) No wonder it is the believer's most precious possession—nothing else can compare with its value (*Phil.* 3: 7–9).

32. BEING A CHRISTIAN

Question: What are the benefits and privileges of being a Christian?

Answer: The benefits and privileges of being a Christian are, principally, union with Christ, adoption by God into His family, Christian liberty, a spiritual right to the sacraments of the new covenant, the fellowship of all Christians, and the resurrection of the body.

1. Union with Christ.

(a) The purpose of all that Christ did was that Christians might be united with Him (*I Thess.* 5: 10):

(i) They were crucified with Him (*Rom.* 6: 6);

(ii) They were buried with Him (*Rom.* 6: 4; *Col.* 2: 12);

(iii) They died with Him (*Rom.* 6: 8; *II Tim.* 2: 11);

(iv) They were made alive with Him (*Col.* 2: 13);

(v) They were raised with Him (*Col.* 2: 12; 3: 1);

(vi) They are made joint-heirs with Him (*Rom.* 8: 17);

(vii) They are to suffer with Christ (*Rom.* 8: 17);

(viii) They shall be glorified with Him (*Rom.* 8: 17);

(ix) They shall be enthroned with Him (*Col.* 3: 1; *Rev.* 20: 4);

(x) They shall reign with Him (*II Tim.* 2: 12; *Rev.* 20: 4).

(b) The union is like that of a Head and a Body:

(i) Christ is the Head of the Body, the Church (*Col.* 1: 18), and Christians, like so many limbs and organs in a single body, constitute the one body of Christ (*I Cor.* 12: 12);

(ii) Christians are meant to grow up in every way into Christ, the Head (*Eph.* 4: 15).

(c) The union is like that of a Husband and Wife:

(i) Christ is the Head of the Church, even as the man is the head of the woman (*Eph.* 5: 23);

(ii) Christians are betrothed to Christ, to be as a pure bride to her husband (*II Cor.* 11: 2; *Eph.* 5: 25–27; *Rev.* 21: 9).

(d) The union is like that of a foundation to a building:

(i) Christ is the rock upon which we are built (*Matt.* 16: 18);

(ii) We become part of God's spiritual building or house, as we are joined to Christ, the chief corner stone, through faith (*Eph.* 2: 20–22; *I Pet.* 2: 4–7).

(e) The Holy Spirit brings the Christian into his living relationship and union with Christ, and there can be no such experience without the Holy Spirit (*Rom.* 8: 9, 11).

(f) It is through being in Christ that God gives us every possible spiritual benefit (*Eph.* 1: 3).

2. Adoption by God into His family.

(a) Before the foundation of the world God chose Christians to become, in Christ, His holy and blameless children, living within His constant care (*Eph.* 1: 4, 5).

(b) God's love has caused Him to bestow upon those who receive His Son the right to become His children (*John* 1: 12, 13; *I John* 3: 1).

(c) Christians receive the spirit of sonship, so that they are rightly able to cry, "Abba! Father!" (*Rom.* 8: 15–17).

(d) As God's children, Christians share His treasures, and all that Christ claims as His will belong to all of them as well (*Rom.* 8: 17).

(e) Christians wait for that redemption of their bodies which will mean that at last they will have realised their full sonship in Christ (*Rom.* 8: 23).

(f) The whole creation may be described as being on tiptoe to see the wonderful sight of the sons of God coming into their own (*Rom.* 8: 19).

3. Christian Liberty.

(a) Christ came to proclaim liberty to the captives, and the opening of the prison to those who are bound (*Isa.* 61: 1, 2; *Luke* 4: 18, 19): when Christ sets us free, we are free indeed (*John* 8: 32, 34, 36; *Gal.* 5: 1).

(b) Christ sets us free from the fear of death (*I Cor.* 15: 55–57; *Heb.* 2: 14, 15).

(c) Christ delivers from that slavish attitude of fear which so easily can characterise life without God (*Rom.* 8: 15).

(d) Christ has redeemed believers from the curse of the Law's condemnation, by Himself becoming a curse for them when He was crucified (*Gal.* 3: 13): no condemnation now hangs over the head of those who are in Christ Jesus (*Rom.* 8: 1).

(e) The burden of all the Jewish ceremonial is removed through Christ (*Acts* 15: 10, 11; *Gal.* 3, 4, 5).

(f) Christ makes us free from slavery to sin (*John* 8: 32, 34, 36): once the servants of sin, having honestly responded to the message of the gospel, Christians are released from the service of sin, and enter the service of righteousness (*Rom.* 6: 17, 18).

(g) The Christian's freedom, however, is not a freedom to do wrong, but a freedom to serve God (*I Pet.* 2: 16).

(h) The Christian is freed from the bondage of the law, but it remains for him a rule of life and holiness: God puts His law within the Christian and writes it upon his heart (*Jer.* 31: 31–33).

(i) The Christian no longer lives under the law, but under grace (*Rom.* 6: 14).

(j) The law is not undermined by the insistence on faith; rather the law is given its proper place (*Rom.* 3: 31).

4. A Spiritual Right to the Sacraments of the New Covenant.

(a) The first sacrament of the New Covenant is baptism:

(i) It was appointed by Christ Himself for all disciples (*Matt.* 28: 19, 20; *Mark* 16: 15, 16);

(ii) It is administered in the name of the Trinity (*Matt.* 28: 19);

(iii) It is a symbol of the individual's reception of the gospel (*Acts* 2: 37, 38, 41; 8: 12; 16: 14, 15);

(iv) It symbolises repentance and faith in the Lord Jesus (*Acts* 2: 38);

(v) It symbolises confession of Christ's Lordship (*Acts* 19: 5);

(vi) It symbolises admittance into the family of God (*Acts* 2: 38, 41, 47; 8: 12; 9: 18; *I Cor.* 12: 13);

(vii) It symbolises entry into all the benefits of Christ's death and resurrection (*Rom.* 6: 3, 4).

(b) The second sacrament of the New Covenant is the Lord's Supper:

(i) The Lord's Supper is a proclamation of the Lord's death by words and symbols (*I Cor.* 11: 26);

(ii) It was established and commanded by Christ (*Matt.* 26: 26–28; *I Cor.* 11: 23);

(iii) It continually reminds Christians of Christ's sacrifice for them (*Luke* 22: 19; *I Cor.* 11: 26);

(iv) By means of it Christians acknowledge their sharing in the benefits of Christ's death (*I Cor.* 10: 16, 17; 11: 25);

(v) In it Christians have fellowship with Christ and with one another (*I Cor.* 10: 16, 17, 21);

(vi) In it Christians make their thanksgiving to God (*I Cor.* 10: 16; *Rom.* 12: 1);

(vii) The Lord's Supper is to be continued until Christ returns (*I Cor.* 11: 26).

5. The Fellowship of all Christians.

(a) God has given His people one heart and one way (*Jer.* 32: 39).

(b) The people of God are one even as the Father and the Son are one (*John* 17: 22)—and Jesus' prayer to His Father had this unity as a main petition (*John* 17: 11, 21).

(c) Jesus, the Great and Chief Shepherd, has one flock to which all Christians belong (*John* 10: 16).

(d) The fellowship of believers—sometimes called "the communion of saints"—arises from Christians belonging to one Body, of which there is one Spirit (*Eph.* 4: 4).

(e) All Christians are baptised by the Spirit into one Body, whether Jews, Gentiles, slaves or free men, and they all have had experience of the same Spirit (*I Cor.* 12: 13).

(f) Though many, Christians are one body in Christ, and individually members one of another (*Rom.* 12: 5; *I Cor.* 12: 12).

(g) The fellowship or communion of believers, therefore, is the sense of identity and belonging we have with all believers through our common allegiance to the Lord Jesus, the truth (*Eph.* 4: 13; *II John* 1).

(h) The fellowship Christians have together arises from their fellowship with the Father and the Son (*I John* 1: 3).

(i) Christians should seek to express their fellowship and union outwardly by avoiding all dissensions among themselves, being united in the same mind and the same judgment (*I Cor.* 1: 10, 11; *Phil.* 2: 1, 2; *I Pet.* 3: 8).

(j) This fellowship of all Christians is given practical expression in the fellowship of the local church according to the pattern revealed in the New Testament (*Acts* 11: 26; 20: 17, 28; 14: 23; *I Cor.* 4: 17; *Heb.* 13: 17; 10: 25).

6. **The Resurrection of the Body.**

(a) God does not give the believer up to hell, but shows him the path of life, which leads to fullness of joy in God's presence, and pleasures for evermore at God's right hand (*Ps.* 16: 9–11).

(b) The believer has the assurance of the resurrection of the body through his living Redeemer (*Job* 19: 25–27; *I Thess.* 4: 14).

(c) The resurrection of the dead will be the first event of Christ's second coming (*I Thess.* 4: 16).

(d) Believers will be made alive through Christ (*I Cor.* 15: 22).

(e) Harvest provides us with a good illustration of the kind of thing that will happen: what you sow is not the body which is to be (*I Cor.* 15: 37); just as to every kind of creature and thing God has given a particular body, so He has determined the particular nature of the resurrection body (*I Cor.* 15: 38–42).

(f) The body characterised by decay, dishonour, weakness, and suited only for this present life, shall be raised an imperishable, glorious body, full of power, and perfectly fitted for life in the world to come (*I Cor.* 15: 42–44).

(g) The transformation will take place in a moment (*I Cor.* 15: 51, 52).

(h) The assurance of the resurrection of the body is a tremendous comfort and encouragement to the Christian (*I Thess.* 4: 18; *I Cor.* 15: 58).

(i) And after the glorious event, Christians shall be with Christ for ever (*I Thess.* 4: 17).

33. ASSURANCE

Question: How can we be sure that we are Christians?

Answer: By the conviction we have from the Holy Spirit, through our obedience to the gospel, that we are children of God and heirs of eternal life. The genuineness of this conviction is demonstrated by right belief in Christ, righteous conduct and love for other Christians.

1. First, we need to be clear as to what being sure includes.

(a) The spiritual benefits concerning which Christians are encouraged to be sure are many and include:

(i) Election (*Ps.* 4: 3; *I Thess.* 1: 4; *II Pet.* 1: 10);

(ii) Salvation and redemption (*Isa.* 12: 2; *Job* 19: 25; *Rom.* 5: 9; *I Cor.* 1: 30; *I Thess.* 5: 9);

(iii) Peace with God by Christ (*Rom.* 5: 1);

(iv) Adoption into the family of God (*Rom.* 8: 16; *I John* 3: 1, 2, 9, 10; 4: 4; 5, 2, 18, 19);

(v) Knowing God (*I John* 2: 3; 5: 20);

(vi) Union with God and Christ (*I Cor.* 6: 15; *II Cor.* 13: 5; *Eph.* 5: 30; *I John* 2: 5; 3: 24; 4: 13);

(vii) Membership of God's kingdom (*Col.* 1: 13; *Heb.* 12: 28);

(viii) Inseparability from the love of God (*Rom.* 8: 38, 39);

(ix) Deliverance from all evil (*Ps.* 3: 6, 8; 27: 3–5; 46: 1–3; *II Tim.* 4: 18);

(x) God's continuing and perfecting work in the life (*Phil.* 1: 6);

(xi) The right to pray and the assurance of God's answer (*I John* 3: 22; 5: 14, 15);

(xii) God's help in affliction (*Ps.* 73: 26; *II Cor.* 4: 8–10, 16–18);

(xiii) God's sure help in death (*Ps.* 23: 4; *Acts* 7: 59; *Phil.* 1: 23);

(xiv) A glorious resurrection (*Job* 19: 26; *Ps.* 17: 15; *Phil.* 3: 21; *I John* 3: 2);

(xv) Eternal life (*I John* 5: 13).

2. The grounds of our being sure that we are Christians, and all that this includes, as seen above.

(a) Firstly, God wants us to be sure (*II Cor.* 13: 5): His will is that those who believe in the name of the Son of God may know that they have eternal life (*I John* 5: 13).

(b) Secondly, the basis of any assurance we have concerning being Christians is that God has spoken to us through His Son Jesus Christ (*Heb.* 1: 1, 2), and all that He wants us to know is contained in the Scriptures, the Word of God (*II Tim.* 3: 15, 16; *I John* 1: 1–3).

(c) The Scriptures give to us the promises of God in Christ through which assurance comes (*II Cor.* 1: 20, 21).

(d) Understanding of God's truth brings a wealth of assurance through the knowledge of God Himself which comes to us as a result (*Col.* 2: 2).

(e) Thirdly, assurance springs from an understanding of God's character: for example, His holiness (*I John* 1: 5), His faithfulness (*I John* 1: 9), and His love (*I John* 4: 8, 9, 10, 16, 19).

(f) The Christian's assurance is not in himself, and not in the truth of God's Word alone, but in God Himself—"I know Whom I have believed . . ." (*II Tim.* 1: 12).

(g) Fourthly, assurance is particularly related to a full understanding of the gospel as being not the word of man, but the Word of God (*I Thess.* 2: 13; *I John* 2: 20, 21).

(h) In particular, our understanding concerns the Lord Jesus Christ and His finished work upon the Cross (*I John* 1: 1–3; 2: 22, 23; 4: 2, 3, 15; 5: 5, 10, 13, 20): Christ fully satisfied the Law's demands for us; Christ is freely offered to all who hear the gospel; all who receive Him and depend upon Him shall be saved (*I John* 2: 1, 2, 12; 3: 5, 8, 16; 4: 10; compare *John* 1: 12; 3: 16).

(i) Fifthly, a further ground of assurance is the awareness that we do believe in the manner God commands (*I John* 3: 23; 5: 13).

(j) Assurance is the result of faith in Christ (*Eph.* 3: 12; *Heb.* 11: 1).

(k) It is most important to realise that the work of assurance is the Holy Spirit's: He witnesses to us, in the first place, that the gospel message is true (*I John* 2: 20, 27; 3: 24; 4: 13); He gives an inward assurance to us that our response to the gospel is real (*I Thess.* 1: 5).

(l) His presence in our life is the proof that our response to the gospel has been genuine (*Acts* 2: 38, 39; 5: 32; 15: 8; *Rom.* 8: 15 f; *Gal.* 3: 2; 4: 6; *Eph.* 1: 13, 14; 4: 30).

(m) Assurance springs from the witness of the Holy Spirit within us (*I John* 3: 24; 5: 6, 8, 9, 10): we may know that we dwell in God and He in us because of the presence of His own Spirit in our life (*I John* 4: 13).

3. The tests to be applied to our conviction that we are Christians to prove its genuineness.

(a) It is necessary to apply these tests because a false assurance is possible; therefore, tests, such as an examination of the quality of our daily life (*Tit.* 1: 16), are to be applied.

(b) The first test is whether we possess right belief concerning the Lord Jesus Christ (*I John* 3: 23; 5: 13).

(c) Those who have right belief confess that Jesus is the Christ (*I John* 2: 22; 5: 1); that He is the Son of God (*I John* 3: 23; 5: 5, 10), and that He came in the flesh (*I John* 4: 2; *II John* 7).

(d) The second test is whether we are marked by righteous conduct: those who are born of God act righteously (*I John* 2: 29; 3: 10).

(e) Righteous conduct is described in many different ways:

(i) Walking in the light (*I John* 1: 7);

(ii) Obedience to God's commandments (*I John* 2: 3, 4, 5, 6; 3: 24);

(iii) The desire to live as Christ lived (*I John* 2: 6);

(iv) Deliverance from the spirit of this world (*I John* 2: 15–17; 3: 14–18; 5: 5, 19);

(v) Self-purification (*I John* 3: 3);

(vi) Ceasing to sin habitually (*I John* 3: 5, 6, 9; 5: 18).

(f) The third test is whether we love other Christians (*I John* 3: 10, 11, 12, 14, 15, 16, 17; 4: 7, 8, 11, 12, 20, 21): we know that we have passed from death to life because we love the brethren (*I John* 3: 14).

(g) By loving one another we show that we know God and are abiding in Him (*I John* 3: 23, 24; 4: 7).

(h) When our life stands up to

these tests we may assure our hearts before God that we are indeed Christians and children of God, even when we are conscious of our natural sinfulness (*I John* 3: 19).

(i) When, however, the application of these tests does not produce a satisfactory proof of genuineness any assurance people may seem to have is unjustified (*I John* 1: 6; 2: 4, 9–11, 23; 3: 6–10; 4: 8, 20; *II John* 9; *III John* 11).

4. The results of being sure that we are Christians.

(a) Joy (*I Pet.* 1: 8; *I John* 1: 4).

(b) The banishment of any unworthy fear of God (*I John* 4: 17–19).

(c) The avoidance of sin (*I John* 2: 1).

(d) Confidence in God and boldness before Him (*I John* 3: 19–22; 5: 14, 15; compare *Heb.* 10: 19–22).

34. PERSEVERANCE

Question: Can a true Christian go so far from God as to become lost?

Answer: A true Christian cannot go so far from God that he becomes lost, although he may backslide. He holds fast to the end because he is held fast by the Lord. Apostasy proves a person was never a true Christian.

1. The Christian must hold fast to the end—this is commanded.

(a) The Christian must hold fast to the end (*Matt.* 24: 13; 10: 22; *Mark* 13: 13).

(b) It is by standing firm that the Christian wins the well-being of his soul (*Luke* 21: 19, R.V.; cf. *Heb.* 10: 39).

(c) Continuance in the word of Christ is the proof of discipleship (*John* 8: 31).

(d) To him who by perseverance in well-doing seeks for glory and honour and immortality, the Lord will give eternal life (*Rom.* 2: 7).

(e) To him who is victorious Christ gives the right to eat of the tree of life (*Rev.* 2: 7).

(f) The Christian shares in all that Christ promises so long as he steadily maintains until the end the trust with which he began (*Heb.* 6: 11, cf. 3: 6, 14).

(g) The perseverance of the Christian is a condition of his reigning with Christ (*II Tim.* 2: 12).

(h) We are not left in any doubt as to the nature of this perseverance; it is perseverance in:

(i) Holiness (*Rom.* 8: 29; *II Thess.* 2: 13; *I Pet.* 1: 2);

(ii) The knowledge of God (*Col.* 1: 10);

(iii) The faith—i.e. being firm on the Christian foundations, never to be dislodged from the hope offered in the gospel (*Col.* 1: 23);

(iv) Christian conduct (*Col.* 1: 10);

(v) Loyalty to Christ (*Rev.* 14: 12);

(vi) Obedience (*Rev.* 14: 12; *Col.* 1: 9);

(vii) Running the race of the Christian life in faith and obedience (*Heb.* 12: 1, 2);

(viii) Good works (*Gal.* 6: 9; *Eph.* 2: 10; *I Thess.* 1: 3);

(ix) Fruitfulness (*Col.* 1: 10);

(x) The Lord (*Phil.* 4: 1).

2. The true Christian will hold fast to the end.

(a) Having begun a good work in the Christian's life, God brings it to completion, right up to the day of Jesus Christ (*Phil.* 1: 6; cf. *I Cor.* 1: 8).

(b) Stirred by the exhortations of the Bible, the true Christian will make every effort to enter into the promises of God, thus confirming his calling and election, adding to his assurance that there will be an abundant entrance for him into the eternal kingdom of our Lord Jesus Christ (*II Pet.* 1: 11).

(c) The warnings God has given against apostasy are used by the Holy Spirit to keep the true Christian from it (*Heb.* 2: 1; 6: 9; 10: 39).

(d) The testing of true faith brings perseverance (*Jas.* 1: 3—A.V. translates it "patience")—the reaction of the true Christian to testing gives proof of his spiritual sonship (*Rom.* 5: 3–5; *II Thess.* 1: 4; *Heb.* 10: 36; *Rev.* 13: 10).

(e) A fight there will be, but perseverance also (*Eph.* 6: 13).

(f) It is the Father's will that the Son should lose none of those whom He has given to Him (*John* 6: 39; 10: 27–29).

(g) The gifts and calling of God are irrevocable (*Rom.* 11: 29).

(h) Nothing is able to separate God's elect in Christ from His love (*Rom.* 8: 30–39).

3. The true Christian is not immune from backsliding although he cannot commit apostasy.

(a) Perseverance does not rule out backsliding, but it does rule out apostasy (*Rev.* 2: 2, with 4–7; 2: 9, with 20–29).

(b) The Christian may backslide (as some of the Hebrew Christians did) but he can never apostatise (*Heb.* 5: 11–6: 12, especially 6: 9).

(c) Though the Christian falls, he is restored through the help of the Lord (*Ps.* 37: 24).

4. The true Christian holds fast to the end because he is held fast by the Lord.

(a) The Christian does not keep himself; he is kept by the power of God, through faith unto salvation (*I Pet.* 1: 5; *Rom.* 14: 4).

(b) God will never forsake His people: His justice and His faithfulness forbid that He should (*Ps.* 37: 28; *II Thess.* 3: 3).

(c) He will fulfil His purposes for His people, and nothing can hinder them (*Ps.* 138: 8; *Rev.* 7: 1–8; cf. *John* 10: 27–29; *Ezek.* 9: 3–6).

(d) Even in the times of His people's ignorance and stupidity the Lord keeps His hand upon them (*Ps.* 73: 21–24).

(e) He sustains them to the end, according to His faithfulness and calling (*I Cor.* 1: 8, 9).

(f) Perseverance is the result of being strengthened by the Lord with all power, according to His glorious might (*Col.* 1: 11; *Eph.* 6: 13, 18).

(g) Satan's desires to have the Christian are not permitted by the Lord—Peter's case, for example (*Luke* 22: 31, 32).

(h) The glory or praise for the Christian's perseverance is entirely God's (*II Tim.* 4: 18).

(i) The Christian, therefore, may be sure of his security (*II Tim.* 4: 18; *Ps.* 37: 28; 73: 24).

(j) This fact should not lead to slackness but to diligence in the Christian life (*II Pet.* 1: 10; *Phil.* 2: 13).

5. Apostasy means a person was never a true Christian.

(a) Straightforward apostasy is the proof that a man was never, in fact, a Christian, although he appeared to be such (*I John* 2: 19).

(b) The parable of the sower indicates that perseverance is the test of reality (*Mark* 4: 3–8).

(c) Cases of falling away, or apostasy, are recorded (*I Tim.* 1: 19; *II Tim.* 2: 17, 18), but in no case is there proof that the persons concerned were true believers (*I John* 2: 19).

(d) We are reminded, therefore, that not everyone who calls himself a child of God is necessarily such (*Matt.* 7: 21–23; *Rom.* 9: 6–8).

6. Fundamental doctrines of the Christian faith underline the truth of what we call final perseverance.

(a) It follows on from election (*Jer.* 31: 3; *Matt.* 24: 22–24; *I Thess.* 1: 2–4).

(b) It follows from the covenant by which God the Father gave His people to His Son as the reward of His obedience and suffering (*Jer.* 32: 40; *John* 17: 2–6).

(c) It springs from the once-for-all nature of Christ's atoning death (*Heb.* 10: 14).

(d) It follows from the union of Christians with Christ (*Rom.* 8: 1; *Gal.* 2: 20; *John* 17: 19).

(e) It follows from the presence of the Holy Spirit in the Christian for ever (*John* 14: 16; *II Cor.* 1: 21, 22; *II Cor.* 5: 5; *Eph.* 1: 13, 14).

(f) It follows from the effectiveness of Christ's intercession for His people (*John* 17: 11, 15, 20; *Rom.* 8: 34; *Heb.* 7: 25; cf. *Luke* 22: 31, 32).

35. SANCTIFICATION

Question: What does God require of us most of all when we have become Christians?

Answer: The comprehensive words which sum up what God requires of us are sanctification and holiness. Sanctification is the process of which holiness is the completed state. In sanctification, God's will is that sinful attitudes and actions should be put to death in the Christian's life, his nature and character renewed after the image of God in Christ, his obedience to God increased, so that he lives to please God. All these things take place through the power and help of the Holy Spirit.

1. Sanctification and holiness.

(a) God's will for us is our sanctification (*I Thess.* 4: 3; *I Pet.* 1: 16).

(b) God's call to the Christian is to holiness (*I Thess.* 4: 7).

(c) The necessity for holiness springs from the fact that the Lord our God is holy (*Lev.* 11: 44; *I Pet.* 1: 16).

(d) That we might serve the Lord, without fear, in holiness and righteousness, all the days of our life is the purpose of God's redemption and of the gift of His Spirit (*Luke* 1: 75; *Ezek.* 36: 27).

(e) The supreme aim of the Christian is to be the achieving of holiness (*Heb.* 12: 14).

2. Sanctification—of which holiness is the completed state—is a continuous process.

(a) It is the continual endeavour to bring holiness to completeness (*II Cor.* 7: 1).

(b) It is a progressive work (*I Thess.* 5: 23), and involves the complete personality: the spirit, the soul and the body (*I Thess.* 5: 23).

(c) Entire sanctification will not be realised until our bodies are changed to be like Christ's body (*Phil.* 3: 21; *I John* 3: 2).

3. Sinful attitudes and actions are to be put to death in the Christian's life (*Rom.* 8: 13; *Col.* 3: 5).

(a) Belonging to the Lord brings the immediate obligation to depart from iniquity (*II Tim.* 2: 19).

(b) God's judgment and condemnation no longer rest upon the Christian because of his sin (*Rom.* 8: 1), but this does not mean that he may ever regard sin lightly (*Rom.* 6: 1, 2; *I John* 2: 1).

(c) The Christian is to throw off the sinful ways of his old life (*Eph.* 4: 22).

(d) While there is necessarily a battle with indwelling sin (*Rom.* 7: 14–25; *I John* 1: 8; 2: 1), sin is not to have the mastery over the Christian (*Rom.* 6: 12, 13).

(e) Sexual immorality and uncleanness are not to be given any place in the Christian's life (*I Thess.* 4: 3, 7).

(f) The more the Christian's sanctification proceeds the more he hates his sin (*Job* 42: 5, 6; *Isa.* 6: 5; *Rom.* 7: 24).

4. The Christian's nature and character are to be renewed after the image of God in Christ.

(a) Sanctification is a call to share God's moral perfection (*I Pet.* 1: 16).

(b) The goal of sanctification is always presented as likeness to Christ: God has chosen Christians to bear the family likeness of His Son (*Rom.* 8: 29; *Phil.* 1: 9–11; *II Pet.* 1: 5–8).

(c) God's purpose is that we should copy Christ and be like Him (*I Cor.* 11: 1; *Phil.* 2: 5).

(d) As our way of looking at things is made different and renewed by the Holy Spirit, so we are able to put on the new nature of God's creating, which shows itself in a just and devout life (*Eph.* 4: 23, 24).

5. Obedience to God is to grow and increase.

(a) Nothing we do outwardly has value to God without the willing obedience of the heart (*I Sam.* 15: 22).

(b) He requires that His commandments shall be upon our heart (*Deut.* 6: 5).

(c) Practical righteousness is walking (another word for "obeying") in all the commandments and ordinances of the Lord blameless (*Luke* 1: 6).

(d) We please God as we keep His commandments (*I John* 3: 22).

(e) We are to actively obey the Holy Spirit as He reveals to us what God requires (*Gal.* 5: 25).

(f) While our obedience is always imperfect (*Ps.* 130: 3), God will always receive the offering of our obedience and of ourselves to Him as holy and acceptable, when we are His children in Christ (*Rom.* 12: 1; *Phil.* 4: 18; *Heb.* 13: 16).

6. All these things take place by the power and help of the Holy Spirit.

(a) Our confidence as we seek to work out the salvation God has given us is that He Himself is at work in us, giving us the will and power to achieve His purpose (*Phil.* 2: 13).

(b) The Holy Spirit is the agent of our sanctification, even as of our regeneration (*I Cor.* 6: 11; *I Thess.* 4: 7, 8).

(c) Strength for the Christian life comes by the personal indwelling of the Holy Spirit (*Eph.* 3: 16; *II Cor.* 4: 16).

(d) The Holy Spirit assists the Christian in putting sin to death (*Rom.* 8: 13).

(e) The Holy Spirit assists in the gradual transformation of the Christian's character to that of Christ (*II Cor.* 3: 18; cf. *Rom.* 8: 29): He takes what is Christ's and declares it to the Christian (*John* 16: 14).

(f) The Holy Spirit assists believers in actual obedience: He implants a supernatural habit and principle in the believer enabling him to obey God's will (*Rom.* 8: 2).

(g) The Holy Spirit strengthens the believer's will to obey God's commandments (*I Pet.* 1: 2; *I John* 3: 24).

7. The instrument the Holy Spirit uses principally for our sanctification is the Word of God.

(a) It is declared to be God's chosen instrument (*John* 17: 17).

(b) Our way of life can be kept pure by guarding it according to God's Word (*Ps.* 119: 9).

(c) Holiness comes from instruction in God's ways, and walking in His paths (*Isa.* 2: 2–5).

(d) It is for this reason that Christ gives, by His Spirit, gifts to enable the people of God to be instructed in the Word of God (*Eph.* 4: 11–16; *I Tim.* 5: 17).

(e) Our sharing in God's holiness involves chastisement on occasions and some of the experiences which lead to greater sanctification are not always pleasant at the time (*Heb.* 12: 10, 11).

8. Many incentives and motives for holiness and sanctification are set before the Christian.

(a) Reverence and respect for God (*II Cor.* 7: 1; *I Pet.* 1: 17).

(b) The mercies of God to us in Christ (*Rom.* 12: 1, 2).

(c) The promises of God (*II Cor.* 7: 1).

(d) The freedom to which we have been called in Christ, enabling us to please God (*Gal.* 5: 13–15).

(e) The prospect of Christ's return (*Tit.* 2: 12, 13; *I John* 3: 3).

(f) God's gift of the Holy Spirit to us and the implications of that gift (*Gal.* 5: 16–26; *I Thess.* 4: 8).

36. BAPTISM

Question: What is baptism?

Answer: It is an act of obedient discipleship, appointed by Christ, administered in the name of the Trinity, which symbolises repentance, faith in the Lord Jesus Christ, the confession of His Lordship, admittance into the family of God, entry into all the benefits of His death and resurrection, and the

desire to live a new life through the power of the Holy Spirit.

1. Baptism was appointed by Christ Himself for all disciples.

(a) Christ Himself was baptised, thereby setting an example to all who would follow Him (*Mark* 1: 9–11; *Matt.* 3: 13–17; *Luke* 3: 21–22).

(b) Speaking of His own baptism, He declared it a rightful act of submission in order to conform to all that God requires (*Matt.* 3: 15).

(c) Baptism was a practice of Christ with regard to those who became His disciples during His ministry (*John* 3: 22, 26; 4: 1)—although Christ did not Himself baptise, leaving it to His disciples (*John* 4: 2).

(d) Baptism was part of the great commission, given to the apostles, after the Resurrection, to be the first thing in which believers were to be instructed of all that Christ commanded (*Matt.* 28: 19, 20; *Mark* 16: 15, 16).

2. It is administered in the name of the Trinity.

(a) It is to be administered always in the name of the Father, the Son and the Holy Spirit (*Matt.* 28: 19).

(b) The identity of the baptiser is unimportant (*John* 4: 2; *I Cor.* 1: 14–17)—this fact may explain why our Lord refrained from baptising disciples (*John* 4: 2), and why Paul appears to have done the same (*I Cor.* 1: 14–16; *Acts* 10: 48).

3. It is a symbol of the individual's reception of the gospel.

(a) It is the consequence of the Lord having opened the individual's heart to give heed to the gospel (*Acts* 16: 14, 15).

(b) It is a mark of a person's reception of the gospel—of the Word of the Lord (*Acts* 2: 37, 38, 41; 8: 12).

(c) It should follow immediately upon confession of faith in Christ (*Acts* 2: 38).

(d) It is the first act of obedient discipleship (*Acts* 9: 18; 16: 14, 15, 33; 22: 16).

(e) It is a badge of discipleship (*Matt.* 28: 19; *John* 3: 22).

(f) It is an experience which every Christian is to share (*Eph.* 4: 5).

(g) It is taken for granted in the New Testament that all believers will be baptised (e.g. *I Cor.* 1: 13; 6: 11; 10: 1 ff).

4. It symbolises repentance and faith in the Lord Jesus Christ.

(a) Baptism is an outward sign of repentance—of turning with contrition from sin to God (*Acts* 2: 38).

(b) It is the personal expression of faith in the Lord Jesus Christ and His gospel (*Mark* 16: 15, 16; *Acts* 8: 12, 13, 37; 16: 31–33).

5. Participation in baptism is the confession of Christ's Lordship.

(a) Baptism is always associated with Christ's name, in that the individual makes a confession concerning Him (*Acts* 2: 37, 38; 8: 16; 22: 16).

(b) It is the acknowledgment of Jesus as Lord (*Acts* 2: 38; 8: 37).

(c) It implies entrance into committed fellowship and allegiance to Christ (*Acts* 2: 38; 10: 48; *Gal.* 3: 27).

(d) It is the public testimony of the individual that he has become Christ's property (*Acts* 16: 15; 19: 5)—the expression "in the name" of someone being used commercially for the transfer of property.

(e) As Lord, Christ's command is to be obeyed (*Mark* 16: 16); to Him the believer must be faithful (*Acts* 16: 14, 15).

6. It symbolises admittance into the family of God.

(a) It marks the believer's admittance into the family of God, or the Church of Christ (*Acts* 2: 38, 41, 47; 8: 12 f, 36, 38; 9: 18, 19; 16: 33; 22: 16; *I Cor*. 1: 14–17).

(b) It is the outward sign of the believer's new birth into God's family (*John* 3: 5).

(c) It is a mark of his entry into the membership of Christ's body (*I Cor*. 12: 13).

7. It symbolises entry into all the benefits of Christ's death and resurrection.

(a) Baptism is a visual aid of the gospel, in that it portrays Christ's death and resurrection and the salvation which comes to men and women as they turn in repentance and faith to Christ (*Rom*. 6: 3, 4).

(b) It is a picture of an individual entering into the benefits of the new covenant, sealed with Christ's blood, even as Noah, believing the promises of God to him, entered the ark (*I Pet*. 3: 18–22).

(c) It is, therefore, a picture of the Christian's cleansing from sin through Christ's death (*Acts* 2: 38)—it is the outward and visible sign of inward and spiritual cleansing (*Acts* 22: 16; *Heb*. 10: 22).

(d) It speaks symbolically of the gift and blessing of new life by the gift and indwelling of the Holy Spirit (*Acts* 2: 38). In order to experience the reality of what baptism signifies, the individual must be born again of God's Spirit (*John* 3: 5; *I Cor*. 12: 13).

8. Participation in baptism expresses the desire the individual has to live a new life through the power of the Holy Spirit.

(a) It signifies his deliverance from the bondage of sin (*Rom*. 6: 3).

(b) It is a symbolical burial of the believer's old life (*Rom*. 6: 3, 4; *Col*. 2: 12), and renunciation of his old relationship to sin, because Christ's death has become his death by faith (*Rom*. 6: 12).

(c) It is a symbol of the beginning of the new life in Christ, of participation in the resurrection life of the Lord Jesus Christ, which is possible by the help and power of the Holy Spirit (*Rom*. 6: 4, 5; *Col*. 2: 12).

(d) It is a symbol of the believer's willingness to present his body to God as an instrument for the doing of God's will (*Rom*. 6: 13).

(e) It symbolises the end of a person's service of sin, and the beginning of his committed service to God (*Rom*. 6: 16, 17).

37. THE LORD'S SUPPER

Question: What is the Lord's Supper?

Answer: The Lord's Supper is the symbolic meal which Christ established and commanded; in which Christians remember Christ's sacrifice continually; in which they acknowledge their sharing in the benefits of His death; at which they

have fellowship with Christ and with other Christians; and make their thanksgiving to God.

1. The Lord's Supper is a symbolic meal.

(a) The Lord's Supper is a proclamation of the Lord's death by words and symbols (*I Cor.* 11: 26).

(b) Christ's body is represented by the bread (*I Cor.* 11: 24).

(c) Christ's blood is represented by the wine (*I Cor.* 11: 25).

(d) The bread is broken and the wine is poured out as symbols of Christ's death upon the Cross (*Matt.* 26: 26; *Mark* 14: 22; *Luke* 22: 19, 20; *I Cor.* 11: 24, 25).

(e) Both the bread and the wine are to be distributed to Christians as they sit at the Lord's Table (*Matt.* 26: 26, 27; *Mark* 14: 22–28; *Luke* 22: 19, 20; *I Cor.* 11: 23, 24, 26).

(f) The Lord's Supper was prepared for, in symbol, by the Jewish Passover (*I Cor.* 5: 7, 8; *Ex.* 12: 21–28): even as the Passover proclaimed the mercy of God in redeeming His people under the old covenant, so the Lord's Supper proclaims God's redeeming mercy under the new covenant (*I Cor.* 11: 26).

(g) The Lord's Supper took place at the Passover feast and was established on the pattern of the Passover (*Matt.* 26: 17–19; *Mark* 14: 1, 2, 12–16; *Luke* 22: 14–20; *John* 13: 21–30; compare *Ex.* 12).

(h) The bread that was eaten with the lamb in the Passover feast was put to a new use (*Matt.* 26: 26).

(i) The third cup of the Passover, "the cup of blessing" (compare *I Cor.* 10: 16) was also put to a new use (*Matt.* 26, 27, 28).

(j) By reason of its significance, the Lord's Supper must be regarded as quite distinct from all other meals (*I Cor.* 11: 29).

2. The Lord's Supper was established and commanded by Christ.

(a) The Lord Jesus Christ established this regular act at the Last Supper on the night of His betrayal (*Matt.* 26: 26–28; *I Cor.* 11: 23).

(b) Christ gave certain actions to be imitated every time the symbolic meal was repeated (*I Cor.* 11: 23 ff).

(c) The Lord's Supper, in its institution, was a meal which Christ earnestly desired to share with His disciples (*Luke* 22: 15).

(d) In establishing the symbolic meal Christ commanded that it should be continually repeated (*Luke* 22: 19b; *I Cor.* 11: 25).

(e) Because Christ established the meal it is called the Lord's Supper (*I Cor.* 11: 20), and also the table of the Lord (*I Cor.* 10: 21). It is also described as the breaking of bread (*Acts* 2: 42; 20: 7) because Christ broke the bread (*Luke* 22: 19; 24: 30, 35). It is also called the "eucharist" or "thanksgiving" (*I Cor.* 10: 16) because Christ gave thanks when He took the cup (*Matt.* 26: 27).

(f) The apostle Paul received a direct revelation from Christ regarding the institution of the Lord's Supper and the importance of its continuation (*I Cor.* 11: 23; cf. *Gal.* 1: 12; 2: 2).

(g) We are not surprised, therefore, that the Lord's Supper was a regular act of the early church (*Acts* 2: 42); they used to assemble on the first day of the week for the breaking of bread (*Acts* 20: 7).

3. By means of the Lord's Supper Christians remember Christ's sacrifice continually.

(a) The Lord's Supper sets forth Christ's death for us (*I Cor.* 11: 26).

(b) The purpose is that we should recall to mind Christ's sufferings on our behalf (*Luke* 22: 19; *I Cor.* 11: 24, 25).

(c) It is a remembrance, or a memorial, meal (*I Cor.* 11: 23–25).

4. By means of the Lord's Supper Christians acknowledge their sharing in the benefits of Christ's death.

(a) The Lord's Supper declares that the new covenant that God promised has been established through the saving work of His Son (*I Cor.* 11: 25).

(b) It reminds us of our sharing by faith in the benefits of His death (*John* 6: 53, 63; *I Cor.* 10: 16).

(c) The Lord's Supper is a symbol of our sharing or partaking of Christ (*I Cor.* 10: 17).

5. In the Lord's Supper Christians have fellowship with Christ and with other Christians.

(a) The Lord's Supper is an act of communion with Christ (*I Cor.* 10: 16).

(b) Christians, therefore, who take part in the Lord's Supper should be in uncompromised fellowship with the Lord Jesus Christ (*I Cor.* 10: 21).

(c) The Lord's Supper is an act of fellowship with other Christians: it is the time when Christians "come together" (*I Cor.* 11: 17, 18, 20, 33, 34; *I Cor.* 10: 17; *Acts* 20: 7).

(d) The Lord's Supper expresses the union of Christians with one another (*I Cor.* 10: 17; 12: 13).

(e) The fellowship which believers have with the Lord Jesus Christ in the Lord's Supper is a pledge of the fulfilled fellowship they will have in the kingdom of God (*Mark* 14: 25; *Luke* 22: 16).

6. In the Lord's Supper Christians make their thanksgiving to God.

(a) The Lord's Supper is a reminder of the death of Christ to bring forth our thanksgiving (*I Cor.* 11: 24, 25).

(b) We are to give thanks for the bread and wine as Christ did, remembering that they are symbols of His broken body and of His outpoured blood (*I Cor.* 11: 23, 24).

(c) Thus the Lord's Supper is the particular time when we offer our thanksgiving to God for Christ and His redeeming work (*I Cor.* 10: 16).

(d) Being more aware of God's mercies towards us at the Lord's Supper than at any other time the sacrifice of thanksgiving should include the offering of ourselves to God (*Rom.* 12: 1).

(e) Christians who take part in the Lord's Supper should be willing to dedicate themselves completely to Christ (*I Cor.* 10: 21).

(f) To take part properly in the Lord's Supper we need to have done with our old kind of life and to be living to the full our new life in Christ (*I Cor.* 5: 7, 8): renewed dedication of ourselves to this end is part of our thanksgiving.

7. The Lord's Supper is a tremendous help to the spiritual life of Christians.

(a) The Lord's Supper strengthens our faith and refreshes our souls—this fact is true every time we consider the love of God to us (*I John* 3: 1–3; *Rom.* 8: 35–39).

(b) At the Lord's Supper we may feed spiritually upon Christ (*John* 6: 32, 33, 35, 50, 51): those who rightly receive the bread and the wine, by living faith, receive Christ and the benefits of His passion (*I Cor.* 10: 16).

8. Unfortunately, it is possible for Christians to take part in the Lord's Supper unworthily.

(a) The Lord's Supper needs to be entered upon with care (*I Cor.* 11: 27).

(b) Christians should examine their lives before they eat their share of the bread and drink from the cup (*I Cor.* 11: 28).

9. The Lord's Supper is to be continued until Christ returns.

(a) The Lord's Supper looks forward to the Lord's return (*I Cor.* 11: 26).

(b) The Lord's Supper will no longer be necessary when Christ returns (*I Cor.* 11: 26).

38. THE CHURCH

Question: What is the Church of Christ?

Answer: The Church consists of those of every race, every land and every age who have been chosen by God the Father, purchased by Christ's blood and sanctified by the Holy Spirit.

1. The Descriptions given of the Church in the Bible.

(a) God's very own people (*Ex.* 6: 7; *II Cor.* 6: 14–18; *Rev.* 21: 2, 3).

(b) The new and true Israel, established in Christ (*Gal.* 3: 29; 6: 16; *I Pet.* 2: 9).

(c) The company of those whom the Lord has called to Himself (*Acts* 2: 39).

(d) Those who are in Christ (*Phil.* 1: 1).

(e) The company of those who in every place call upon the name of Jesus Christ the Lord (*I Cor.* 1: 2).

(f) The company of those who believe (*Acts* 4: 31, 32).

(g) The household of God (*Heb.* 10: 21), and the household of faith (*Gal.* 6: 10).

(h) God's building (*I Cor.* 3: 10).

(i) God's temple (*I Cor.* 3: 16, 17), i.e. the temple of the Spirit (*Eph.* 2: 22).

(j) Christ's flock (*Heb.* 13: 20; *Acts* 20: 28).

(k) The Body of Christ (*I Cor.* 12: 14–27; *Eph.* 1: 23; 5: 30; *Col.* 1: 24).

(l) The bride of Christ (*Eph.* 5: 21–33; *Rev.* 21: 2, 9; 22: 17).

2. The members of the Church are chosen by God the Father.

(a) They were chosen in Christ before the foundation of the world (*Eph.* 1: 4).

(b) They were destined in God's love to be His sons in Jesus Christ (*Eph.* 1: 5).

(c) Being chosen, they are called by God to be members of Christ's Church (*Rom.* 8: 28–30; 9: 11, 24; 11: 5; *Gal.* 1: 15; *I Thess.* 1: 4).

(d) The Church is made up of those who have been called of God, out of darkness into His marvellous light (*Rom.* 1: 5, 6; *II Tim.* 1: 9; *I Pet.* 2: 9).

3. The members of the Church are cleansed from sin through Christ's blood.

(a) The Church was purchased by the blood of Christ (*Acts* 20: 28; *Eph.* 5: 25; *Heb.* 9: 12).

(b) Christ loved the Church and gave Himself up for her, that she might be cleansed and sanctified (*I Cor.* 6: 11; *Eph.* 5: 25–27).

(c) Christ gave Himself to redeem her members from all iniquity (*Tit.* 2: 14).

(d) Thus the Church is made up of those who were once alienated from God by sin but have been brought nigh to Him through the blood of Christ (*Eph.* 2: 11–13).

(e) They are members of the Church through the blood of the new and eternal covenant (*Heb.* 13: 20).

4. The members of the Church are sanctified by the Holy Spirit who lives within them to this end.

(a) Members of Christ's Church were chosen that they should be holy and blameless before God (*Eph.* 1: 4), conformed to the image of God's Son (*Rom.* 8: 29), and purified (*Tit.* 2: 14).

(b) This work of sanctification is the Holy Spirit's, which He never ceases to perform throughout the Christian's life (*I Pet.* 1: 2; *I Thess.* 4: 7, 8; *Phil.* 1: 6).

(c) Thus the Church is the company of those who have received the Holy Spirit through faith in the Lord Jesus Christ (*Rom.* 8: 9; *Acts* 11: 17), who have been born again of God's Spirit (*John* 3: 5–8).

5. Some of the conclusions the Bible draws for us.

(a) The Church belongs to God (*Gal.* 1: 13; *I Tim.* 3: 15).

(b) God alone knows exactly who are the true members of the Church (*II Tim.* 2: 19).

(c) The sole right of adding new members to the Church is the Lord's (*Acts* 2: 47).

(d) The Church is made up of those of every race who have been brought together in Christ, and are indwelt by the Holy Spirit (*Eph.* 2: 11–22; *Rev.* 5: 9, 10).

(e) Thus the Church of Christ ignores all divisions of race or social distinctions, making all its members one (*I Cor.* 12: 13).

39. BECOMING A MEMBER OF THE CHURCH

Question: How do we become members of the Church?

Answer: Through the new birth by living faith in Jesus Christ.

1. Christ is the foundation of the Church.

(a) There is no other foundation save Jesus Christ (*I Cor.* 3: 11).

(b) The Church is built upon Him (*Matt.* 16: 18).

2. Living faith in Christ, therefore, is essential.

(a) It is by coming to Him, the living foundation stone of the Church, that we become part of God's spiritual building — the Church (*I Pet.* 2: 4, 5).

(b) As we believe that Jesus is the

Son of God and confess Him as Lord, through the help of the Holy Spirit, we become members of the Church of Christ (*Matt.* 16: 16, 17; *John* 20: 31; *I Cor.* 12: 3).

(c) Those who thus hear God's call to become members of Christ's Church do so by means of the Word of God and the work of the Holy Spirit (*John* 3: 8; *Acts* 16: 14; *I Cor.* 4: 15; *I Pet.* 1: 23).

3. Such living faith means that the new birth has taken place.

(a) We become members of the Church by new birth (*John* 3: 5–8).

(b) We belong to Christ and His Church through our possession of the Holy Spirit (*Rom.* 8: 9).

(c) All believers are brought into the one Body of Christ—the Church—by the one and the same Holy Spirit (*I Cor.* 12: 13).

4. The Church of Christ is made up, therefore, of those who have a personal relationship to Christ.

(a) They know Him (*Phil.* 3: 10; *II Pet.* 3: 18).

(b) He is their Shepherd (*John* 10: 14; *I Pet.* 2: 25; 5: 4).

(c) As members of His Body, they have a living relationship to Him, the Head (*Eph.* 4: 14–16).

40. BELONGING TO THE CHURCH

Question: What does belonging to the Church of Christ involve?

Answer: It involves, first and foremost, obedience to Christ's control, and the recognition in practice of the implications of the relationship we have towards all other members of the Church: fellowship; caring for one another; submitting to necessary discipline; maintaining spiritual unity; and offering together spiritual sacrifices acceptable to God.

1. Membership of the Church of Christ involves, first and foremost, obedience to Christ's control.

(a) The Church is His Body (*Eph.* 1: 23).

(b) The Church, therefore, is to be subject to Christ in everything (*Eph.* 4: 15, 16; 5: 24).

(c) Christ is to be reverenced in the heart as Lord (*I Pet.* 3: 15).

(d) The love of the members of the Church for Christ, the Head, is seen in their obedience to His commandments (*John* 14: 15); for example, in their zeal for good works (*Matt.* 5: 16, compared with *Tit.* 2: 14).

2. Membership of the Church of Christ involves recognising the relationship we have to all other Christians.

(a) We are members of the same Body (*I Cor.* 12: 4–27; *Eph.* 1: 23; 5: 30; *Col.* 1: 24); and, therefore, individually members one of another (*Rom.* 12: 5).

(b) We constitute together the people of God (*I Pet.* 2: 9, 10).

(c) We belong to the same family or household (*Gal.* 6: 10; *Heb.* 10: 21).

(d) We are sheep of the same flock (*Heb.* 13: 20; *Acts* 20: 28).

(e) We are citizens of the same kingdom (*Phil.* 3: 20; *Heb.* 11: 16; 12: 28; *Rev.* 21: 2, 3).

(f) We are together a chosen race, a royal priesthood and a holy nation (*I Pet.* 2: 9, 10).

3. Membership of the Church of Christ involves fulfilling the implications of this relationship which we have with all other Christians.

(a) By living in fellowship (*Acts* 2: 42–47; *Heb.* 10: 24; *I John* 1: 3, 7; 2: 19).

(b) By caring for one another (*I Cor.* 12: 7; *Gal.* 6: 10; *I Pet.* 5: 2; *I John* 3: 16, 17).

(c) By accepting the family discipline (*I Cor.* 5: 12, 13; *Heb.* 13: 17; *Rev.* 2: 12–29).

(d) By maintaining spiritual unity (*Eph.* 4: 2, 3; *Phil.* 2: 1, 2).

(e) By offering together the spiritual sacrifices of our spiritual priesthood which are acceptable to God by Jesus Christ (*I Pet.* 2: 5): for example, praise (*Heb.* 13: 15), thanksgiving (*Ps.* 50: 14; 107: 22), prayer (*Ps.* 141: 2), the dedication of our bodies to Him (*Rom.* 12: 1), doing good and sharing what we have with others (*Heb.* 13: 16).

41. THE WORK AND DESTINY OF THE CHURCH

Question: What is the work of the Church? And what is going to happen to the Church?

Answer: The work of the Church—in brief—is to proclaim the gospel of Christ, making disciples of all who believe, until, as the bride of Christ, she is presented to Christ at His return.

1. The work of the Church is to proclaim the gospel of Christ.

(a) Christians are to declare the wonderful deeds of Him who has called them out of darkness into His marvellous light—principally by the change which the gospel has brought into their lives (*I Pet.* 2: 9).

(b) The main function of the Church is testimony to Jesus Christ (*Rev.* 11: 7; 12: 11, 17).

(c) The purpose the Lord Jesus Christ had for the Church from the beginning was the preaching of repentance and forgiveness of sins in His name to all nations (*Luke* 24: 47; *Mark* 16: 15; *Acts* 1: 8).

2. The work of the Church is to make disciples of all who believe the gospel.

(a) Believers are to be baptised in the name of the Father, and of the Son, and of the Holy Spirit (*Matt.* 28: 19).

(b) They are to be taught to observe all that Christ has commanded (*Matt.* 28: 20).

(c) They are to be warned and instructed, according to all that God would have them know, so that they are brought to their full maturity as members of Christ's Body, the Church (*Col.* 1: 28).

3. The end always in view is the return of Christ and the presentation of the Church to Him as His bride.

(a) No matter how dark the days may be, and how apparently hopeless the Church's situation may appear, she shall triumph and the powers of hell will not prevail against her (*Matt.* 16: 18).

(b) Christ loves the Church, and He will demonstrate that love before the enemies of the Church (*Rev.* 3: 9; compare *II Thess.* 1: 5–10).

(c) The Church will be gathered from every part of the earth, with no member missed, at Christ's return (*Matt.* 24: 31; *Mark* 13: 27; *Luke* 21: 28).

(d) Her destiny is to be presented glorious before Him at the last (*Eph.* 5: 27), His bride (*II Cor.* 11: 2; *Rev.* 21: 2).

42. MEMBERSHIP OF A LOCAL CHURCH

Question: Why belong to a church?

Answer: The teaching of the New Testament takes it for granted that every Christian will join together with other Christians in the membership of a local congregation for only then can the implications of common membership of the Church of Christ find expression—that is to say, in fellowship, mutual care, submission to necessary discipline, the maintenance of spiritual unity, and the offering together of spiritual sacrifices acceptable to God—and the work of the Church be effectively carried out—that is to say, in the proclamation of the gospel and the making of disciples in a particular area.

1. The New Testament gives an essential place to the local church in the life of the Christian.

(a) The local church is not to be despised by the Christian (*I Cor.* 11: 22).

(b) The New Testament refers to patterns of behaviour in the church, meaning the local church (*I Cor.* 14: 19, 28, 35); and the directions given by the apostles were given in the first place to churches (*I Cor.* 16: 1).

(c) As the work of evangelism progressed in the first century, Christians were gathered together as soon as possible into churches (*Acts* 13: 1; 14: 23; 15: 41; 20: 17; *Rev.* 1: 11).

(d) Usually, wherever Christians were to be found there were ordained elders (*Acts* 14: 22, 23), and a local situation was defective where elders had not been appointed (*Tit.* 1: 5).

(e) Christians were assumed to be in such a close relationship together that they acknowledged certain men as leaders (*Heb.* 13: 7), and the latter knew themselves to be guardians of the local company of Christians (*Acts* 20: 28).

(f) The New Testament takes it for granted that Christians living in the same locality will have regular fellowship, assembling together as a company of believers (*I Cor.* 1: 2; 14: 23; *II Cor.* 1: 1; *I Tim.* 3: 15).

(g) Christians are instructed not to neglect meeting together (*Heb.* 10: 25).

(h) The early Christians were in such an established relationship with one another that they could speak of some who "went out from us" who "were not of us" (*I John* 2: 19).

(i) Christians are to strive to excel in building up the local church (*I Cor.* 14: 12).

(j) The instinctive act of Paul after his conversion was to identify himself with the Christians in Damascus, and with those at Jerusalem on his arrival there (*Acts* 9: 19, 26).

2. The Descriptions the Bible gives of the Church as a whole demand that Christians meet together as ordered congregations in their localities.

(a) The flock of God gathers together under the leadership of the under-shepherds whom the Chief Shepherd, Christ, has appointed (*Heb.* 13: 20; *I Pet.* 2: 25; 5: 2, 4).

(b) The members of the Body of Christ are members of one another and are intended, therefore, to be in the closest possible association together (*I Cor.* 12: 26, 27).

(c) The picture of the church as the household of faith implies a close relationship together (*Gal.* 6: 10).

(d) A brick is only a building as it is together with other bricks, properly joined to them: so too with the Christian (*I Pet.* 2: 4, 5).

3. To belong to a church is a practical demonstration of the recognition of our relationship in Christ to our fellow-believers.

4. It enables us to live in fellowship.

(a) The logical consequence of receiving the Holy Spirit is to want to live in fellowship with other Christians (*Rom.* 8: 9; *Phil.* 2: 1).

(b) Constant fellowship is possible through the local church as in no other way (*Acts* 2: 42).

(c) The fellowship is to be so close that mutual encouragement can be given both to love and to do good works (*Heb.* 3: 13; 10: 24).

5. It enables us to fulfil Christ's command to remember His death and its meaning by means of the Lord's Supper.

(a) To do this together is a vital part of Christian fellowship (*Acts* 2: 42; *I Cor.* 10: 16, 17).

(b) The early Christians gathered together on the Lord's Day to break bread in remembrance of Christ's death (*Acts* 20: 7).

(c) Christians need to come together regularly in the local church for the Lord's Supper (*I Cor.* 11: 23–34).

6. It enables us to get to know our fellow-believers and thus to care for one another.

(a) We may do good effectively to those who are of the household of faith only as we know who they are by coming together in the fellowship of the local church (*Gal.* 6: 10).

(b) By close association with one another Christian love is able to find the positive and practical expression it needs (*John* 13: 35).

(c) Through church-membership we are able to strengthen one another (*Luke* 22: 32), restore one another when fallen (*Gal.* 6: 1), and bear one another's burdens (*Gal.* 6: 2).

(d) By means of the local church the exercise of spiritual gifts to the benefit of one another is made possible (*I Cor.* 12: 24–28).

7. It shows our acceptance of the family discipline of the Church, expressed, as it can only be, through the local church.

(a) The Lord Jesus Christ taught that the local church was essential for maintaining the right kind of discipline amongst God's people (*Matt.* 18: 15–20).

(b) It is taken for granted in the New Testament that all Christians will be so committed to a local church that they will be within the discipline of that church (*I Thess.* 5: 12; *I Tim.* 5: 17; *Heb.* 13: 17; *I Pet.* 5: 1–5).

(c) Christians are to be in such an association of membership together that they can discipline members who bring dishonour to Christ (*I Cor.* 5: 2, 4, 12, 13).

8. It is a practical expression of spiritual unity.

(a) Christians feel within themselves the desire to express the oneness there is in Jesus Christ (*Gal.* 3: 28).

(b) No effort is to be spared to make fast with the bonds of love the unity which the Spirit gives (*Eph.* 4: 2, 3).

(c) The common life Christians have in Christ brings a common care for unity (*Phil.* 2: 1, 2).

9. It enables us to offer regularly the corporate spiritual sacrifices which honour God.

(a) By means of the local church, Christians make their praise and prayers corporate (*Heb.* 13: 15; *Acts* 2: 42, 47; 12: 5, 12).

(b) Through the knowledge Christians have of one another's needs, associated as they are in the local church, they are able to do good and share what they have with others (*Heb.* 13: 16).

(c) They are able to fulfil their financial obligations too to the work of Christ's Church (*I Cor.* 16: 2; *Phil.* 4: 14–19).

10. It is the instrument God uses to proclaim the gospel of Christ in an area.

(a) The testimony of the corporate life of a local church should be such a powerful influence for evangelism, that the Lord adds to the number of His people (*Acts* 2: 42–47).

(b) The local church is the means of sounding forth the word of the Lord in an area (*I Thess.* 1: 1, 8).

11. It is the provision God has made for the instruction of believers that they should be mature disciples.

(a) Christians are to be instructed in all that the Lord Jesus Christ commanded that they should do and observe (*Matt.* 28: 19): to this end God gives to local churches pastors and teachers, so that Christians may be fed and built up by the Word of God (*Acts* 20: 28; *Eph.* 4: 12, 15, 16; *I Pet.* 2: 2; 5: 2).

(b) The most important part of the elders' work is the ministry of the Word of God (*I Tim.* 5: 17; *I Pet.* 5: 2).

(c) Christians are expected to be in a situation where they will be contributing to the financial support of those who give themselves to preaching and teaching (*Gal.* 6: 6; *I Tim.* 5: 17, 18).

(d) The local church, faithfully taught, is one means God uses to preserve the pure teaching and preaching of the gospel (*II Tim.* 2: 2).

43. THE DEVIL

Question: What do we know about the devil?

Answer: The devil is the great enemy of God and man, the opposer of all that is good and the promoter of all that is evil. He has been defeated already by Christ's death and resurrection, and this defeat will be complete and clear to all at the end of this present age.

1. The devil's history.

(a) He is one of the fallen angels exalted in rank and power above all the rest (*Jude* 6; *II Pet.* 2: 4).

(b) He fell from the truth in which he once stood (*John* 8: 44).

(c) He is represented as a star fallen from heaven to earth (*Rev.* 9: 1).

(d) He sinned probably by reason of pride (*I Tim.* 3: 6).

(e) From the time of his first rebellion against God, the devil has sinned continuously (*II Pet.* 2: 4; *I John* 3: 8).

2. He is called by many names.

(a) He is called Satan (*Matt.* 16: 23; *Luke* 22: 31; *Rev.* 12: 9; 20: 2).

(b) He is the wicked one (*I John* 2: 13, 14; 3: 12; 5: 18).

(c) He is the prince of the power of the air (*Eph.* 2: 2).

(d) He is the prince of the devils (*Matt.* 9: 34; 12: 24).

(e) He is the god of this world (*II Cor.* 4: 4).

(f) He is called Beelzebub (*Matt.* 12: 24, 27; *Luke* 11: 15, 18, 19).

(g) He is the tempter (*Matt.* 4: 3; *I Thess.* 3: 5).

(h) He is called the old serpent (*Rev.* 12: 9).

(i) He is called the dragon (*Rev.* 12: 3, 4, 7, 9, 13, 16, 17; 20: 2).

3. The devil's power.

(a) He has great power: he showed Christ all the kingdoms of the world in a moment of time (*Matt.* 4: 8; *Luke* 4: 5).

(b) All who are without Christ and the new birth are under the authority and power of the devil and his agents (*Eph.* 6: 12; *I John* 5: 19)—to be outside of the Church of Christ is to belong to Satan (*I Cor.* 5: 5; *I Tim.* 1: 20).

(c) The whole world is in his power (*I John* 5: 19), for he is its ruler (*John* 12: 31; 14: 30; 16: 11; *II Cor.* 4: 4; *Eph.* 2: 2; 6: 12).

(d) Men and women have the devil as their father, and they are his children (*John* 8: 44; *I John* 3: 10).

(e) To be in his power is to be imprisoned, to be spiritually blind, and in spiritual darkness, under God's condemnation (*Acts* 26: 18).

(f) He is likened to a strong man, whose house contains men and women as chattels or goods. He must be bound before his house can be broken into (*Matt.* 12: 29; *Mark* 3: 27; *Luke* 11: 21, 22).

(g) His power is such that Christ prayed against him on behalf of His disciples (*John* 17: 15).

4. Some of the devil's characteristics.

(a) He is the enemy of all righteousness, full of deceit and villainy, whose activity is to make crooked the straight paths of the Lord (*Acts* 13: 10).

(b) He is wicked (*Matt.* 6: 13; *John* 17: 15; *I John* 2: 13, 14; 3: 12; 5: 18, 19).

(c) He is a liar and the father of lies (*John* 8: 44): he has nothing to do with the truth, because there is no truth in him.

(d) He is subtle and deceitful (*Gen.* 3: 1; *II Cor.* 11: 3, 4; *Eph.* 6: 11).

(e) He is proud and presumptuous (*I Tim.* 3: 6; *Job* 1: 6; *Matt.* 4: 5, 6).

(f) He is malignant: he makes malicious accusations and pleads false charges (*Job* 1: 6–12; 2: 4; *Zech.* 3: 1; *Rev.* 12: 9–11).

(g) He is fierce and cruel (*Luke* 8: 29; 9: 39, 42): he prowls around like a roaring lion (*I Pet.* 5: 8).

(h) He is a murderer (*John* 8: 44; *I John* 3: 12).

(i) His activity is ceaseless (*Rev.* 12: 10).

5. His activity in general.

(a) Sin is his characteristic activity (*I John* 3: 8): he was the originator of the Fall (*Gen.* 3: 1, 6, 14, 24).

(b) He is active in doing evil (*Job* 1: 7; 2: 2).

(c) He masquerades as an angel of light (*II Cor.* 11: 14), and so too do his agents (*II Cor.* 11: 15).

(d) He causes false beliefs to arise (*I Tim.* 5: 15): every anti-Christian movement and spirit is a result of his activity (*II Thess.* 2: 9).

(e) He encourages men in lies and deceit (*II Thess.* 2: 10; *Rev.* 3: 9).

(f) He engineers pretended signs and wonders and wicked deception (*II Thess.* 2: 9, 10; *Rev.* 16: 14).

(g) He misapplies the Scriptures to gain his own wicked ends (*Matt.* 4: 6).

(h) Through depending upon human wisdom rather than divine, men can become his agents without being aware of the fact (*Matt.* 16: 23; *Mark* 8: 33): the devil put it into the heart of Judas Iscariot to betray Jesus (*John* 13: 2).

(i) He opposes God's work (*Zech.* 3: 1; *Matt.* 13: 39; *I Thess.* 2: 18): especially the preaching of the gospel (*Matt.* 13: 19; *II Cor.* 4: 4; *Mark* 4: 15; *Luke* 8: 12).

6. His attacks upon Christians.

(a) He does battle against every individual who would keep God's commandments and bear testimony to Jesus (*Luke* 22: 31; *I Pet.* 5: 8, 9; *Rev.* 12: 17).

(b) He is always looking for an opportunity of causing trouble to the Christian (*Eph.* 6: 11; *I Tim.* 3: 7; *Jas.* 4: 7; *Rev.* 12: 10).

(c) He seeks to gain the advantage over believers (*II Cor.* 2: 11): he tells of the pleasures of sin but not of its consequences (*Gen.* 3: 4 f); he tells half-truths for the truth (*Gen.* 3: 5).

(d) He seeks to tempt believers by any means possible, trying one temptation after another (*Matt.* 4: 1–10; *Mark* 1: 13; *Luke* 4: 2, 13).

(e) He tempts along the line of the appetites frequently (*Gen.* 3: 1 ff; *Matt.* 4: 2, 3; *Luke* 4: 2, 3; *I Cor.* 7: 5).

(f) He tempts Christians to use spiritual powers selfishly (*Matt.* 4: 3; *Luke* 4: 3), and to presume upon God's care (*Matt.* 4: 5, 6; *Luke* 4: 9–11).

(g) He encourages doubts and questionings, together with compromise (*Gen.* 3: 1, 4; *Matt.* 4: 8, 9; *Luke* 4: 5, 6, 7).

(h) He gets at the Christians through their lack of balance (*I Cor.* 7: 5).

(i) He seeks to bewitch them so that they take their eyes off Christ crucified (*II Cor.* 11: 14; *Gal.* 3: 1).

(j) He would encourage them in evil—even to lie to the Holy Spirit (*Acts* 5: 3).

(k) He inspires the persecution of Christians (*Rev.* 2: 10, 13).

7. Christ's conquest of the devil at the Cross.

(a) The devil had no power over Christ (*John* 14: 30); his power and authority are inferior to those of Christ (*Mark* 3: 7; *Luke* 11: 19, 20, 21, 22).

(b) Christ partook of flesh and blood that through death He might destroy him who had the power of death, that is, the devil (*Heb.* 2: 14; *I John* 3: 8).

(c) Christ's conflict with the devil came to a head at the Cross: He disarmed the devil and all his powers, and made a public example of them at His resurrection, triumphing over them (*John* 12: 31; 16: 11; *Heb.* 2: 14; *Col.* 2: 15; *I John* 3: 8).

(d) So far as Christ is concerned, the devil is a conquered enemy (*Luke* 10: 18).

(e) Christ's people enter into His victory over the devil (*Rom.* 16: 20).

8. The devil's limits.

(a) The devil's power has been given to him, and can, therefore, be taken away from him by God (*Luke* 4: 6): he knows his time is short (*Rev.* 12: 12).

(b) He is allowed liberty, within bounds, to test and tempt Christians (*Job* 1: 1–12; 2: 1–6; *Luke* 22: 31; *II Cor.* 10: 13; *Rev.* 20: 2, 7).

(c) The Father is able to keep from the evil one those whom He has given to His Son out of the world (*John* 17: 15).

(d) His activity can even be used by God to accomplish some good purpose (*I Cor.* 5: 5; *II Cor.* 12: 7).

9. The devil's end.

(a) His final defeat will take place at the last day, and his ultimate condemnation and punishment are sure at the judgment of that day (*Jude* 6; *Rev.* 20: 10).

(b) He is to be crushed by God (*Rom.* 16: 20).

(c) Eternal fire is prepared for the devil and his angels at the final judgment (*Matt.* 25: 41).

10. Meanwhile, the devil is to be overcome by Christians.

(a) Christians are not to be ignorant of his devices (*II Cor.* 2: 11).

(b) They are dependent upon Christ's protection and activity on their behalf for deliverance from the devil (*Luke* 22: 31).

(c) The devil is overcome by the blood of the Lamb and by the word of Christians' testimony (*Rev.* 12: 11).

(d) As Christians resist the devil, he will flee from them (*Jas.* 4: 7).

(e) The spiritual equipment God provides for the Christian is alone sufficient to enable him to stand against the devil's wiles (*Eph.* 6: 11): using this equipment, the Christian cannot be defeated (*Eph.* 6: 13).

44. THE RETURN OF CHRIST

Question: Will Christ come again?

Answer: Christ will come again, as promised, at a time not told us, in the same way as He was seen to return to heaven.

1. Christ's second coming is clearly promised in the Bible.

(a) The Lord Jesus Christ Himself promised, "I will come again" (*John* 14: 3; *Matt.* 25: 31).

(b) His second coming is promised by the Old Testament prophets (*Dan.* 7: 13; *Zech.* 14: 5).

(c) The apostles bore witness to Christ's second coming (*Acts* 3: 20).

(d) Peter declares that Christ will be revealed (*I Pet.* 1: 13).

(e) John declares that Christ will appear and Christians will see Him (*I John* 3: 2).

(f) Paul preached with urgency in view of the appearing of our Lord Jesus Christ yet to come (*I Tim.* 6: 14).

(g) The Lord's Supper is intended to be a perpetual reminder of the Lord's second coming for it is an "interim" measure—it is "until He comes" (*I Cor.* 11: 26).

(h) A common greeting amongst the early Christians seems to have been "Maranatha"—"the Lord is coming" (*I Cor.* 16: 22).

2. Signs of Christ's coming again are indicated in the Bible.

(a) The second coming of Christ will be preceded by disturbances in nature, and distress among the nations (*Luke* 21: 25).

(b) There will be signs in sun and moon and stars (*Luke* 21: 25; *Matt.* 24: 29).

(c) The second coming will be preceded by concern and fear over coming events: men will faint with fear and with foreboding of what is coming to the world (*Luke* 21: 26).

(d) The second coming will be preceded by the appearance of many antichrists (*I John* 2: 18).

(e) Many shall depart from the faith and false teaching shall be on the increase (*I Tim.* 4: 1–3).

3. The precise time of Christ's second coming is not stated.

(a) It is natural for us to want to know the timing of everything (*Mark* 13: 4).

(b) But no one knows the day or the hour of Christ's second coming, except the Father (*Mark* 13: 32; *Matt.* 24: 36).

(c) We are not intended to know the exact time (*Acts* 1: 6, 7).

(d) Christ shall be sent by the Father at the appointed time (*Acts* 3: 20, 21).

(e) Christ's coming will be at the unexpected moment (*Matt.* 24: 44; *Luke* 12: 40)—in the twinkling of an eye (*I Cor.* 15: 51–52).

(f) His coming will be sudden (*Mark* 13: 36)—like lightning (*Matt.* 24: 27) or a thief in the night (*I Thess.* 5: 2; *II Pet.* 3: 10; *Rev.* 16: 15).

(g) The world will be totally unprepared for the second coming of Christ even as it was unprepared for the coming of the flood (*Matt.* 24: 38).

(h) There is no delay about the Lord's coming (*Heb.* 10: 37): the only reason for any appearance of delay in the Lord's return is His forbearance, in that He does not wish that any should perish, but that all should reach repentance (*II Pet.* 3: 9).

(i) The coming of the Lord Jesus draws near with the passing of each day (*Heb.* 10: 25).

(j) His coming will be soon (*Rev.* 22: 7, 12, 20).

(k) His coming is always to be considered as being at hand (*Rom.* 13: 12; *Phil.* 4: 5; *I Pet.* 4: 7).

4. We are told something of the manner in which Christ will come.

(a) He will come in the same way

as He was seen to go into heaven (*Acts* 1: 9, 11).

(b) He will come from heaven (*Acts* 3: 21; *Phil.* 3: 20; *I Thess.* 1: 10; 4: 16).

(c) He will come visibly (*Matt.* 24: 30; *Mark* 13: 26; 14: 62; *I John* 3: 2; *Rev.* 1: 7).

(d) He will come openly (*Matt.* 24: 27), and personally (*Acts* 1: 11)—His coming will mean His presence after His absence (*John* 14: 2, 3).

(e) He will come in clouds with power and great glory (*Matt.* 24: 30; 26: 64; *Rev.* 1: 7)—the glory of His Father (*Matt.* 16: 27).

(f) He will come with His angels (*Matt.* 16: 27; 25: 31; *Mark* 8: 38; *II Thess.* 1: 7), and with all His saints, in flaming fire (*I Thess.* 3: 13; *II Thess.* 1: 8).

5. **Christ's second coming should influence Christians in their character and conduct continually.**

(a) We are to rest the full weight of our hopes on the grace that will be ours when the Lord Jesus Christ returns (*I Pet.* 1: 13).

(b) We are to anticipate the sight of the Lord Jesus Christ (*I Pet.* 1: 8).

(c) We are to love His appearing (*II Tim.* 4: 8), looking (*Phil.* 3: 20; *Tit.* 2: 13), waiting (*I Cor.* 1: 7; *I Thess.* 1: 10) and praying for it (*Rev.* 22: 20).

(d) Having this hope before us, we shall find ourselves stimulated to pursue holiness (*I Thess.* 3: 13; *II Pet.* 3: 11, 12; *I John* 3: 3).

(e) Our conduct will be influenced and regulated by this truth as it is ever before us (*I Pet.* 4: 7–11).

(f) We shall use the apparent "delay" to bring about men's salvation by the preaching of the gospel (*II Pet.* 3: 15), at the same time hastening the coming of the Lord by this activity (*II Pet.* 3: 12).

(g) We shall aim at being ready for the Lord Jesus when He comes (*Matt.* 24: 42; 25: 6; *Mark* 13: 33, 35–37; *Luke* 12: 40; 21: 36).

(h) We shall always act and live remembering that time is short (*I Cor.* 7: 29).

(i) We need constantly reminding of Christ's coming (*Rev.* 22: 7, 12, 20).

6. **Unbelievers find the Second Coming a cause for scoffing.**

(a) Unbelievers often scoff at Christ's coming (*II Pet.* 3: 3, 4).

(b) Men, who prefer to follow their own passions, scoff at the promise of Christ's coming, deliberately ignoring the Word of God (*II Pet.* 3: 3–7).

(c) Unbelievers shall, nevertheless, be overtaken and surprised by the reality of the Lord's second coming (*Matt.* 24: 37–39; *I Thess.* 5: 2; *II Pet.* 3: 10).

45. THE CONSEQUENCES OF CHRIST'S RETURN

Question: What will happen when Christ returns?

Answer: Christ's glory will be seen, and the resurrection of the dead and the transformation of all believers will take place. The judgment will follow, with the final division of all men and women, either to being with Christ for ever or to suffering the punishment of eternal destruction

and exclusion from the presence of the Lord. The end of all things as we know them will come, and the Father will be glorified in it all.

1. Christ's glory will be seen.

(a) The second coming will be an occasion of glory for Christ (*Matt.* 25: 31).

(b) Everyone will see Him (*Mark* 13: 26; *Rev.* 1: 7).

(c) He will be seen sitting at the right hand of Power, and coming with the clouds of heaven (*Mark* 14: 62).

(d) His glory will be revealed to the world (*I Pet.* 4: 13).

(e) He will be glorified amongst His own and adored among all believers (*II Thess.* 1: 10).

2. The resurrection of the dead will take place, and the transformation of all believers.

(a) Christ's grace will be revealed to believers in a manner unknown before (*I Pet.* 1: 13).

(b) The completeness of the Christian's salvation will be revealed (*Heb.* 9: 28; *I Pet.* 1: 5).

(c) A most important aspect of this completeness will be the resurrection of the dead (*I Cor.* 15: 23, 51–54).

(d) Christians shall be made like Christ (*I John* 3: 2): at His coming the Lord Jesus Christ will change our lowly bodies to be like His glorious body, by the power which enables Him to make all things subject to Himself (*Phil.* 3: 21).

3. Following the resurrection of the dead, believers will be gathered together.

(a) At His coming Christ will gather together all believers (*Matt.* 24: 31; *I Thess.* 2: 19; 3: 13; 4: 15–17; 5: 23; *I John* 2: 28).

(b) Christ will send out the angels and gather His elect from the farthest bounds of earth to the farthest bounds of heaven (*Mark* 13: 27).

(c) Christ will gather His people to Himself (*II Thess.* 2: 1)—both those who had died before His coming and those alive on earth at the time (*I Thess.* 4: 16, 17; *John* 14: 2, 3).

(d) The gathering together of all His people is likened to the gathering in of the harvest (*Rev.* 14: 14–16).

4. Then the judgment will be held.

(a) Every man and woman will acknowledge Christ as the Lord (*Phil.* 2: 9–11) and therefore as the supreme judge (*Acts* 17: 31).

(b) The second coming will be a time of reckoning (*Luke* 12: 40–48).

(c) Christ will be ashamed of those who have been ashamed of Him, and of His words in this adulterous and sinful world (*Mark* 8: 38).

(d) He will bring to light, at His coming, the things now hidden in darkness and will disclose the purposes of the heart (*I Cor.* 4: 5).

(e) His coming will bring distress to some, because of the judgment He will bring (*Rev.* 1: 7).

(f) The Lord's coming will mean the giving of account to Christ by Christians (*I Thess.* 2: 19): this giving account will not be with regard to the condemnation they deserve because of sin (*Rom.* 5: 1; 8: 1) but as to the rewards they shall receive on account of faithfulness to Christ (*I Cor.* 3: 8, 14).

5. The final division of men and women will come after the judgment.

(a) Men and women without the knowledge of God and who have refused to obey the gospel of our Lord Jesus Christ shall suffer the punishment of eternal destruction and exclusion from the presence of the Lord and from the glory of His might (*II Thess.* 1: 8, 9).

(b) The judgment of God will be executed by God's angels on unbelievers (*Rev.* 14: 17–20).

(c) Believers will enter into the full wonder of everlasting life and the enjoyment of God's presence for ever (*II Thess.* 1: 10; *I Thess.* 4: 17).

(d) Christ will take believers to Himself that where He is they may be also (*John* 14: 2, 3).

6. The end of all things as we now know them will take place.

(a) The coming of the Lord will herald the end of things as we know them on this earth (*II Pet.* 3: 7, 10, 11, 12, 13).

(b) The heavens will pass away with a loud noise, and the elements will be dissolved with fire, and the earth and the works that are upon it will be burned up (*II Pet* 3: 10).

(c) After the dissolution of this world, there will be revealed new heavens and a new earth in which righteousness dwells (*II Pet.* 3: 13).

7. The Father will be glorified in all that happens.

(a) All that He ever spoke by the mouth of His holy prophets shall be established (*Acts* 3: 21).

(b) As all men and women will be compelled to confess Christ as Lord, that act will have one great end—the glory of God the Father (*Phil.* 2: 11).

(c) After destroying every rule and every authority and power, there will come the end of all the events connected with Christ's coming, when Christ will deliver the kingdom to God the Father (*I Cor.* 15: 24).

(d) When all things are subjected to Christ, then He Himself will be subjected to the Father who put all things under Christ (*I Cor.* 15: 28).

46. THE JUDGMENT

Question: What will happen at the judgment?

Answer: Christ will be the Judge and all will appear before Him. The perfect justice of God and the undeniable guilt of all men and women will be plain and beyond dispute. Those justified through faith in Christ will be acquitted from the guilt of sin and will receive rewards according to their faithfulness; the unbelieving will receive their final condemnation.

1. The timing of the judgment.

(a) Our Lord Jesus Christ spoke of a judgment which was still future (*Matt.* 12: 41).

(b) Judgment is the certainty which follows men after death (*Heb.* 9: 27).

(c) God has fixed a day on which He will judge the world by righteousness by a man whom He has appointed, and of this He has given assurance to everyone by raising Him from the dead (*Acts* 17: 31; *Rom.* 2: 16).

(d) The judgment will take place at the coming of the Lord Jesus Christ (*Matt*. 25: 31 ff; *II Tim*. 4: 1; *II Pet*. 3: 7).

(e) The judgment will be preceded by the resurrection of the dead (*John* 5: 28, 29).

(f) The day of judgment will be followed by the dissolution, by means of fire, of the heavens and earth that now exist, according to God's promise (*II Pet*. 3: 7).

2. Christ will be the Judge.

(a) God the Father judges no one (*John* 5: 22), but has committed to the Son the task of judging all men and women (*John* 5: 22, 27).

(b) The Lord Jesus Christ is the One ordained of God to be the Judge of the living and the dead (*Acts* 10: 42; *II Tim*. 4: 1).

(c) The separation of the wheat from the chaff (*Matt*. 3: 12; *Luke* 3: 17), and the sheep from the goats (*Matt*. 25: 32, 33) will be His responsibility.

(d) Christ will come the second time, therefore, as Judge (*Matt*. 25: 31–46).

3. All will appear before the judgment seat.

(a) The Old Testament declares that God will judge the righteous and the wicked, for He has appointed a time for every matter and for every work (*Eccl*. 3: 17).

(b) Judgment will be held on all nations (*Matt*. 25: 32; *Joel* 3: 12).

(c) The judgment will include all men and women (*Heb*. 9: 27)—the small and the great (*Rev*. 20: 12), the living and the dead (*II Tim*. 4: 1; *I Pet*. 4: 5).

(d) We must all appear before the judgment-seat of God, so that we may each one receive good or evil, according to our faith and works (*Rom*. 14: 10, 12; *II Cor*. 5: 10).

(e) The fallen angels will also be finally judged at the judgment (*II Pet*. 2: 4; *Jude* 6).

4. The perfect justice of God will be seen.

(a) The judgment is pictured as a harvest—there will be no doubt which is wheat and which is chaff (*Joel* 3: 13; *Matt*. 3: 12; *Luke* 3: 17).

(b) God's just judgment will be revealed (*Rom*. 2: 5; 3: 4–6)—the judgment shall be in righteousness (*Ps*. 98: 9; *Acts* 17: 31).

(c) God's judgment will be a precise and just retribution (*Obad*. 15), perfectly related to people's ways and deeds (*Hos*. 12: 2), and according to God's perfect records (*Dan*. 7: 10; *Rev*. 20: 12).

(d) The judgment will be in proportion to the opportunities and privileges of men and women: every one to whom much has been given will find much is required (*Luke* 12: 48).

(e) The judgment will be individual and personal (*Matt*. 25: 42–45).

(f) God will render to every man according to his works (*Rom*. 2: 6).

(g) Those who have had no opportunity of knowing the law given to Moses, or the gospel, will be judged according to the law of conscience (*Rom*. 2: 12, 14, 15).

(h) All who have had the law of Moses will be judged by it (*Rom*. 2: 12).

(i) Neglected opportunities of repentance and faith increase the condemnation men and women shall experience at the judgment (*Matt.* 11: 20–24; *Luke* 11: 31, 32).

(j) If men and women have sinned deliberately after receiving the knowledge of the truth, their condemnation will be all the worse (*Heb.* 10: 26).

(k) Although all our questions about the judgment cannot be answered now, we know that the Judge of all the earth will do right (*Gen.* 18: 25).

5. The guilt of all will be plain.

(a) Account will be rendered for words spoken (*Matt.* 12: 36).

(b) Every secret thing, including the purposes of the heart, will be brought under judgment (*Eccl.* 12: 14: *I Cor.* 4: 5).

(c) Actions will be judged (*Eccl.* 11: 9; 12: 14; *Rev.* 20: 13) and the ill deeds of men and women shall return upon their heads (*Obad.* 15, 16).

(d) None can stand before such a judgment and deserve to live (*Ps.* 130: 3), for no living man is righteous before God (*Ps.* 143: 2) on the grounds of what he is in himself.

(e) All will be found guilty: those without the law have perverted the light which comes from nature (*Rom.* 1: 21 ff), and those with the law have failed to keep it (*Gal.* 3: 10–12).

(f) No one will have anything to say in self-defence—all excuses will die upon men's lips (*Rom.* 3: 19).

(g) The word of Christ will be a witness against those who have rejected Christ and refused His sayings (*John* 12: 48).

(h) The judgment is clearly a fearful prospect (*Heb.* 10: 27).

(i) The first part of the judgment will be the separation of those who have accepted God's way of salvation from those who have gone about to gain salvation by dependence on their own efforts (*Matt.* 25: 31–33).

(j) Those whose names are in the book of life shall escape the judgment of condemnation on account of sin (*Luke* 10: 20; *Phil.* 4: 3; *Rev.* 20: 12; 21: 27) because, having seen the folly of trusting in their own righteousness (*Isa.* 64: 6), through faith in Christ they have become the righteousness of God in Him (*II Cor.* 5: 21).

6. Acquittal from the guilt of sin will be granted to those who have been justified by faith.

(a) The final judgment will be determined by works and faith in Christ (*Rev.* 20: 13–15).

(b) There is no condemnation for those who are justified by faith in the Lord Jesus Christ (*Rom.* 5: 1; 8: 1).

(c) Christians have complete confidence for the day when Christ shall judge all men and women (*I John* 4: 7; *John* 5: 25); they will not be ashamed at His coming (*I John* 2: 28).

(d) Christ will acknowledge Christians openly in the presence of the Father (*Matt.* 25: 34–40; *Rev.* 3: 5), presenting them guiltless (*I Cor.* 1: 8; *I Thess.* 3: 13), having declared them free from sin (*Rom.* 8: 1, 33, 34).

(e) The key to deliverance from this judgment, therefore, is a personal relationship to the Lord Jesus Christ (*Matt.* 10: 32, 33; *Mark* 8: 38; *Heb.* 10: 29).

(f) Salvation from the judgment

which sin deserves is possible through the Lord Jesus Christ alone (*I Thess.* 5: 9, 10).

(g) Having been acquitted from all guilt, Christians will join with Christ in the judgment of the world (*I Cor.* 6: 2; compare *Matt.* 19: 28; *Luke* 22: 28 ff; *Dan.* 7: 22; *Rev.* 20: 4).

7. Those who have refused to acknowledge God and to obey the gospel of our Lord Jesus Christ will be condemned.

(a) Eternal judgment is a first principle, an elementary doctrine, of the gospel (*Heb.* 6: 2; *Acts* 24: 25).

(b) The children of the wicked one will be revealed and their destiny made known (*Matt.* 13: 24–30, 36–43, 47–50).

(c) The judgment will be a time of misery for those who have rejected the Lord Jesus Christ (*Rev.* 1: 7; *II Thess.* 1: 8, 9).

(d) Those who have disobeyed the truth and obeyed wickedness will experience the wrath of God and eternal punishment (*Rom.* 2: 8; *Jude* 15; *Rev.* 20: 15).

(e) The punishment of evildoers will be final and complete (*Matt.* 13: 40–42; 25: 46).

(f) No one will be able to resist the judgment (*Matt.* 3: 12; *Luke* 3: 17; *Amos* 9: 1–4).

8. Christians will be rewarded by Christ.

(a) To those who by patience in well-doing seek for glory and honour and immortality, Christ will give eternal life (*Rom.* 2: 7; *Jude* 24; *Rev.* 20: 12, 15).

(b) He will come as the righteous Judge, judging His people by the gospel—the law of liberty (*Jas.* 2: 12)—that He may reward them for their faithfulness (*II Tim.* 4: 8; *Jas.* 1: 12; *Luke* 19: 17, 19).

(c) Every Christian's service will be subject to scrutiny and examination (*I Cor.* 3: 9–14): there will be rewards for faithful service (*I Cor.* 3: 9–13; *II Tim.* 4: 8; *Rev.* 11: 18).

(d) Christians will discover the value of the work they have done for Christ (*II Cor.* 1: 14; *Phil.* 2: 16).

9. The effect the knowledge of the coming judgment should have upon Christians.

(a) The certainty of judgment is a great incentive to urgent preaching (*II Cor.* 5: 11; *II Tim.* 4: 1, 2).

(b) Unbelievers are to be warned of the future judgment (*Acts* 24: 25): this warning provides an incentive to repentance (*Acts* 17: 30, 31) and to faith in Christ (*Isa.* 28: 16, 17; *John* 3: 17, 18).

(c) The certainty of the judgment is an incentive to holiness (*II Pet.* 3: 11, 14): the fact that Christians must stand too before the judgment seat of Christ is not to promote fear but the desire to please Him now, so that they may be pleasing to Him then (*II Cor.* 5: 9, 10).

47. THE RESURRECTION OF THE BODY

Question: Will our bodies be raised to life again?

Answer: All will rise from the dead, believers to the resurrection of life, and unbelievers to the resurrection of judgment. Christ's resurrection will be the pattern of the believer's.

1. There will be a resurrection both of the righteous and the wicked.

(a) The resurrection of the dead will take place at the second coming of the Lord Jesus Christ (*I Cor.* 15: 23; *I Thess.* 4: 14).

(b) The resurrection of the dead is a fundamental part of the Christian gospel (*I Cor.* 15: 12, 13; *Heb.* 6: 2).

(c) Many of the details of the resurrection of the dead are not revealed to us (*I Cor.* 15: 51) but it will take place by the power of God (*Matt.* 22: 29), who gives life to the dead and calls into existence the things that do not exist (*Rom.* 4: 17).

(d) The resurrection of the dead will take place in a moment, in the twinkling of an eye (*I Cor.* 15: 52).

(e) The actual fact of resurrection will be true of everyone: all in the tombs and graves will hear Christ's voice, and come forth, those who have done good, to the resurrection of life, and those who have done evil, to the resurrection of judgment (*John* 5: 28, 29).

(f) For some the resurrection of the dead will mean awaking to everlasting life and for some to shame and everlasting contempt (*Dan.* 12: 2).

(g) There will be a resurrection of both the just and the unjust (*Acts* 24: 15), of those whose names are in the book of life and those whose names are not (*Rev.* 20: 11–15).

(h) The Scriptures assure us of the resurrection of the dead (*Matt.* 22: 29).

(i) The resurrection of the dead was anticipated and promised in the Old Testament:

(i) It was hinted at in God's words to Moses, "I am the God of Abraham, the God of Isaac, and the God of Jacob" (*Ex.* 3: 6; *Matt.* 22: 32).

(ii) It was promised that the dead should live, their bodies should rise (*Isa.* 26: 19).

(iii) It was promised that many of those who sleep in the dust of the earth should awake, some to everlasting life, and some to shame and everlasting contempt (*Dan.* 12: 2).

(j) The Lord Jesus Christ spoke of raising up believers at the last day (*John* 6: 39, 40, 44).

(k) By His own resurrection Christ abolished death and brought life and immortality to light through the gospel (*II Tim.* 1: 10)—the Christian confidence concerning the resurrection of the dead springs from Christ's resurrection (*I Cor.* 15: 12, 13, 15, 16).

(1) The apostles preached the resurrection of the dead through Jesus (*Acts* 4: 2).

2. Addressed as it is to Christian believers, the New Testament concentrates on the resurrection of believers.

(a) Christ will raise up at the last day all who have believed in Him and inherited eternal life, according to the will of the Father (*John* 6: 40).

(b) By God's great mercy Christians have been born anew to a living hope through the resurrection of Jesus Christ from the dead (*I Pet.* 1: 3)—Christians are children of the resurrection (*Luke* 20: 36).

(c) Christ's resurrection is the pledge of the believer's resurrection (*II Cor.* 4: 14).

(d) That there should be no

resurrection of the dead is inconceivable in the light of Christ's resurrection (*I Cor.* 15: 12).

(e) Even as Christ was raised from the dead, so shall believers be raised (*I Cor.* 15: 20): by Christ, the man, has come the resurrection of the dead, even as by man came death (*I Cor.* 15: 21).

(f) The precise details of the resurrection of the dead will cause some to question, almost inevitably (*I Cor.* 15: 35)—"How will it happen? With what kind of body do they come?"

(g) The resurrection body will be something quite beyond our present experience (*I Cor.* 15: 35–37): there will, for example, be no marriage after the resurrection, and thus sexual relations will end (*Mark* 12: 25).

(h) Harvest provides us with an illustration of the kind of thing that will happen at the resurrection: the body that is sown is not the body which shall be, but the two are directly related (*I Cor.* 15: 36, 37).

(i) The resurrection body will be a real body: even as to every kind of creature and thing God has given a particular body, so He has determined the particular nature of the resurrection body (*I Cor.* 15: 38–42).

(j) The perishable body sown in death will be raised imperishable (*I Cor.* 15: 42); the body sown in dishonour at death will be raised in glory (*I Cor.* 15: 43); the body sown in weakness will be raised in power (*I Cor.* 15: 43): the physical body sown in death will be raised a spiritual body (*I Cor.* 15: 44).

(k) Even as the physical body bore the image of the man of dust—of Adam—so the spiritual body will bear the image of the man of heaven—Christ (*I Cor.* 15: 49).

(l) Believers will all be changed at the resurrection of the dead (*I Cor.* 15: 51): the imperishable will replace the perishable; the immortal will replace the mortal (*I Cor.* 15: 53).

(m) The dead in Christ shall rise first, being given their resurrection bodies (*I Thess.* 4: 16); and then shall all living believers be caught up together to meet the Lord in the air; and so we shall always be with the Lord (*I Thess.* 4: 17).

(n) Those still alive at Christ's coming will experience the change of body necessary to their entry into heaven (*Phil.* 3: 21)—that is to say, they will be given a body identical with those raised from the dead.

(o) The resurrection of the dead will be followed by entry into God's presence (*II Cor.* 4: 14): from the resurrection of the dead onwards we shall be forever with the Lord (*I Thess.* 4: 17).

3. The resurrection of Christ tells us something of the nature of the resurrection body of the believer.

(a) Christians shall be like Christ (*I John* 3: 2): Christ will change their lowly body to be made like His glorious body by the power which enables Him even to subject all things to Himself (*Phil.* 3: 21).

(b) From what we are told (*I John* 3: 2; *Phil.* 3: 21), we know that the resurrection body will be like Christ's resurrection body.

(c) Our Lord's resurrection body seems to have been similar to His body as it was before:

(i) The disciples were able to hold the Lord Jesus by the feet as they worshipped Him (*Matt.* 28: 9).

(ii) He could be handled (*Luke* 24: 40; *John* 20: 27).

(d) But Christ's body was clearly different in some ways:

(i) His body appears to have passed through the grave clothes (*John* 20: 6, 7).

(ii) When He walked on the road to Emmaus with the two disciples they did not immediately recognise Him (*Luke* 24: 13–35).

(iii) He was able to eat food, if He desired (*Luke* 24: 41–43).

(iv) He was able to pass through shut doors (*John* 20: 19, 26).

(e) Uncertain of so many aspects not yet revealed to us about the resurrection of the body, of the fact of it we are certain, for Christ was the first-fruits, by His own resurrection, of the resurrection of the dead to come (*I Cor.* 15: 20, 23).

4. The encouragement which the assurance of the resurrection brings to the believer.

(a) The resurrection of the dead is a tremendous comfort to the Christian (*I Thess.* 4: 18)—those who have fallen asleep in Christ have not perished (*I Cor.* 15: 18).

(b) The resurrection of the dead is a great encouragement to our continuance in service (*I Cor.* 15: 58).

(c) The assurance of life after death means that life here and now is not thought precious if it is endangered for the sake of the gospel—the reward of this life can be reaped in the life to come (*I Cor.* 15: 32).

(d) The assurance of the resurrection of the dead makes a difference to conduct (*I Cor.* 15: 33).

(e) The assurance of the resurrection of the dead takes away fear of death—it gives men a confidence in the face of death and the terrors which can be associated with it (*I Cor.* 15: 31; *Heb.* 11: 35).

(f) Christians are to be envied indeed for the glorious assurance they have of resurrection on the grounds of Christ's (*I Cor.* 15: 19).

48. LIFE AFTER DEATH

Question: What happens when we die?

Answer: The body returns, as dust, to the earth as it was, and the spirit returns to God. The body may be described as asleep, and for the Christian the return of the spirit to God means to be consciously with Christ.

1. The body sleeps.

(a) The picture of sleep is frequently used of the dead (*Matt.* 9: 24; 27: 52; *John* 11: 11; *I Cor.* 11: 30; *I Thess.* 4: 13).

(b) The description of the dead as asleep would seem to have particular reference to the body rather than the spirit: at death the body returns to dust, and the spirit to God (*Eccl.* 12: 7); whilst the body may sleep (*Acts* 7: 60), the spirit may be with God (*Acts* 7: 59).

(c) To die before the coming again of the Lord Jesus is to leave the flesh (*Phil.* 1: 24).

(d) The human body is but a temporary shelter for the human

spirit, to be replaced by something better (*II Cor.* 5: 1–5).

2. The spirit lives.

(a) It is important to remember that, for the Christian, eternal life has begun already: he who has heard Christ's word and believed God who sent Him, has eternal life; he does not come into judgment, but has passed from death to life (*John* 5: 24).

(b) The soul—"soul" and "spirit" are often used as meaning the same—is not affected by the death of the body (*Matt.* 10: 28).

(c) That the dead lived in spirit was implied in the Old Testament (*Ex.* 3: 6; *Matt.* 22: 32).

(d) Death is gain for the Christian (*Phil.* 1: 21).

(e) When the Christian dies, he lives; in fact, he cannot really die (*John* 11: 25, 26).

3. The Christian's spirit is immediately with Christ from the moment of death.

(a) Jesus told the penitent thief, "Today you will be with Me in Paradise" (*Luke* 23: 43).

(b) Statements made by the apostle Paul have no meaning unless they speak of conscious existence immediately following death:

(i) To be away from the body is to be at home with the Lord (*II Cor.* 5: 8);

(ii) To die and to be with Christ is far better than to continue ordinary human existence (*Phil.* 1: 23);

(iii) The spirit is with Christ, and is made perfect (*Heb.* 12: 23).

(c) In the light of what we have seen from the Scriptures we may say that the Christian who has died before the coming of the Lord Jesus is without his body, but has conscious enjoyment of the Lord's presence. Even as the Lord Jesus Christ was quickened in His human spirit before His body was raised from the tomb (*I Pet.* 3: 19), so the Christian's quickened spirit awaits the day of resurrection when it will be united with the resurrection body.

4. Death holds no fear for the Christian.

(a) Our Lord Jesus Christ has abolished death for the Christian (*II Tim.* 1: 10; *Heb.* 2: 14).

(b) The Christian shall never taste real death (*John* 8: 51; 11: 26).

(c) Death cannot separate the Christian from God (*Rom.* 8: 38, 39).

(d) Death has lost both its victory and its sting (*I Cor.* 15: 55).

(e) Victory over death is so complete that it can be described as belonging to the Christian (*I Cor.* 3: 22).

(f) The Christian's attitude to death is the very opposite of despair (*Phil.* 1: 21–23).

(g) The Christian, seeing things aright, would rather be away from the body, and at home with the Lord (*II Cor.* 5: 8).

49. HEAVEN

Question: What do we know about heaven?

Answer: Heaven is the eternal dwelling place of God and of His angels, the place from which Christ came at His Incarnation and to which He returned at His Ascension.

All the language the Bible uses to describe heaven expresses the perfection of the eternal life which Christians will experience there. With such assurance may Christians regard it as their eternal home that they are described as citizens of heaven whilst here on earth.

1. **Heaven is the eternal dwelling place of God** (*Matt.* 5: 16; 12: 50; *Rev.* 3: 12; 11: 13; 20: 9) **and of His angels** (*Matt.* 18: 10; 22: 30; *Rev.* 3: 5).

(a) The Father is said to be "in heaven" (*Matt.* 5: 45; 6: 1, 9; 7: 11, 21b; 10: 33; 12: 50; 16: 17; 18: 10b, 14, 19; *Mark* 11: 25 f).

(b) He is the architect and maker of heaven (*Heb.* 11: 10)—He is the Lord of heaven (*Dan.* 5: 23; *Matt.* 11: 25).

(c) He reigns in heaven (*Ps.* 11: 4): He does according to His will in the host of heaven and among the inhabitants of the earth (*Dan.* 4: 35; *Ps.* 135: 6).

(d) He fills heaven (*I Kings* 8: 27; *Jer.* 23: 24); His glory (*Acts* 7: 55) and His majesty (*Heb.* 8: 1) are manifested there.

(e) Heaven is the place from which God speaks to men today (*Heb.* 12: 25); He answers His people from heaven (*I Chron.* 21: 26; *II Chron.* 7: 14; *Neh.* 9: 27; *Ps.* 20: 6).

(f) God sends His judgments from heaven (*Gen.* 19: 24; *I Sam.* 2: 10; *Dan.* 4: 13, 14; *Rom.* 1: 18).

2. **Christ came from heaven and returned to heaven.**

(a) From heaven Christ came to become Incarnate (*John* 3: 13, 31, 32; 6: 38, 42, 50; *I Cor.* 15: 47).

(b) At His Ascension He returned to heaven (*Mark* 16: 19; *I Pet.* 3: 22).

(c) Heaven, since the Ascension, is the scene of His present life and activity (*Acts* 7: 55; *Eph.* 6: 9; *Heb.* 8: 1).

(d) At God's right hand, He pleads the cause of His people (*Rom.* 8: 34; *Heb.* 9: 24).

(e) He prepares a place in the Father's house for His people (*John* 14: 2, 3).

(f) He is all-powerful in heaven (*Matt.* 28: 18): angels, authorities, and powers have been made subject to Him (*I Pet.* 3: 22).

(g) He is the King of heaven (*Matt.* 25: 40).

(h) From heaven He will descend at His second coming (*I Thess.* 4: 16; *Phil.* 3: 20; *Matt.* 24: 30; *II Thess.* 1: 7).

3. **Heaven is not part of this creation and is quite different from it** (*Heb.* 9: 11). We must distinguish "heaven" from "the heavens" where birds, clouds, sun and stars, etc., are to be found.

(a) Heaven is the place of the "real" (*Heb.* 8: 5).

(b) Heaven is a place of peace (*Luke* 19: 38).

(c) Heaven is holy (*Deut.* 26: 15; *Ps.* 20: 6; *Isa.* 57: 15).

(d) Heaven is everlasting (*Ps.* 89: 29).

(e) Heaven is indescribable in its happiness and satisfaction (*Rev.* 7: 17).

4. **Descriptions given of heaven to aid our understanding.**

(a) It is described as paradise (*II Cor.* 12: 2, 4).

(b) It is likened to a granary—

Christians being the wheat (*Matt.* 3: 12).

(c) It is called the Father's house (*John* 14: 2).

(d) It is described as a city, prepared by God for His people (*Heb.* 11: 16)—Mount Zion, the city of the living God, heavenly Jerusalem (*Heb.* 12: 22).

(e) It is described as a heavenly country—better than anything known on earth (*Heb.* 11: 16).

(f) It is described as a rest (*Heb.* 4: 9).

(g) It is described as the Christian's inheritance (*I Pet.* 1: 4; *Matt.* 25: 34).

5. The grounds of entry into heaven.

(a) The inheritance of heaven is not by legal right but by promise (*Gal.* 3: 18).

(b) Those who inherit it will recognise that they do not deserve to do so by reason of their own merits (*Matt.* 25: 37–39).

(c) All who gain entry into heaven do so on the grounds of the mediation of Jesus Christ and the efficacy of His sacrifice (*Heb.* 12: 24).

(d) Heaven will be made up of those of every nation and tongue who have been redeemed by Christ (*Matt.* 25: 32; *Rev.* 5: 9, 10).

6. Entry into heaven is impossible for some.

(a) Entry is impossible for those who are not "born again" (*John* 3: 3).

(b) Those whose lives are characterised by the works of the flesh have no place there (*Gal.* 5: 19–21; *Eph.* 5: 5).

(c) The devil and his angels can have no place in heaven (*Matt.* 25: 41).

7. What heaven will mean to the Christian.

(a) To enter heaven will be to be blessed of the Father (*Matt.* 25: 34).

(b) There he shall have the things he has hoped for (*Col.* 1: 5).

(c) In heaven he will be perfect and holy, and thus able to see the Lord (*Heb.* 12: 14).

(d) In heaven he will have his glorified body (*II Cor.* 5: 1).

(e) He will be able to look upon Christ's glory (*John* 17: 24).

(f) He will receive his reward (*Matt.* 5: 12; 25: 34–40; *Heb.* 10: 34, 35).

(g) He will enjoy never-failing treasure which he has laid up for himself (*Matt.* 6: 20; *Luke* 12: 33).

(h) The partial will have vanished and wholeness will have come (*I Cor.* 13: 10).

(i) His knowledge will be whole, like God's knowledge of him now (*I Cor.* 13: 9, 10).

(j) All the puzzles of this human life will be resolved (*I Cor.* 13: 12).

8. The relationship of the Christian to heaven now.

(a) He is an heir of heaven: since the foundation of the world God has been preparing it for him and all like him redeemed by Christ (*Matt.* 25: 34).

(b) His name is enrolled in heaven (*Luke* 10: 20; *Heb.* 12: 23)—a ground for true rejoicing.

(c) He is a citizen of heaven (*Phil.* 3: 20).

(d) He knows heaven to be his true home (*Heb.* 13: 14).

9. The effect the fact of heaven should have upon the Christian.

(a) There should be a great longing for heaven in his heart (*Heb.* 11: 16; cf. 11: 10).

(b) He should set his standards by those of heaven—as he knows them from the Scriptures—rather than by those of this world for he knows his citizenship is in heaven (*Phil.* 3: 20).

(c) He should hold loosely to his earthly possessions, never allowing them to be all-important (*Heb.* 10: 34).

(d) He should let his thoughts dwell on that high realm, where Christ is, rather than on this earthly life (*Col.* 3: 2).

50. HELL

Question: What do we know about hell?

Answer: Hell is the place of everlasting punishment and banishment from God's presence, the future dwelling place of all who have neglected God and disobeyed the gospel of Christ.

1. Hell is the place of banishment and punishment.

(a) Hell is the place of banishment from God's presence (*Matt.* 7: 23; 25: 41).

(b) It is the sphere of the manifestation of the wrath to come, from which Christ delivers the believer (*I Thess.* 1: 10); there there will be the revelation from heaven of the wrath of God against all ungodliness and unrighteousness (*Rom.* 1: 18).

(c) To be cast into hell is to be separated from Christ, to be cursed, to be cast into the eternal fire prepared for the devil and his angels, and to be eternally punished (*Matt.* 25: 41, 46).

(d) Hell means eternal exclusion from the radiance of the face of the Lord and the glorious majesty of His power (*II Thess.* 1: 9).

(e) A person's presence in hell is the direct result of his choices made during his earthly life (*Luke* 16: 19–31).

(f) It is the dwelling place of all who have lived their human life neglecting God (*Ps.* 9: 17).

(g) The cowardly, the faithless, and the vile, murderers, fornicators, idolators and liars of every kind will be cast into hell (*Rev.* 21: 8), that is to say, those who do not know God and do not obey the gospel of our Lord Jesus Christ (*II Thess.* 1: 8, 9).

(h) The body suffers in hell (*Matt.* 5: 29).

(i) The soul suffers also in hell (*Matt.* 10: 28).

(j) The punishment of hell is eternal (*Isa.* 33: 14; *Rev.* 20: 10).

(k) There is no transfer from hell to heaven (*Luke* 16: 26).

(l) We are born on the road to hell, and the majority remain upon it (*Matt.* 7: 13, 14).

2. The descriptions given of hell in the Bible.

(a) Hell is described as a dark imprisonment (*II Pet.* 2: 4) and outer darkness (*Matt.* 22: 13).

(b) It is like a bottomless pit (*Rev.* 9: 1).

(c) It is a place of bondage, darkness and weeping (*Matt.* 22: 13).

(d) It is like fire—everlasting burnings (*Isa.* 33: 14), unquenchable *Matt.* 3: 12; *Mark* 9: 44), a furnace (*Matt.* 13: 42), devouring (*Isa.* 33: 14), everlasting (*Matt.* 18: 8; 25: 41), a lake of fire (*Rev.* 20: 14).

(e) It is a place of torment (*Luke* 16: 23)—there is no rest, day or night (*Rev.* 14: 10, 11).

3. The right attitude to hell.

(a) God has no desire that men should remain on the road to hell but that they should reach repentance (*II Pet.* 3: 9); our desire for them should be the same.

(b) Christ came to deliver men from hell (*John* 3: 16).

(c) He who is wise avoids hell (*Prov.* 15: 24).

(d) Christians should seek to save men and women from the road to hell (*Jude* 23).

BIBLE DEFINITIONS

ADOPTION is an act of God by which He bestows on those who are justified in Christ, the status or standing of His sons and daughters (*John* 1: 12). They are made members of His family, and possess all the privileges of that family. The Holy Spirit is the Spirit of adoption because He makes believers the sons and daughters of God and enables them to call God their Father and to have the feelings towards God which go with the relationship (*Rom.* 8: 15).

ADVOCATE is a title given to both our Lord Jesus Christ and the Holy Spirit. The word carries the idea of calling someone alongside to help, and was used in legal matters for the counsel for the defence. In the references to the Holy Spirit in John's Gospel, where the word is translated "Comforter", "Helper" would be the most apt word (*John* 14: 16, 26; 15: 26; 16: 7). In *I John* 2: 1, where it is used of the Lord Jesus Christ, it is translated "Advocate", indicating its more legal use.

An advocate does two things: first, he stands and pleads on behalf of his client; secondly, he advises his client how to speak when he has to. Christ acts for believers in the first sense: He appears in God's presence on our behalf, interceding there by His presence and on the basis of His finished work on the Cross (*Heb.* 7: 25).

The Spirit acts for believers in the second sense: He comes alongside believers in prayer, for example, and puts pleas and words into their mouths (*Rom.* 8: 26–27).

ALIENATED describes the condition of men in relation to God before reconciliation. They are cut off from the life of God through sin and ignorance (*Eph.* 4: 18). The evil in their lives makes them God's spiritual enemies (*Col.* 1: 21).

ANGEL OF THE LORD. This angel appears in the Old Testament as a messenger of God, but constantly acts and speaks in a way which implies that He is Himself God. All divine titles are given to Him, and worship is offered also (*Gen.* 16: 10–13; 18: 13, 14, 19, 25, 33; 22: 11 ff; 48: 15, 16; *Ex.* 3: 2, 6, 14; 13 : 21; 14: 19; 23: 20; *Josh.* 5: 13–15; *Judg.* 6: 11; 13: 3 ff). As the Old Testament revelation unfolds, this angel or messenger of the Lord is called the Son of God, the Messiah (*Isa.* 42: 1 ff; *Mal.* 3: 1).

The angel of the Lord is spoken of quite differently in the New Testament (*Luke* 1: 19). Many hold, with reason, that the angel of the Lord in the Old Testament was none other than the Son of God, who later became flesh as Jesus.

ANGELS are created beings, who act as God's messengers (*Acts* 7: 53; *Gal.* 3: 19; *Heb.* 2: 7), and as God's heavenly servants (*Heb.* 1: 14). Their presence with God always represents the glorious nature of God (*Rev.* 5: 11). There are evidences of a fall amongst the angels, with Satan as their leader (*Job* 4: 18; *Matt.* 25: 41; *II Pet.* 2: 4; *Rev.* 12: 9).

ANTICHRISTS are opponents or adversaries of the Messiah who appear in the last days. They are men who put forth teaching which fundamentally opposes and denies Christ (*I John* 2: 18, 22; 4: 3; *II John* 7). Such teaching may be deceitful in that it pretends to be true Christian teaching (*II John* 7: 8).

APOSTATE, APOSTASY, APOSTATISE. Apostasy is falling away from allegiance to Christ, departing from the faith (*I Tim.* 4: 1). The apostate is a person who having shown all the outward signs of faith in Christ and obedience to Him, then loses all interest and even becomes hostile to Christ and His claims (*Heb.* 6: 6).

It is persistence in sin, sinning wilfully after knowing the truth as it is in Christ (*Heb.* 10: 26). It is the result often of a superficial profession of Christ (*Matt.* 13: 5, 6, 20, 21).

To "apostatise" is to become an apostate. See *Question* 34.

APOSTLES. The word "apostle" means a person sent by another. The title belongs strictly in the New Testament to the twelve apostles and Paul who joined their number later. They were chosen, called and sent forth by Christ Himself (*John* 6: 70; 13: 18; 15: 16, 19; *Gal.* 1: 6); they were His witnesses, especially of His resurrection (*Acts* 1: 8, 22; *I Cor.* 9: 1; 15: 8; *Gal.* 1: 12; *Eph.* 3: 2–8; *I John* 1: 1–3). In a particularly marked sense they knew the help of the Holy Spirit, who led them into all truth (*Matt.* 10: 20; *John* 14: 26; 15: 26; 16: 7–14; 20: 22; *I Cor.* 2: 10–13; 7: 40; *I Thess.* 4: 8). God confirmed the value of their work by signs and miracles (*Matt.* 10: 1, 8; *Acts* 2: 43; 3: 2; 5: 12–16; *Rom.* 15: 18, 19; *I Cor.* 9: 2; *II Cor.* 12: 12; *Gal.* 2: 8).

ASCENSION. See *Question* 22.

ASSURANCE is the conviction Christians have from the Holy Spirit (*Rom.* 8: 15, 16; *I John* 3: 24), through their obedience to the gospel, that they are children of God and heirs of eternal life (*I John* 5: 13). The genuineness of this conviction is demonstrated by right belief in Christ (*I John* 2: 22; 5: 1), righteous conduct (*I John* 2: 3–6; 3: 3) and love for other Christians (*I John* 3: 10–17; 4: 7–12, 20, 21). See *Question* 33.

BACKSLIDE, BACKSLIDING. Backsliding describes the state of the believer when his spiritual life declines and he loses his spiritual vitality through deliberate disobedience to the Lord. It consists of faithlessly turning or drawing back from what the Lord demands (*Jer.* 3: 6–14; *Hos.* 11: 7).

BAPTISED, BAPTISM. See *Question* 36.

BELIEVE is the verb from which we obtain the noun "faith" expressing confidence in God. It describes awareness of God's existence (*Heb.* 11: 6), assurance concerning His trustworthiness, active confidence in His help and self-committal to His care (*John* 3: 16; *Acts* 16: 31, 34; 27: 25; *Rom.* 10: 9, 10; *II Tim.* 1: 12).

BELIEVER is the name given to those who believe and trust in Christ as the only Saviour and the Lord (*Acts* 2: 36), and who find themselves added to the Lord and to His Church (*Acts* 5: 14; 2: 41, 44, 47). See BELIEVE.

BLASPHEMY is some open insult to the majesty of God. At first specific words of reviling and defamation were thought of, as offending in this way (*Lev.* 24: 16; *Mark* 2: 7), but it came to be realised that words which encroach upon God's sole rights in some way are blasphemy. This explains the false charge which the religious authorities made concerning the Lord Jesus Christ (*Mark* 14: 64). It is never a mark of the Holy Spirit's influence (*I Cor.* 12: 3) but rather it is characteristic of the devil and his agencies (*Rev.* 13: 1, 5, 6).

BLOOD OF CHRIST is an expression often used in the New Testament to express the fact of Christ's death as a sacrifice for sins. It is a particularly apt way of describing His death in view of the ceremonial offerings of the Old Testament which had prepared the way for it by their symbolism (*Heb.* 10: 1–17). His blood purges the conscience of moral guilt, and provides the forgiveness which gives the sinner peace (*Heb.* 9: 13, 14). Its power to cleanse is continuous, enabling the believer to maintain fellowship with God (*I John* 1: 7).

BODY. The body represents many aspects of human life, besides describing man's purely physical being: the main characteristic of life is that it is "in the body" (*II Cor.* 5: 8). The body is the organ of man's activity (*I Cor.* 6: 20; *Rom.* 12: 1), the instrument of human experience and suffering (*II Cor.* 4: 10; *Gal.* 6: 17), and the seat of the sexual function during man's present earthly life (*Rom.* 4: 19; *I Cor.* 7: 4).

The Christian's present lowly body is destined to be changed into a glorious body—even as Christ's glorified body—at the resurrection from the dead on Christ's return (*Phil.* 3: 21; *I Cor.* 15: 44).

The word "body" is also used to describe the community of Christians, the Church as a unified body, especially as the body of Christ (*Rom.* 12: 5; *I Cor.* 10: 17; 12: 13, 27; *Eph.* 1: 23; 2: 16; 4: 12, 16; 5: 23, 30; *Col.* 1: 18, 24; 2: 19; 3: 15).

BOOK OF LIFE a pictorial expression of the fact, often expressed, that the Lord knows those who belong to Him (*II Tim.* 2: 19), and that their entry into the full enjoyment of eternal life is absolutely certain (*Phil.* 4: 3; *Rev.* 3: 5).

BORN AGAIN or "regeneration", as it is called, is the supernatural work of the Holy Spirit by which those who were dead in trespasses and sins are made spiritually alive (*John* 3: 3, 6, 7, 8; *Eph.* 2: 1; *Jas.* 1: 18; *I Pet.* 1: 23). See *Question* 26.

CALLED, CALLING, CALLS. Calling is an act of God alone by which the elect are brought into fellowship and union with Christ (*I Cor.* 1: 9) so that they benefit from all the fruits of His redeeming and saving work on their behalf. It is the first step in the application of God's salvation to the individual (*Rom.* 8: 28–30; cf. *Acts* 16: 14). The call carries with it the grace of God sufficient to enable the individual to answer the call and to believe on the Lord Jesus Christ and be saved (*Acts* 16: 31). This grace is, in fact, what we call regeneration.

There is also the "call" to service. It is the individual's duty to recognise that call, and for the local church, when involved at all, to recognise it also and to act accordingly (*Acts* 13: 2; 16: 10).

CHASTISEMENT is the careful and gracious disciplining and correcting of our characters by means of unpleasant circumstances and trials. God's object in chastisement is always the spiritual development and maturity of the believer (*Heb.* 12: 5–7). A company of people, or a local church, or a single individual may all be the subjects of it.

CHOSEN. In the Old Testament the expression was used of the Israelites (*I Chron.* 16: 13; *Ps.* 89: 3) whom God chose from the peoples of the world, not for any merit, to fulfil His eternal purposes in the world (*Deut.* 7: 6, 8; *Isa.* 42: 1; 43: 20, 21).

In the New Testament it is a designation of those whom God has chosen from all mankind, apart from race and nation, and drawn to Himself through living faith in His Son, Jesus. The word reminds Christians that their faith rests on the work of God in them, and not on their own merits, and that they are chosen for God's own purposes (*Eph.* 1: 4; 5: 27; *Col.* 1: 22).

CHRIST is a Greek word meaning "The Anointed One"—the meaning of the word "Messiah". Anointing was a symbol of being set apart for a special task by God. The Jews looked for the coming of a Great One, called the Messiah, who would accomplish God's purposes for His people. Jesus accepted the title but only infrequently, for it would appear the Jews thought mainly of the Messiah as a political deliverer and Jesus had not come as such (*Matt.* 16: 16, 17; *Mark* 14: 61, 62; *John* 4: 26; cf. *Matt.* 1: 18; 2: 4; *Luke* 2: 11, 26).

CHRISTIAN. Christians are those who are connected with Christ—Christ's men and women. Believers were first called Christians in Antioch (*Acts* 11: 26). To believe the apostolic message of the gospel was to become a Christian (*Acts* 26: 28). To be known as a Christian, in some circumstances, became the basis for persecution (*I Pet.* 4: 16).

CHURCH. The word "church" is used mainly in two ways: first, of the whole company of those redeemed through Christ (*Matt.* 16: 18; *Acts* 9: 31; *I Cor.* 6: 4; 12: 28; *Eph.* 1: 22; 3: 10, 21; 5: 23 ff, 27, 29, 32), and secondly, of a company of professing believers in a particular area or district (*Matt.* 18: 17; *I Cor.* 1: 2; 10: 32; 11: 16, 22; 15: 9; *II Cor.* 1: 1; *Gal.* 1: 13; *I Thess.* 2: 14; *II Thess.* 1: 4; *I Tim.* 3: 5, 15; *Acts* 20: 28).

CLEANSED, CLEANSING is what we need from our sin (*Ps.* 51: 2). It normally describes physical cleansing, but it has another meaning in the Bible. Sin pollutes the soul, and makes it an object of dislike to God. The removal of sin, both in its condemning and corrupting influences, through the blood of Christ, is very appropriately described as cleansing (*Heb.* 1: 3). This cleansing is continuously available to the Christian as he endeavours to live in obedience to God, confessing all known sins as they arise (*I John* 1: 7–9).

COMFORTER. By its Latin derivation, and in older English, the word meant "encourager". The same Greek word is translated elsewhere in the New Testament as "Advocate" (*John* 14: 16, 26; 15: 26; 16: 7). See ADVOCATE.

COMMUNION is sharing and participating, and translates the same word in the New Testament which we more often translate as "fellowship". Communion is a particularly apt word for describing the Lord's Supper because by participating in it, not only does the Christian express his own personal fellowship with Christ and sharing in the benefits of His completed atoning work, but he does so in fellowship with other

Christians because of the essential spiritual unity and identity of all who share the benefits of Christ's redeeming work (*I Cor.* 10: 16, 17).

COMMUNION OF SAINTS is another way of expressing the fellowship of Christian believers. This fellowship, or communion, of believers is the identity, sympathy and belonging we have with all believers through our common allegiance to the Lord Jesus Christ (*Eph.* 4: 6, 13). The more fellowship with God the Father and the Son is enjoyed, the more is communion with God's people experienced (*I John* 1: 3).

CONDEMNATION, CONDEMNED. Condemnation describes the result of man's sinful condition before God. Deserving the wrath of God, sinners are sentenced to just punishment—death (*Ezek.* 18: 4; *John* 3: 16–19). Through Christ, the believer's sin is adequately and finally dealt with, and all condemnation is removed (*Rom.* 8: 1; *I John* 4: 10).

CONFESS, CONFESSION. The same word is used with regard to a few different matters. First, confession is the acknowledgment before God of our individual sins; and upon such confession depends our experience of His forgiveness and cleansing (*I John* 1: 9). Secondly, confession is our consistent declaration before men that Jesus is the Son of God and has become our Saviour and Lord, to whom we give total allegiance (*Rom.* 10: 9, 10; *Phil.* 2: 11; cf. *Matt.* 10: 32; *Luke* 12: 8). Thirdly, confession is the acknowledgment we make and the witness we give to the truths of the faith (*I Tim.* 6: 12; *Heb.* 10: 23).

CONSCIENCE is that part of us which registers disapproval when we go against what we know is right, and approval when we do the right thing. Like a witness, it declares facts (*Rom.* 2: 15; 9: 1; *II Cor.* 1: 12), like a trusted adviser, it prohibits evil (*Acts* 24: 16; *Rom.* 13: 5), and like a judge, it assesses what is deserved (*Rom.* 2: 15; cf. *I John* 3: 20 f). Conscience on its own is not the standard of right and wrong; it needs to be instructed and informed by the Word of God and the Holy Spirit. Before a person is a Christian, conscience tends to be either bad or asleep. When the work of conviction begins a man's conscience is made sensitive, and he knows he has a bad conscience before God. When he is reconciled to God, as a gift from God, his conscience is purged through the effectiveness of the blood of Christ on his behalf (*Heb.* 9: 14). A conscience "void of offence" (*Acts* 24: 16) is maintained as he seeks to do God's will and allows no sin to remain unconfessed (*I John* 1: 6–10).

CONTRITION is brokenness of spirit through a right appreciation of the sinful nature of sin. A man's pride is properly humbled by this appreciation and he is in a fit position then to receive the grace and forgiveness of God (*Ps.* 34: 18; 51: 17; *Isa.* 57: 15; 66: 2).

CONVERSION. See *Question* 27.

CONVICTION is the work of the Holy Spirit, who, through the Scriptures as they are preached, convicts the conscience of its sin before God, bringing a conviction of the justice and certainty of God's wrath upon sin, and a hatred of sin on the part of the individual (*John* 16: 8, 9; cf. *Acts* 2: 37; *I Thess.* 1: 5, 9, 10).

CORRUPTION is used first in a physical sense of the body decaying and dying (*Ps.* 16: 10; cf. *Acts* 2: 27), and secondly in a spiritual sense of man's state before God as a consequence of his sinful rebellion (*Ps.* 14: 1). Left to himself man gets worse and worse, and everything he does is infected by his sin.

COVENANT. A covenant is a compact or a contract. When the word is used in connection with God, it has the idea of a one-sided arrangement made by a superior party. In the covenant with Adam, for example, God placed him on probation, promising life, if he were obedient (*Gen.* 2: 17).

The word is used particularly, however, of those obligations which God imposes upon Himself, for the reconciliation of sinful men and women to Himself (*Gen.* 17: 7; *Deut.* 7: 6–8; *Ps.* 89: 3–4; *Heb.* 13: 20).

CREATION. The God and Father of our Lord Jesus Christ is the creator of all things (*Neh.* 9: 6; *Ps.* 90: 2; *Isa.* 42: 5; *Acts* 17: 24, 25;

I Cor. 8: 6). God the Son and God the Holy Spirit were active in the creation (*Gen.* 1: 2; *Job* 26: 13; *John* 1: 3; *Col.* 1: 16; *Heb.* 1: 2), and God the Father has ordained that all creation shall ultimately belong to the Son (*Heb.* 1: 2). In the final analysis, the absolute creation of all things by God is a matter for faith rather than scientific proof (*Heb.* 11: 3). See *Question* 9.

CROSS. The cross was an upright stake or beam used in punishing and executing criminals, particularly by the Romans. The word describes the painful form of death Jesus endured, but it is more often used as a one-word summary of the good news of salvation, that Jesus "died for our sins". "The word of the cross" is "the preaching of the gospel" (*I Cor.* 1: 17 ff).

CURSE is a sentence of destruction called down upon someone because of a misdemeanour. In the Bible it does not refer to blasphemous language as today. It is used of the Lord Jesus Christ who is said to have become a curse for sinners. The failure of sinners to keep God's law brings upon them the curse of God which, in fact, is death (*Gal.* 3: 10; *Rom.* 6: 23). Christ willingly stood in the place of sinners at the Cross, taking their death upon Himself. In this way He became a curse for them (*Gal.* 3: 13).

DAY OF JUDGMENT. See JUDGMENT.

DEPRAVED is used to describe man's corrupt state before God as a result of his sin. Man is said to be totally depraved, not in the sense that he is as bad as he can possibly be, but rather that sin has corrupted every part of his being, his mind, will and affections. Men's hearts are full of evil and madness (*Eccl.* 9: 3; *Matt.* 15: 11, 15–20; *Mark* 7: 15, 20–23), and correction sometimes only makes him sin the more (*Zeph.* 3: 7).

DESTRUCTION describes the eternal death, damnation and ruin which is the punishment of the wicked (*Matt.* 7: 13; *Rev.* 17: 8, 11).

DEVIL. See *Question* 43.

DISCIPLE was something of a technical term used of a person who attached himself to a particular teacher. A disciple is someone under instruction. Jesus chose the twelve, to bring them under His instruction so that they should be able to convey His teaching later to others (*Matt.* 28: 20; cf. *II Tim.* 2: 2). But many more besides the twelve were called "disciples" (*Luke* 10: 1 ff) and the term was given generally to all professing Christians (*Acts* 11: 26). Jesus requires faithfulness and obedience to what He says as the major condition of discipleship (*John* 8: 31).

DISOBEDIENCE can describe either the deliberate and obstinate rejection of the will of God (*Eph.* 2: 2; 5: 6) or the refusal to hear God's words (*Jer.* 11: 10; 35: 17). It can, of course, describe both aspects at once.

ELDERS were the spiritual leaders of the early Christian churches. They were appointed from the earliest times (*Acts* 11: 30). Their precise functions are not clear, although pastoral care and rule fell to them as their particular responsibilities and some had the further task of teaching and preaching the Word of God. The qualifications for elders and bishops are more or less identical (*Tit.* 1: 6–9; *I Tim.* 3: 1–7) and it is generally agreed that the two titles were interchangeable, referring to the same spiritual office.

ELECT, ELECTION. Election is God's eternal, unconditional choice of guilty sinners to be redeemed and born again of His Spirit so that they may be brought at the last to His everlasting glory (*Rom.* 8: 30; *Eph.* 1: 3–12; *I Pet.* 1: 2). The believer's experience of salvation, sanctification, and glory all flow from God's election (*II Thess.* 2: 13, 14) which had no regard at all to any works or merit on the believer's part (*Rom.* 11: 6; *II Tim.* 1: 9).

ETERNAL always conveys the idea of something which is without end (*Luke* 16: 9; *Acts* 13: 46), and, sometimes, when God is spoken of, of that without beginning (*Gen.* 21: 33; *Isa.* 26: 4; *Rom.* 16: 26; *Heb.* 9: 14).

ETERNAL LIFE, EVERLASTING LIFE is never-ending life, the very opposite of death and corruption (*Rom.* 6: 22; *Gal.* 6: 8). It is the gift of God, and the present possession of the Christian through believing in the Lord Jesus Christ (*Rom.* 6: 23; *John* 3: 16; 10: 28). Its essence is everlasting fellowship with God (*John* 17: 3).

EVIL describes that which is bad, and contrary to law, such as crime, sin and wrong-doing. It begins in the human heart (*Matt.* 9: 4), and unchecked leads to further evil (*Eccl.* 8: 11).

EVIL ONE is a name given to the devil because of his wicked, bad, base and vicious activities (*Matt.* 13: 19; *John* 17: 15; *Eph.* 6: 16; *I John* 2: 13 f; 5: 18, 19).

EXPIATE, EXPIATION. To expiate is to pay the penalty of sin, and to make amends for it. Christ is the expiation for our sin in that to Him were transferred our sins, and He died for our sins, so that we might be brought near to God (*I Pet.* 3: 18). By giving up Himself sacrificially, Christ annulled the power of sin to separate between God and the believer (*Heb.* 2: 17; *Rom.* 3: 25).

FAITH. See *Question* 29.

FALL, The. See *Question* 13.

FATHER (See **GOD**). The word is the distinguishing name of the first Person of the Trinity in relation to the second Person—the Son (*John* 14: 6; 20: 17; *Rom.* 15: 6; *II Cor.* 1: 3). The relationship has no like anywhere, and is beyond our understanding.

The word is used, secondly, of the relationship God the Father has with those who believe in His Son (*Rom.* 1: 7; *I Cor.* 1: 3; *II Thess.* 2: 16). Such are taught by the Holy Spirit to call Him "Father" (*John* 1: 12; *Rom.* 8: 15; *I John* 3: 1).

The relationship which God has to men in general is seldom spoken of as fatherhood, indeed the opposite is the case (*John* 8: 44).

FELLOWSHIP is a favourite Christian word and is the name for the common sharing of Christians in the grace of God, the salvation Christ brings, and the indwelling Holy Spirit which is the spiritual birthright of all Christians. The fellowship which Christians have with one another, therefore, springs from the fellowship they have with the Father, Son and Holy Spirit (*I John* 1: 3). Fellowship with God is a relationship in which Christians receive from, and respond to, all three Persons of the Trinity in a relation of friendship (*John* 14: 23; *Rom.* 5: 5; 8: 16; *Eph.* 4: 30). Such fellowship is the life of heaven begun on earth (*I Pet.* 1: 8).

FLESH is used to describe an important part of our bodies, and as such no blame is attached to it (*I Cor.* 15: 50; *Luke* 24: 39).
But generally it is used to describe the sinful and corrupt nature of men. It represents the lower part of man's nature, where his natural desires have unhindered scope, leading to all kinds of sin (*Rom.* 7: 18; *Gal.* 5: 19–21; *Eph.* 2: 3). In the person who is born again, the deeds of the flesh are put to death as the Holy Spirit is obeyed. But in those who are not Christians, the flesh dominates (*Rom.* 8: 4–9, 12, 13).

FORGIVENESS is the cancelling by God (*Micah* 7: 19; *Eph.* 1: 7) of the sinner's debt and guilt on the basis of Christ's death for sinners (*Matt.* 26: 28; *Mark* 14: 24). The conditions are repentance and faith in Christ (*Acts* 2: 38; 5: 31; 10: 43; *I John* 1: 9).

GENTILES was, to begin with, a term for "nations". The Jews knew themselves to be distinct from all other peoples and they used this term to describe all such peoples. In the New Testament the term usually has the Greeks especially in mind, and now, of course, it covers all who are not of Jewish race.

GLORY is used of God Himself to sum up the perfection of all that He is and all that He does, not least His grace, power and righteousness—the latter revealing especially how far short men fall of God's standards (*Rom.* 1: 23; *Eph.* 1: 17; *Jude* 24).

The word is also used to describe the eternal happiness which Christians are to enjoy in the life to come (*Rom.* 8: 18, 21; *I Pet.* 5: 1, 10).

GOD is Spirit (*John* 4: 24): invisible (*I Tim.* 6: 15, 16; *John* 1: 18), personal (*Ex.* 3: 14), great beyond human estimation (*Isa.* 40: 18; 45: 6; *Rom.* 11: 33–34), life-giving (*Gen.* 1; *John* 5: 26; *Acts* 17: 25) and supremely powerful (*Ps.* 115: 3; *Isa.* 40: 15, 17).

There is but one God (*Deut.* 6: 4), but one in three Persons, Father, Son and Holy Spirit (*Matt.* 28: 19; *II Cor.* 13: 14).

Although no one has ever seen God the Father (*John* 1: 18), God has given clues to His existence both in creation (*Gen.* 1: 1; *Ps.* 19: 1; *Acts* 17: 24; *Rom.* 1: 18–20) and in the nature of man (*Ps.* 139: 14; *Rom.* 2: 14, 15), and in the glorious revelation of Himself in the Person of His Son, Jesus Christ (*II Cor.* 4: 6; *John* 1: 14, 18; 14: 9; *Col.* 1: 15–17; *I John* 1: 1–3).

Added to these evidences, there is the witness of the Bible (*II Tim.* 3: 16), and of those who have found God (*Acts* 4: 20; *I John* 5: 20).

GOD (god) is a word used of divine beings generally, and of the one true God, the God and Father of our Lord Jesus Christ. It is also used of idols who are so-called "gods", and of Satan who is the god of this world (*II Cor.* 4: 4). In using this term to describe idols and evil spirits the Bible does not acknowledge their deity—indeed the opposite is the case—but it recognises the false worship which men may foolishly give to them.

GODHEAD is an expression standing for the very being of God, or His essential nature; an alternative word is deity (*Acts* 17: 29; *II Pet.* 1: 3, 4).

GOOD WORKS are the good actions which are to be produced in the Christian's life following upon his experience of being justified (*Eph.* 2: 10). Even as the health of a tree is shown by its fruit, so too is the health of a Christian shown by his good works (*Matt.* 5: 16; 7: 15–20). They necessarily contain imperfections but they are pleasing to God because they arise from living faith in Christ.

Good works are worthless, however, as a means of justification and for gaining merit before God (*Eph.* 2: 9; *Tit.* 3: 5).

GOSPEL means "good news"—the good news concerning God's Son Jesus Christ. The good news is that Christ died for sinners, and that through repentance and faith in Christ sinners can possess His righteousness before God, and receive the gift of the Holy Spirit and everlasting life.

GOSPELS. The four gospels—Matthew, Mark, Luke and John—are the books in which the story of Christ's life and teaching is found. They are not so much biographies of Jesus as written copies of the apostles' preaching and teaching, putting the emphasis on the events through which God's salvation was made available to men and women—the "good news" after which the gospels are named. According to the four gospel writers, there is but one gospel—the gospel of Jesus Christ, the Son of God—delivered to, and preached by the apostles (*Acts* 2: 42; *I Cor.* 15: 1–4).

GRACE is the undeserved love of God to men revealed in Christ, giving them through Him help and countless gifts and benefits which they could never merit (*Rom.* 3: 24; 5: 15; 6: 1; *Eph.* 1: 6; 2: 5, 7, 8).

GUILT is the deserving of punishment because of law-breaking or failure to do something required. All men, since the first rebellion of man (*Rom.* 5: 12), are guilty before God since all have sinned and fallen short of His glory (*Rom.* 3: 23) and are accountable to Him (*Rom.* 3: 19). Salvation rescues from guilt (*Eph.* 1: 7), the sacrifice of Christ completely removing the guilt of sin (*Heb.* 10: 4, 18).

HEART covers the whole inward life of a man: his thinking, feeling and will (*Matt.* 13: 15). Sin has its roots in the heart (*Matt.* 15: 19, 20) and it is in the hearts of men, therefore, that God's work of salvation begins (*Matt.* 13: 19; *Rom.* 2: 15; *II Cor.* 3: 3; *Heb.* 8: 10) so that men believe in their own heart (*Acts* 15: 9; *Rom.* 10: 9, 10).

HEATHEN. Used in the Bible, the word means "nation". Being the sole people in the Old Testament to whom God had revealed Himself in a covenant relationship, the Jews regarded other nations as completely separate and different. All other peoples, not having the covenant relationship with God, were the heathen. The term "heathen" describes men and women everywhere who are without the true knowledge of God.

HEAVEN. See *Question* 49.

HELL. See *Question* 50.

HOLINESS, HOLINESS OF GOD. Holiness is a term which above all others expresses the perfection of God's character. He is entirely free from moral evil, and possesses infinite purity. He is absolutely distinct from all His creatures, and is exalted above them in infinite majesty. The idea behind the word "holy" and "holiness" is that of being cut off, separated, or set apart. God sets apart His people from other peoples, and He calls them to separate themselves from all that displeases Him and is contrary to His will. He calls them to be like Himself (*I Pet.* 1: 15, 16).

HOLY GHOST is another way of describing the Holy Spirit. Both "Spirit" and "Ghost" are translations of the same word in the New Testament. "Spirit" is a better word than "Ghost" for other uses are inclined to mislead us when we think of the Holy Spirit by the title of "Ghost".

HOLY SPIRIT. The Holy Spirit is the Lord (i.e. Himself God) and the Giver of life, the third Person of the Trinity, to be worshipped and glorified with the Father and the Son (*Matt.* 28: 19; *I Cor.* 12: 4–6; *II Cor.* 13: 14; *Eph.* 4: 4–6). He is most commonly presented to us as the Executor of God's purposes, whether in creation (*Gen.* 1: 2; *Job* 26: 13), revelation (*II Tim.* 3: 16; *II Pet.* 1: 21) or redemption (*Luke* 1: 35; *John* 3: 5, 6; *Acts* 2: 24; *I Cor.* 12: 3). He is the gift of the Father and the Son to the believer to live within him (*John* 14: 16; 15: 26; 16: 7): giving him spiritual life (*Gal.* 5: 25; *Eph.* 2: 1); assuring him of his sonship (*Rom.* 8: 16); and communicating to him the benefits of the gospel (*Rom.* 5: 5; 15: 13). See *Questions* 23, 24.

HOPE as used in the New Testament, has behind it no idea of clinging to a mere possibility, but rather the happy and confident expectation of enjoying some unseen and future promise of God. The living hope of the resurrection from the dead and the inheritance to follow are examples (*I Pet.* 1: 3–4).

IMMORTALITY is deathlessness, and belongs to God alone. Christians receive it as a gift, but God Himself is the source (*I Tim.* 6: 16). Immortality is not merely the survival of the soul after the death of the body, but the self-conscious existence of the whole person, body and soul together, in a state of eternal happiness (*I Cor.* 15: 53 f).

IN CHRIST is a characteristic description of Christians, signifying the spiritual union which every Christian has with Christ, from which springs his experience of all the benefits of Christ's finished work and the knowledge of Christ living within him by the Holy Spirit (*John* 15: 4, 5; *Rom.* 8: 9–11; *I Cor.* 1: 30; *II Cor.* 5: 17; *Gal.* 2: 20; *Phil.* 1: 1).

INCARNATION. The word itself comes from Latin, meaning "becoming-in-flesh", and describes the amazing fact of Christ, the Son of God, becoming flesh (*John* 1: 14). In both the Old and New Testaments Christ is declared to be both God and man (*Ps.* 2; 22; 45; 72; 110; *John* 1: 1–3, 14; *Col.* 2: 9). His perfect deity and perfect humanity are essentials of the Christian faith (*I John* 2: 22–25; 4: 1–6; 5: 5–12; *II John* 7), although these glorious facts are beyond the understanding of the human mind (*I Tim.* 3: 16). See *Question* 19.

INFINITE describes that which is boundless, endless and very great. It is used commonly of God because no limitation can be set to His being. He is far greater in His being and perfection than we can know or think.

INHERITANCE. In the Old Testament the land of Canaan, promised to Abraham and his descendants, was called the "inheritance" (*I Kings* 8: 36).

In the spiritual sense, the Lord Himself is said to be His people's inheritance (*Jer.* 10: 16) and the Lord speaks of His true people as His inheritance (*Deut.* 4: 20; 32: 9; *Ps.* 2: 8).

In the New Testament the "inheritance" is the kingdom of God with all its benefits (*Matt.* 25: 34; *I Cor.* 6: 9; *Gal.* 5: 21; *I Pet.* 1: 3, 4). As the children of God through faith in Christ, believers are to share God's treasures and Christ's glory (*Rom.* 8: 17).

INIQUITY is persistent wickedness and disobedience to God's laws (*Isa.* 53: 6; *Rom.* 6: 19; *Tit.* 2: 14).

INSPIRED, INSPIRATION. The word used in the New Testament for "inspired" means "God-breathed" (*II Tim.* 3: 16). The Scriptures came about not by the impulse of man, but through men being moved by the Holy Spirit to speak from God (*II Pet.* 1: 21). The responsibility of such men was to transmit what they received (*I Pet.* 1: 10–12). The authority of the Bible springs from its divine inspiration (*II Tim.* 3: 16, 17). The conviction that the Scriptures are the Word of God is brought about in the heart of the Christian by the Holy Spirit (*I Cor.* 2: 4, 5; *I Thess.* 1: 5; 2: 13).

INTERCESSION is the continuing work of Christ in heaven for Christians. On the grounds of His sacrifice on their behalf, He unfailingly claims every spiritual benefit for them, secures forgiveness for all their sins and makes their worship and service acceptable to God (*Rom.* 8: 34; *Heb.* 7: 27; 9: 24; 13: 15; *I John* 2: 1).

A different kind of intercession is the Holy Spirit's work in the Christian by which He disposes, teaches and helps the Christian to pray according to God's will. The Spirit gives both the inclination and the ability to pray (*Rom.* 8: 26, 27).

ISRAEL was the name given by God to the patriarch Jacob (*Gen.* 32: 28; 35: 10) and to all the descendants of Jacob. The name was given then to the whole nation of Israel. In the New Testament it is used also of Christians, whether Jews or Gentiles, as the true nation of Israel (*Gal.* 6: 16) for whom circumcision is a matter of the heart, not of the body (*Rom.* 2: 29).

JESUS is the Greek form of the Hebrew name Joshua, meaning "God is salvation" or "God is the Saviour". In obedience to God's command, it was given to the Son of God when He became man, as a symbol of God's promise that Christ would rescue God's people from the guilt and power of their sins (*Matt.* 1: 21; *Luke* 1: 31; 2: 21).

JEWS. The title "Jew" was used first for members of the tribe of Judah or of the two tribes of the Southern Kingdom (*II Kings* 16: 6; 25: 25). Later it was used of any Hebrew who returned from the Captivity. Now it covers all of the Hebrew race anywhere in the world (*Esth.* 2: 5; *Matt.* 2: 2).

JUDGE, The. Sometimes God the Father is spoken of as the Judge (*Heb.* 12: 23), and sometimes the Lord Jesus Christ (*Acts* 10: 42; *II Tim.* 4: 1, 8). God the Father has fixed a day on which He will judge the whole world in justice by Christ the Judge whom He has appointed (*Acts* 17: 31).

JUDGMENT, JUDGMENT DAY. Judgment is the condemnation of God which rightly falls upon sinners (*Rom.* 2: 2) and which will be executed at the judgment when Christ will be the Judge and all will appear before Him (*Matt.* 25: 31–46; *John* 5: 22, 27). The perfect justice of God and the undeniable guilt of all will be plain and beyond dispute (*Gen.* 18: 25; *Acts* 17: 31; *Rom.* 2: 5, 6). Those justified through faith in Christ will be acquitted from the guilt of sin and will receive rewards according to their faithfulness (*Rom.* 5: 1; *I Cor.* 3: 9–13; *II Tim.* 4: 8); the unbelieving will receive their final condemnation (*Rom.* 2: 8; *II Thess.* 1: 8, 9; *Jude* 15; *Rev.* 20: 15).

The day of judgment is the day when Christ returns (*I Thess.* 5: 4; *Heb.* 10: 25; *I Cor.* 3: 13), when all these things will take place. See *Question* 46.

JUDGMENT SEAT. Both Greek and Roman judges sat on either a raised platform or seat in a public place and justice was seen to be done. Because of the absolutely fair and public nature of the last judgment, the picture is taken up to illustrate the judgment day when Christ shall publicly and justly judge all men (*Rom.* 14: 10; *II Cor.* 5: 10).

JUST describes men who are upright or righteous in that they conform to the laws of God and man; this is only possible to us through the new birth (*I John* 2: 29). It is used of God Himself to describe the perfect fairness of His judgment of men and nations (*Ps.* 7: 11; *II Tim.* 4: 8). It is used of Jesus, who is the perfect standard of obedience and uprightness (*Matt.* 27: 19; *Acts* 7: 52; *I Pet.* 3: 18).

JUSTIFICATION, JUSTIFY. See *Question* 31.

KINGDOM, KINGDOM OF GOD, KINGDOM OF HEAVEN. The kingdom of God or the kingdom of heaven, is spoken of in two ways: first, as that of which Christians are members because Christ, through the new birth (*John* 3: 3, 5), actively rules as King in their hearts; and secondly, as that which they possess as an inheritance in the future (*Matt.* 25: 34; *Luke* 22: 16; *II Tim.* 4: 18; *Heb.* 12: 28).

LAMB is a picture used of Christ to set Him forth as the One promised in the Old Testament to obtain for others deliverance from God's judgment by the sacrifice of Himself for sin (*John* 1: 29; *I Pet.* 1: 19). In the Old Testament the lamb was the principal sacrificial animal, and all such sacrifices looked forward to the one sacrifice which would deal with sin once and for all—the sacrifice of Jesus as the Lamb of God (*Heb.* 10: 1–14). While meekness characterised Jesus as the Lamb of God in His earthly ministry (*Isa.* 53: 7; *I Pet.* 2: 22, 23), the symbol is used in the Book of Revelation to express His position as the Conqueror and the Mighty One (*Rev.* 5: 6; 7: 14 ff; 12: 11).

LAST DAY, LAST DAYS. The Last Day is usually a reference to Christ's second coming (*John* 6: 39, 40, 44, 54) and the events which will then occur, principally the judgment and the resurrection of the dead.

The last days are sometimes thought of as beginning with the birth of Christ (*Heb.* 1: 2) in that God's new and final order of things through the redeeming work of His Son, and the consequent birth of the Church, then comes into operation.

The last days also describes the period of history immediately preceding the second coming of Christ (*II Tim.* 3: 1), the great event which will mark the completion of the present age.

LAW is used to describe the whole of the Scriptures (*Josh.* 1: 8; *Ps.* 119: 97) and more particularly the Law of God, as summed up in the Ten Commandments (*Ex.* 20: 1–17). It is the Law of God which makes us aware of our sin against God (*Rom.* 3: 20) and thus drives us to realise our need of the salvation achieved by Christ for sinners (*Gal.* 2: 15, 16, 21). See *Question* 16.

LORD describes God, and is the word used in the Greek translation of the Old Testament to render the name of God, "Jehovah". It is used regularly of Christ, meaning that He is divine Lord, having the highest place of all, worthy of our worship, service and obedience (*Acts* 2: 36; *I Cor.* 16: 22; *Phil.* 2: 9–11; *Col.* 3: 24). It is also used of the Spirit (*II Cor.* 3: 18).

Significantly, references to the LORD God in the Old Testament are applied to Christ in the New Testament (*Isa.* 40: 3; cf. *Matt.* 3: 3; *Isa.* 44: 6; *Rev.* 1: 17).

LOST is used to describe the condition of men and women who live without Christ and therefore without the hope of eternal life. Like lost sheep, they are separated from the Shepherd they need (*Matt.* 10: 6; *Luke* 15: 4; 19: 10). The lost need to be found and saved through Christ, or else they will perish (*Matt.* 18: 12–14; *John* 3: 16).

LOVE is the foremost characteristic of God, together with His holiness (*I John* 1: 5; 4: 8). It is a love which is utterly independent of the merits of those loved, a fact so perfectly illustrated in the Cross, when Christ died for us, while we were yet sinners (*John* 3: 16; *Rom.* 5: 8). Christ perfectly expressed the love of God for men (*II Cor.* 5: 14; *Eph.* 2: 4; 3: 19; 5: 2).

Christian love is the fruit of the Holy Spirit's presence in the Christian (*Gal.* 5: 22). Love for God is seen in obedience to His commandments (*John* 14: 15, 21, 23; 15: 10; *I John* 2: 5; 5: 3; *II John* 6). Love for others is seen in seeking their best interests, irrespective of the attitude or response received (*Rom.* 15: 2; *I Cor.* 13; *Gal.* 6: 10).

MEDIATOR, MEDIATION. A Mediator, literally, is a go-between. He mediates between two parties to produce peace by removing disagreement.

Christ is the one Mediator between God and men (*I Tim.* 2: 5). He was uniquely qualified to mediate being Himself both God and man. Christ voluntarily took His stand between the offended God and the offending sinner, so as to deliver the sinner by taking upon Himself the wrath of God which the sinner deserved.

By His unique sacrifice for sins on behalf of men peace between God and man was made possible. Christ Himself is our peace (*Eph.* 2: 14).

MERCY is warm affection demonstrated to the needy, helpless and distressed. In sending Christ to be the Saviour of sinners, the amazing mercy of God was shown (*Luke* 1: 78; *Tit.* 3: 5). His abundant mercy is seen in the manner in which He blots out the penitent sinner's transgressions (*Ps.* 51: 1).

MESSIAH means "Anointed" and was the name given to the coming deliverer promised in the Old Testament. The word indicated that the deliverer or saviour was to be specially consecrated for his tasks, in the same way as a king or a priest might be. Among the Greeks the title Messiah was translated "Christos", or "Christ" as we spell it.

Jesus accepted the title (*Matt.* 16: 16) but He used it cautiously to describe His mission, for many of the Jews looked upon the Messiah as merely a political deliverer rather than a spiritual Saviour. He always emphasised the sufferings which had to be His as the Messiah before He could enter upon His glory (*Matt.* 16: 16, 20, 21).

MIND represents man's ability to think, his understanding—and the word "understanding" often translates the Greek word for "mind" in the New Testament. The mind of the unregenerate man is described as blinded (*II Cor.* 3: 14; 4: 4), darkened (*Eph.* 4: 18), alienated (*Col.* 1: 21), puffed up (*Col.* 2: 18), corrupt (*I Tim.* 6: 5), and defiled (*Tit.* 1: 15). Regeneration brings a new awakening of the mind to love God, to understand His will and to do it (*Rom.* 12: 1, 2; *Eph.* 4: 23; *I Pet.* 1: 13).

MIRACLE. A miracle is an act or a work of supernatural origin or character, which would not be possible by ordinary or natural means. The deeds of power of Jesus were miracles in this sense (*Matt.* 13: 54, 58; *Luke* 19: 37).

NEW BIRTH. See *Question* 26.

NEW COVENANT, NEW TESTAMENT. The word "testament" means "covenant" rather than our modern "testament". The term "New Testament" came into general use in the later part of the second century to describe these twenty-seven writings which fall into four divisions: the four gospels; the Acts of the Apostles; twenty-one letters; the Book of Revelation.

The great message of the New Testament is that God's promises of redemption have been fulfilled in the life, death and resurrection of Jesus His blood has secured the provision of a new covenant, according to God's will, so that all who believe and obey become God's people and Christ's Church.

OBEDIENCE, OBEY. Obedience is the obeying of God's voice in His commandments (*Josh.* 22: 2; *Ex.* 19: 5; *Jer.* 17: 23; *Deut.* 5: 10). The revelation God has given us in the Scriptures is to be the rule of the individual's whole life (*II Tim.* 3: 16, 17). Christ is the perfect example of obedience (*John* 15: 10; *Heb.* 10: 7).

Obedience is, in effect, our response to the Word of God (*Matt.* 13: 23). It is almost identical with a sensitive conscience, constantly educated and informed by the Holy Spirit through the Scriptures, and consistently obeyed (*Acts* 23: 1; 24: 16; *II Tim.* 1: 3).

Obedience is the work of God in the Christian, as a result of the new birth, for God inspires both the will and the deed, for His own good pleasure (*I Pet.* 1: 2, 14; *Phil.* 2: 13, 14).

By obedience we please God (*I John* 3: 22), dwell in Christ's love (*John* 15: 10), sustain our fellowship with God (*John* 14: 23–24; *I John* 1: 3, 7), grow in holiness (*Luke* 1: 6; *I Pet.* 1: 14–16), and perfect our love for God (*I John* 2: 5).

OFFERING. Sacrifices and offerings

are linked in the Old Testament (*Heb*. 10: 5; *Ps*. 40: 6). The "sacrifices" were animal offerings and the "offerings" vegetable offerings. The word "offering" carried with it the idea of drawing near. It was that with which a man drew near to God. The sin of man is such that he cannot enter into the presence of God without some preparation: to this fact the offerings bore witness.

Leviticus 1–7 describes them. They are of great interest because we know how the Lord Jesus fulfilled their deepest significance for us by the one offering of Himself, opening up the way for us into the presence of God by His blood (*Heb*. 10: 10, 19–22).

OLD TESTAMENT. The word "testament" means "covenant" rather than our modern "testament". The term "Old Testament" came into general use in the later part of the second century to describe the writings we know by that title.

The thirty-nine books were arranged by the Jews in three divisions: the Law, the Prophets and the Writings. They deal particularly with the promises, or covenant that God made with Israel. They are the record of the working out of God's redemption on behalf of His people, and they always look forward to the spiritual redemption to take place in the future with the coming of the Messiah.

OMNIPOTENCE means possessing all power, and is characteristic, therefore, of God alone who can do all things so that no purpose of His can be thwarted (*Job* 42: 2). There is no power higher than God's (*Ps*. 135: 6; *Rev*. 1: 8). His limitless power is expressed in the title "God of Sabaoth" or "Lord of hosts" (*Jas*. 5: 4; cf. *Judg*. 5: 20; *II Kings* 6: 17; *Isa*. 5: 9; *Rom*. 9: 29; *Isa*. 1: 9).

OMNIPRESENCE means being everywhere at the same time and is an ability and quality possessed by God alone (*Amos* 9: 2–4; *Ps*. 139: 7–12).

OMNISCIENCE means possessing all knowledge and wisdom and is a characteristic of God alone. Nothing can escape the knowledge of God (*Ps*. 139: 2, 3, 6; 145: 7). He is the only wise God (*Rom*. 16: 27).

PARADISE is an oriental word, first used by the Persians of an enclosed garden or park. It was taken over by the Greeks and it expressed the idea of a place of supreme happiness above the earth. Our Lord used it of the heavenly home to which the believer's spirit goes at death (*Luke* 23: 43).

PASSOVER was the name given to the feast appointed by God to keep in memory the deliverance of the Israelites from Egypt (*Ex*. 12). It was so called because the Lord "passed over" or "spared" the Israelites when He punished the Egyptians. The Israelites had to offer up a lamb or a kid in order that the destroying angel might pass over them. The passover lamb is a picture of Christ, and He is called "our Passover" (*I Cor*. 5: 7) because His death has saved us from the judgment of God's wrath which we deserve.

PEACE is harmony with God restored, made possible by the reconciliation God has already accomplished through the death of Christ (*II Cor*. 5: 20, 21), into which we enter by faith (*Rom*. 5: 1). This peace brings with it glorious access to God (*Rom*. 5: 2).

PENTATEUCH is the name given to the first five books of the Bible (Genesis, Exodus, Leviticus, Numbers, Deuteronomy), the actual word itself meaning a five-volumed book. In the Old Testament, the Pentateuch is described as the Law (*Josh*. 8: 34; *Neh*. 8: 2) or the book of the Law of God (*Josh*. 24: 26; *Neh*. 8: 18), and sometimes as the book of Moses (*Ezra* 6: 18; *Neh*. 13: 1), in view of his responsibility in writing down God's revelation and dealings with God's people.

In the New Testament also, these first five books are associated particularly with God's law (*Gal*. 3: 10; *Matt*. 12: 5; *Luke* 16: 16; *John* 7: 19; *Luke* 2: 23, 24) and with Moses (*Luke* 2: 22; *Mark* 12: 26; *John* 7: 23; *Luke* 20: 28).

The period covered by the Pentateuch is from the creation to the beginning of Joshua's leadership, after the death of Moses.

PERISH means to die, with all the consequences of death, and eternal separation from God—the opposite, in fact, of everlasting life (*John* 3: 16).

PERSEVERANCE describes the New Testament teaching that once a man is truly saved, he remains saved for ever (*John* 6: 39; 10: 27–29; *II Tim.* 4: 18). God does not keep a man living the Christian life, however, without exertion, diligence and watchfulness on the man's part (*John* 8: 31; *I Tim.* 2: 15; *II Pet.* 1: 11). The strength to persevere in the faith is from God alone (*Phil.* 1: 6). The believer holds fast to the end because he is held fast by the Lord (*I Pet.* 1: 5). Apostasy proves a person was never a true Christian.

PRAYER is not simply making requests of God, but rather conversation with God. In prayer God makes Himself known to the soul, revealing His glory and His love. Christians must endeavour always to pray in the way God has laid down: through Christ and the Holy Spirit. Through Christ Christians have confidence to come before God (*Heb.* 10: 19) and by the Holy Spirit they are enabled to offer true prayer (*Rom.* 8: 9, 26, 27).

PRESERVATION is a term used to describe, first, God's preserving and maintaining the creation which He made so that it continues to exist and function (*Neh.* 9: 6). The Son and the Holy Spirit are also spoken of as having their functions to fulfil in the upholding and continuing of God's creation (*Ps.* 104: 30; *Heb.* 1: 3).

The term is used, secondly, for describing God's preserving or keeping of believers in faith and grace, even using trials and difficulties to the strengthening of their faith (*Phil.* 1: 6; 2: 13; *II Tim.* 4: 18; *I Pet.* 1: 6, 7; *Jude* 24).

PROPHECIES, PROPHECY. Prophecy in the Bible represents the speaking forth of the mind and counsel of God. Although prophecies sometimes referred to future events, prophecy was not necessarily foretelling the future. Rather it was the setting forth of truth which could not be known by natural means. Prophecy apparently passed away when all the Bible books were available to the Christian church. Teaching from the whole Scriptures has taken the place of the prophecy which was necessary before the complete Scriptures were available (cf. *II Pet.* 2: 1).

PROPHETS were God's spokesmen: individuals supernaturally instructed in God's will, and inspired and commissioned to make known that will to men, both as to present and future events (*Jer.* 1: 9; *Isa.* 51: 16; *II Pet.* 1: 20, 21). The Holy Spirit who inspired them caused some to write down their messages for the benefit of future generations.

PROPITIATION. To propitiate is to "placate" or "appease". The reaction to sin of God's holiness is wrath, displeasure and vengeance. The purpose of propitiation is the removal of God's displeasure. By His death upon the Cross for our sins, Christ propitiated the wrath of God and rendered God well disposed to His people—and this He did as the provision of God the Father's great love for the sinner (*I John* 4: 8, 9, 10).

PROVIDENCE is God's good, kind, and unceasing activity and control of all things, working out everything in agreement with the counsel and design of His own will (*Ps.* 100: 5; *Eph.* 1: 11). Wars, suffering, and such like, are permitted by Him only in so far as they may serve to fulfil His purposes; His final and sure purpose being that they shall cease.

PSALMS means "praises" and gives its name to the longest book in the Bible. The 150 psalms came from different authors, although many—73—are said to have been written by David. They were like a hymnbook for Solomon's temple. Reflecting as they do so many different varieties of experience amongst God's people, strength and help is readily found in them by the Christian believer in his own particular experience.

RECONCILE, RECONCILED, RECONCILIATION. The idea behind the word "reconciliation" is that of making peace again after a quarrel, the bringing together of two parties who have been estranged. The harmony which man knew with God in the beginning has been completely spoiled by man's sin, so that God's attitude of wrath is the only right one man can deserve. Men constitute themselves God's enemies (*Rom.* 5: 10; *Col.* 1: 21), because God's demand for righteousness means that He is always opposed to evil.

Reconciliation, in this situation, is

effected by God's dealing with the root cause of the quarrel—human sin. By the death of His Son God dealt with sin finally and effectively (*Rom.* 5: 10, 11). God caused Christ, who Himself knew no sin, actually to be sin for sinners, so that in Christ they might be made righteous and acceptable to Him (*II Cor.* 5:21). Man may now be reconciled to God as he responds to God's gracious offer in Christ (*II Cor.* 5: 20).

REDEEM, REDEMPTION. Redemption is a term by which Christ's work for sinners may be viewed. Redemption is deliverance from captivity, bondage or death, by purchase. The Biblical picture behind it is that of slavery. By nature we are slaves to sin, deserving the punishment of death (*John* 8: 34). The price paid to purchase sinners from the slavery of sin was the death of the Lord Jesus Christ (*I Cor.* 6: 20; *Eph.* 1: 7). Through Christ, believers become free from the power of sin and death, but they have a privileged obligation, as a consequence, to glorify God in their bodies (*I Cor.* 6: 20).

REGENERATION. See *Question* 26.

REPENTANCE is turning from sin to God (*Ezek.* 33: 11; *Acts* 3: 19; 26: 20), as a result of a change of mind and heart about sin.

RESURRECTION. God the Father raised Christ from the dead (*Acts* 2: 24; 3: 15; *Eph.* 1: 20; *Col.* 2: 12), in fulfilment of the Scriptures (*Ps.* 16: 10; cf. *Acts* 13: 34, 35; *Luke* 24: 44) and Christ's promises (*John* 2: 19–22; *Matt.* 16: 21; 20: 19; *Mark* 9: 9; 14: 28), declaring Christ to be His Son (*Rom.* 1: 4), and His acceptance of Christ's redemptive work (*I Cor.* 15: 14, 17, 19), guaranteeing the justification of all believers (*Acts* 26: 23; *I Cor.* 15: 20, 23, 49).

RESURRECTION OF THE BODY. See *Question* 47.

RESURRECTION OF THE DEAD. This event will take place at Christ's return (*I Thess.* 4: 14–16). All will rise from the dead, believers to the resurrection of life, and unbelievers to the resurrection of judgment (*Dan.* 12: 2; *John* 5: 28, 29; *Acts* 24: 15; *Rev.* 20: 11–15). The resurrection of the dead is a fundamental of the Christian message (*I Cor.* 15: 12, 13; *Heb.* 6: 2; *II Tim.* 2: 18).

RETRIBUTION is generally recompense for evil, although sometimes for good. The wheels of God's vengeance may appear to move slowly (*Eccl.* 8: 11) but vengeance belongs to God, and He will righteously recompense evil (*Rom.* 12: 19; *Rev.* 18: 6). At His return, Christ will carry His recompense with Him, to repay everyone according to his deeds (*Rev.* 22: 12).

REVELATION is God's making known of Himself and His will to men in a way which otherwise they could not themselves discover. It is God speaking to us so that we both know what He is like, and come to know Him.

God has revealed facts about Himself in His creation (*Ps.* 19: 1–4; *Rom.* 1: 20 f), and His providence (*Ps.* 145: 9; *Matt.* 5: 45; *Acts* 14: 16 f), and in man's conscience (*Rom.* 1: 32; 2: 14 f). These things all men everywhere may discern, and they do not bring a knowledge of God's salvation. God speaks to men in a supernatural way through the Scriptures, called "the Word of God", and through His Son, who is also called "the Word"—the One through whom God perfectly reveals Himself to man (*John* 1: 1; *Heb.* 1: 1, 2).

REWARDS have nothing to do with the earning of salvation, for salvation is a free gift (*Rom.* 6: 23; *Eph.* 2: 8). When the gift of salvation has been received, however, God is graciously pleased to give rewards for faithful service (*Matt.* 19: 28; *Mark* 10: 29–30; *Luke* 18: 28, 29).

The parable of the talents teaches that where there is unequal ability but equal faithfulness, the reward will be the same in both cases (*Matt.* 25: 14–30).

The parable of the pounds teaches that where there is equal ability but unequal faithfulness, the reward will be graded (*Luke* 19: 11–27).

RIGHTEOUS, RIGHTEOUSNESS is a characteristic of God, expressing the rightness of all that He is and does (*Rom.* 3: 5). It is used to describe, too, whatever is pleasing to God (*Matt.* 3: 15; 5: 6, 10, 20). The most important use is when it describes the right relationship men are brought into with God when they believe in Christ (*Rom.* 10: 10). They are made righteous in Him, that is to say, they become in Christ all that God requires a man to be (*I Cor.* 1: 30; *II Cor.* 5: 21).

SACRAMENT. A sacrament is an outward sign by which God confirms to believers' consciences His promises of goodwill towards them. The sacraments provide believers with an opportunity of declaring their devotion and allegiance to God.

The two commonly accepted sacraments of the Christian Church are baptism and the Lord's Supper. Most Protestants maintain that these are the only two because our Lord Jesus specifically ordained them (*Matt.* 28: 19; *I Cor.* 11: 23–25). Some prefer the word "ordinances" in place of "sacraments", therefore, because baptism and the Lord's Supper were "ordained" by the Lord.

SACRIFICE, SACRIFICES. A sacrifice was an act of worship by which an offering was made to God of some object belonging to the worshipper, the purpose being to please God and to obtain His favour.

The animal sacrifices of the Old Testament were intended by God to teach the method of salvation. They always had the idea of cleansing behind them and the indispensable element was the shedding of blood (*Heb.* 9: 22, 23) but their repetition only served to point out their effectiveness (*Heb.* 10: 2). Thus the sacrifices reminded men of sin, revealed the need of atonement, and prepared the way for the coming of Christ.

The expression is used of the sacrificial death of Christ, for He offered for all time a single sacrifice for sin (*Heb.* 10: 12), doing what the Old Testament sacrifices could never do. His sacrifice is effective for all time, guaranteeing perfect forgiveness (*Heb.* 9: 26).

SACRIFICE, SACRIFICES (Spiritual). Christ's single sacrifice for sin for all time has completely done away with the need for animal and ceremonial sacrifices.

But God still requires sacrifices of another kind from those who are saved through Christ's one perfect sacrifice. As spiritual priests, Christians may offer to God acceptable spiritual sacrifices (*I Pet.* 2: 5, 9) by means of praise, thanksgiving, prayer, contrition, obedience, sharing and doing good to others (*Ps.* 50: 14; 51: 17; 107: 22; 141: 2; *Rom.* 12: 1; *Heb.* 13: 15, 16; *Jas.* 1: 27). By such means we worship God in the Spirit, for these are all part of the Holy Spirit's activity in the Christian (*Phil.* 3: 3).

SAINT serves as a name for all believers, and is not given in the Bible only to people of outstanding holiness and saintliness.

The word means "separated" or "dedicated". Christians are called upon to separate themselves from evil (*II Tim.* 2: 19), and to dedicate themselves to God's service (*Rom.* 12: 1, 2), because He has set them apart to be His own possession (*I Pet.* 2: 9, 10). For these reasons Christians are called "the saints".

SALVATION is deliverance from the guilt and penalties of sin to enjoy, instead, the unchanging favour of God for ever through repentance and faith in the Lord Jesus Christ (*Acts* 4: 12; *Rom.* 10: 10). It is known and felt in the present by the gift of the Holy Spirit (*Acts* 2: 38) and the forgiveness of sins (*I John* 1: 9), but it will be completely disclosed in the future in the full enjoyment of everlasting life and all its benefits (*Acts* 2: 38–40; 16: 30, 31; *I Thess.* 5: 8, 9, 10; *I Pet.* 1: 5, 13).

SANCTIFICATION. See *Question* 35.

SANCTIFIED when applied either to persons or to things indicates their consecration, dedication, or inclusion in the inner circle of what is holy, because of their association with God in some way. Thus Christians, because of their relationship to God through Christ which sets them apart as His, are described as "sanctified" or as "saints", as the word is sometimes translated.

SATAN is the name of the prince of evil, the adversary, commonly called the devil. He is the great enemy of God and man, the opposer of all that is good and the promoter of all that is evil. He has been defeated already by Christ's death and resurrection, and this defeat will be complete and clear to all at the end of this present age. See *Question* 43.

SAVIOUR. A Saviour is a deliverer or preserver, and as a title for Christ is especially appropriate because of His saving work on the Cross on behalf of sinners, promised by God throughout the centuries (*Luke* 2: 11; *Acts* 13: 23; *Phil.* 3: 20). As the Saviour He offers forgiveness of sins on true repentance (*Acts* 5: 31), and life and immortality (*II Tim.* 1: 10).

SCRIPTURES. The word means simply "writings", and in the New Testament is used to refer to the Old Testament (*Luke* 24: 44, 45; *I Cor.* 15: 3 f). The term is often used by Christians to describe both the Old and New Testaments.

SEPARATION FROM GOD. God's holiness demands that He shall be entirely separate from sin. Men's iniquities make a separation between them and God so that fellowship is impossible (*Isa.* 59: 2). The reality of that separation which sin brings is probably best illustrated in the cry of separation which Jesus uttered upon the cross (*Matt.* 27: 46; *Mark* 15: 34), when He who knew no sin was made to be sin, so that in Him we might become the righteousness of God (*II Cor.* 5: 21).

SIGN. A sign, like a miracle, is a work or an event which is contrary to the usual course of nature.

The miracles of Jesus in John's Gospel are all described as "signs" for besides being supernatural in nature, they provided direct evidence of His deity, sufficient to bring a man to living faith in Jesus (*John* 20: 30, 31).

SIN. See *Question* 12.

SON, SON OF GOD was an expression Jesus rarely used, although He spoke of Himself sometimes as "the Son" (*Matt.* 11: 27; *Mark* 13: 32). He is not the Son in the same sense as men may become sons of God through faith (*Matt.* 11: 27; *Luke* 2: 49; *John* 20: 17). He is uniquely God's one Son, His well-beloved (*Mark.* 12: 6), in a way no one else can be. He and the Father are one, a fact which the disciples fully appreciated at the resurrection (*John* 20: 28; *Rom.* 1: 3, 4). All the works, glory and perfection of God may be attributed to Him (*John* 1: 3; *Col.* 1: 16, 17; *Heb.* 1: 2; *Mark* 2: 5, 7). He is one with His Father, He is equal with God.

SOUL is, firstly, the seat and centre of the inner life of a man in its varied aspects, and it can represent man's feelings and emotions. But, secondly, it is also the seat and centre of that life that goes beyond this life. As such, the soul can receive God's salvation (*Jas.* 1: 21; *I Pet.* 1: 9). Men cannot harm it, but God can give it over to destruction (*Matt.* 10: 28).

It is because it is capable of partaking of the nature of God (*I Pet.* 1: 22; cf. *II Pet.* 1: 4) that its worth is so tremendous—indeed nothing man possesses is more precious (*Matt.* 16: 26; *Mark* 8: 37).

SOVEREIGNTY is supreme authority and absolute dominion.

Such sovereignty by right is God's alone. He accomplishes all things according to the counsel of His own will (*Eph.* 1: 11). He is over all things and He does what He will (*Rom.* 9: 5, 18).

SPIRIT is sometimes used in place of the word "soul" (*Luke* 23: 46; *Acts* 7: 59; *I Cor.* 5: 3, 5; *Eccl.* 12: 7), and compared with the body is the more important, being that part of us which thinks, feels and wills and lives for ever (*Matt.* 16: 26; *II Cor.* 5: 8; *II Tim.* 4: 22).

It is also used to describe God's nature: He is spirit, that is to say, there is nothing material in His nature (*John* 4: 24), He has no body. Like the wind—the same word, in fact—spirit is invisible, immaterial, and powerful, and these characteristics perfectly belong to God.

SPIRIT OF CHRIST is a title given to the Holy Spirit, the Third Person of the Trinity, on several occasions in the New Testament (*Rom.* 8: 9; *Gal.* 4: 6; *Phil.* 1: 19; *I Pet.* 1: 11).

The title expresses the close link that exists in the Bible between the two Persons. The Spirit was promised by the Son as well as by the Father (*John* 14: 17, 26). It is by the Spirit that Christ lives in believers' hearts (*Eph.* 3: 16, 17). The ministry of the Spirit has been and is, to take of the things of Christ and to make them known to men (*I Pet.* 1: 11; *John* 16: 14).

TEMPTATION is used both in a good and a bad sense, and can have the meaning of test as much as tempt. In the good sense God tests men so that they may prove themselves true (*Heb.* 11: 17) and in this sense Christ was tested by God (*Heb.* 2: 18; 4: 15).

In the bad sense there is the enticement to sin, which is the devil's work (*I Cor.* 7: 5; *Matt.* 4: 1; *Gal.* 6: 1; *Jas.* 1: 13).

TESTAMENT. A testament, like a covenant, is an undertaking or engagement made between God and man, at God's initiative through His promises.

The Old Testament relates to the promises, relating principally to this life, which God made to the Jews. The Old Testament was built upon the keeping of God's law.

The New Testament relates to those everlasting promises which God makes in Christ throughout all the Scriptures. This testament is built on faith and not on works (*John* 3: 16).

TESTING describes the use God makes of varying and difficult circumstances to make known to men their real character, and often to prove to them the reality and strength of their faith and obedience (*Gen.* 22: 1, 12; *Heb.* 11: 17; *I Pet.* 1: 7; 4: 12).

TRANSFIGURATION is the term used in the gospels to record what three of the apostles witnessed of Christ's glory. For a few moments the heavenly glory of Christ, which was usually hidden by the conditions of Christ's human life, shone through His body and its clothing (*Matt.* 17: 2; *Mark* 9: 2). This revelation was accompanied by a statement of God's approval of His Son.

TRANSGRESSION is the violation of God's law, the picture behind the word being the stepping over the bounds laid down by the law. When we do what God's law forbids, we transgress—we step over the bounds God has set (*Dan.* 9: 11).

TRESPASS. To trespass is to make a false step, to turn aside from right and truth, to sin either against men (*Matt.* 6: 14, 15) or against God (*Rom.* 5: 15, 17; *Gal.* 6: 1).

TRINITY. See *Question* 8.

UNJUST is used to describe those who do contrary to what is right in the sight of God—all men, by nature, find themselves rightly so described (*Matt.* 5: 45; *Acts* 24: 15; *I Pet.* 3: 18).

UNRIGHTEOUSNESS is wrongdoing or the persistent doing of that which is wrong—the characteristic of man as a sinner (*I John* 1: 9; 5: 17). See **INIQUITY** which is almost identical.

WASHED is a description of the Christian when forgiveness of sins is thought of in terms of inward and spiritual cleansing (*Acts* 22: 16; *I Cor.* 6: 11; *I John* 1: 7–9).

WICKED describes a person or a thing that is evil, bad, base, worthless, vicious or degenerate. The wicked man's life is governed by transgression; he has no fear of God (*Ps.* 36: 1). The prosperity he appears to enjoy is a fleeting experience (*Ps.* 37: 13).

WICKED ONE. See **EVIL ONE.**

WICKEDNESS is baseness, maliciousness and sinfulness. It is the characteristic of this present age (*Gal.* 1: 4) and comes from within man, from the heart (*Mark* 7: 22). Wickedness multiplies and its intense multiplication will be a mark of the end (*Matt.* 24: 11).

WILL is the ability we possess as persons to decide or think ourselves as deciding upon action, without any other cause. It represents the act of willing or desiring. This exercise of will is necessary to our personality and to our responsibility as rational beings. The will is always free, and we have the power of choice. We also have to say, however, that the will is not always good, for, since the fall of man, it is diseased, impaired and always prone to evil.

WORD OF GOD, The. The expression is used in three particular senses. Firstly, our Lord Jesus Christ is called the Word of God (*John* 1: 1), in that God has spoken to us in Christ, giving us His final and complete revelation in Him (*Heb.* 1: 1, 2).

Secondly, the gospel is called the Word of God (*Mark* 4: 14; *Luke* 5: 1; 8: 11; 11: 28) because it is God's message to sinful men (*Rom.* 1: 16; 15: 16).

Thirdly, the Scriptures are the Word of God. Christ and the apostles spoke of the Old Testament and quoted it as God's Word (*Mark* 7: 13; *Acts* 3: 22–25; *Rom.* 1: 2; *II Tim.* 3: 16).

And then the Word of God taught by the Lord and the apostles is the content of the New Testament, thus constituting the whole Bible the Word of God. This fact makes the Bible the sole authority in everything which concerns faith and life. When the Bible speaks, God speaks. See *Questions* 3, 4.

WORKS (Human) i.e. deeds of men. A man cannot be made acceptable to God by what he does or achieves (*Rom.* 3: 20, 28; *Gal.* 2: 16; *Eph.* 2: 8, 9). His acceptance by God depends upon his relationship to Christ. But good works are the demanded and expected result of a right relationship with God through Jesus Christ (*Eph.* 2: 10; *Tit.* 2: 7, 14; 3: 1, 8).

WORLD is used sometimes simply to describe the world in a geographical sense (*John* 1: 10), or the men and women of the world (*John* 3: 16, 17). Most frequently, it refers to the life of men as dominated and organised by the god of this world, Satan (*II Cor.* 4: 4; *I John* 2: 15–17).

WORSHIP is the acknowledgment by the believer of the worth-ship of God with every part of his being (*Rom.* 12: 1, 2). Such worship is only acceptable to God as it is offered through Christ, the Mediator and our great High Priest (*Heb.* 13: 15, 16). This worship cannot be separated from practical conduct bearing out what has been professed by the lips (*Jas.* 1: 27).

WRATH is the inevitable reaction of the holiness of God against sin, which demands that He, the righteous Judge, shall finally reckon with it (*John* 3: 36; *Rom.* 1: 18; *I Thess.* 1: 10; 5: 9).